Naming Canada:
Stories about Place Names from *Canadian Geographic*

⟨ **W9-ANZ-208**

How did your city/town/village get its name? For that
matter, how did Canada find itself with some of the most
unusual place names in the world? Names like Miramichi,
Flin Flon, Medicine Hat, Saskatoon? Or some of the most
mellifluous – Keremeos, Similkameen, Twillingate, or
Margaree?

Since 1983 Alan Rayburn has been writing a popular
column called 'Place Names' for *Canadian Geographic*.
In it he delves into the sources of Canadian place names,
and in so doing reveals a treasure trove of Canadian history
and myth. This volume brings together over sixty columns
Rayburn has written; it is at the same time a fine and ac-
curate reference for Canadian place names and a collection
of colourful anecdotes.

Covering everything from how our national parks were
named to places with names that are acronyms, such as
Arvida and Kenora, *Naming Canada* is a delightful addition to the library of anyone who has puzzled over the
strange and unusual names that abound in Canada.

ALAN RAYBURN, a former Orangevillian, and a Nepeanite
since 1961, is a geographer who specializes in the study
of place names. He was Executive Secretary of the Canadian Permanent Committee on Geographical Names
from 1973 to 1987.

A co-publication of the University of Toronto Press and
the Royal Canadian Geographical Society, publisher of
Canadian Geographic.

Naming
Canada

Stories about
Place Names from
Canadian Geographic

Alan Rayburn

UNIVERSITY OF TORONTO PRESS
Toronto Buffalo London

© University of Toronto Press Incorporated 1994
Toronto Buffalo London
Printed in Canada

Reprinted 1997

ISBN 0-8020-0569-1 (cloth)
ISBN 0-8020-6990-8 (paper)

Printed on acid-free paper

Canadian Cataloguing in Publication Data

Rayburn, Alan
  Naming Canada

  Includes index.
  ISBN 0-8020-0569-1 (bound)
  ISBN 0-8020-6990-8 (pbk.)

  1. Names, Geographical – Canada.   I. Title.

  FC36.R38 1994   917.1′0014   C94-930823-4
  F1004.R38 1994

University of Toronto Press acknowledges the financial assistance to
its publishing program of the Canada Council and the Ontario Arts
Council.

Contents

Preface ix
Acknowledgments xiii
Introduction 3

**Looking at Canada's Places from the Atlantic to the
   Pacific, and to the Arctic**
Canada: A Native Name from the Land 11
How Canada Lost Its 'Dominion' 15
Canada: The North, South, East, and West of It 18
High Points Across the Land 22
How Our National Parks Got Their Names 25
A Medley of Favourite Names 29
Riding Names: Some Gratifying, Some Grating 34

Scrutinizing Political Issues and Language Problems
Of Hatters and Capers, Townies and Trifluviens, and
   Other Monikers People Call Themselves 41
Pronouncing Names as the Locals Do 44
Sorting Out the Sound-alikes and Look-alikes 47
Standard Spelling Eliminates Confusion ... Usually 50
Who's to Blame for Mistake Names? 54
Acronyms ... Such as Kenora, Koocanusa, and Snafu
   Creek 58
Avoid the Apostrophe ... But Not Always 60

When Names Become Politically Incorrect 63
Hot and Bothered by 'Disgusting' Names 67
Castle Mountain and Its Thirty-five-Year Eisenhower
   Hiatus 71

**Receiving Names from Overseas and Exporting Names
   Abroad**
Touring the Middle East without Leaving Canada 75
Capitalizing on Foreign Capitals 79
Anzac to Zealandia: Names from Down Under 83
A Touch of Portuguese on the East Coast 87
Spanish Names Along Our West Coast 90
Crimean Victories Commemorated Across Canada 93
On the Western Front: Names from First World War
   Battles 97
Heavenly Places from Coast to Coast 100
Canadian Names Around the World 103

**Revealing Special Characteristics of Place Names and
   Generic Terms**
Cities: Source of Pride, Broken Dreams 108
Legacy of the Voyageurs on the Prairies 112
Of Tickles and Rips, Barachois and Bogans 115
Christmas Creek ... and Other Yuletide Honours 118
Of Valentines and Other Matters of the Heart 122
Giving the Devil His Due 126
A Giggle, er, Gaggle of Ha!Ha!s 130

**Adopting Names of Native Origin and Acknowledging
   Names Used by Indigenous Peoples**
Native Place Names: We All Have Our Favourites 134
Native Names for Native Places 136

Miramichi: Jacques Cartier in the 'Land of the
   Micmacs' 140
Saskatoon: A Home-made Name from a Home-grown
   Fruit 142
Medicine Hat: Mystery, Romance, and Hints of Magic
   Below 145
In Canso, Survival Is a Tradition 148
We Have 'Honoured' the Moose 662 Times! 151

Examining the Names of Particular Places
Cupids, Nfld.: Britain's First Canadian Colony 156
Acadia: A Land without Boundaries 159
Montréal: A People's City Beneath a King's Mountain 162
Meech Lake – of Accord Fame – and Other Lakes
   Nearby 165
Flin Flon: A Strange 'Professor' on Even Stranger
   Ventures 168
Lake Laberge (Rhymes with Marge) and Other Yukon
   Names 170

Observing Selected Names in Particular Regions
Captain Vancouver's Legacy 173
Mackenzie Expeditions Left a Trail of Names 177
'88 Olympics: Calgary, Kananaskis, and Mount Allan 182
The Thousand Islands: There Are Really 1,149 185
Relocating the Lost Villages 189
Great Divide Passes in the Rockies 193

**Commemorating Prominent Individuals and Honouring
   Certain Family Names**
Fraser, a Thoroughly Geographic Name 198
George Dawson, Inspiration for More Than Twenty-five
   Names 204

viii   Contents

Victoria: The Most-Honoured Name in Canada 208
Fit for the Prince of Wales 211
Vanier: Places Honouring an Illustrious Statesman 213
A Mountain for Michener, a Lake for Léger 218
Laurier, Most-Commemorated Canadian 221
Remembering John F. Kennedy 225
Smith: We Are Blessed with 439 of Them! 228

Index 233

Preface

A passion for maps and places and names has its roots in my preschool days in the late 1930s outside the town of Orangeville, Ontario. During my years of attendance in the schools of Orangeville from 1939 to 1952, my love for geography and history was nurtured by numerous helpful and dedicated teachers.

The joy of studying Canadian and world history continued during several years at university, first at Waterloo College (in the mid-1950s, part of the University of Western Ontario, but now Wilfrid Laurier University), and later at the University of British Columbia, the University of Kentucky, and l'Université Laval. It was at the University of Kentucky that my interest in pursuing a career in place-name study received a dramatic boost. My thesis adviser, Thomas Field, was usually a mild-mannered gentleman, but he revealed considerable excitement, and sometimes animosity, when discussing the background and merits of certain place names in the state. Through his inspiration, I resolved to take up the study of toponymy, if not as a profession, at least as an avocation.

In 1957, I joined the staff of the Geographical Branch of the federal Department of Mines and Technical Surveys. Until 1964, I was involved in land-use studies in the Maritime provinces, Québec, and Sri Lanka. In 1961, the staff serving the Canadian Permanent Committee on Geographical Names was transferred from the topographical survey division of the Surveys and Mapping Branch to the Geographical Branch. Norman Nicholson, who was both the director of the branch and the chairman of the committee, announced that a new toponymy research division would be set up in the branch, with Keith Fraser as its chief and as executive secretary of the committee.

Soon after joining the toponymy division in 1964, I undertook a place-names study of Renfrew County, a huge area of 5,000 square kilometres in the Upper Ottawa Valley. The main aims of the study were to assess the accuracy of names on topographical maps and to gather previously unrecorded names. The study revealed an error factor of 15 per cent among the official names; and for every name already in official use, at least one other new local name for another geographical feature was found to be in use.

The approach and the results of the Renfrew study appealed to the designated-names authorities in New Brunswick and Prince Edward Island, and they invited me in 1967 to undertake similar comprehensive field investigations in those provinces. The stock of approved names in New Brunswick in 1967 amounted to approximately 7,500. During an exhaustive two-year study, some 1,500 of those names were found to be incorrect as to local usage, spelling, or placement on maps; and 8,000 additional names in local usage were picked up. During the Prince Edward Island study, the stock of names was increased from 1,200 to 2,200, and 300 corrections were made. A similar study of Nova Scotia's names was undertaken by Michael Munro of the toponymy division's staff in 1973, with even more dramatic results.

In 1967, the Geographical Branch published *Geographical Names of Renfrew County* (74 pages) as part of its Geographical Paper series. Revisions of this book were privately published in 1989 and 1990. The Surveys and Mapping Branch (when the Geographical Branch had been disbanded by the Department of Energy, Mines and

Resources in 1967, the toponymy division had been transferred to the Surveys and Mapping Branch) published
Geographical Names of Prince Edward Island (135 pages)
in 1973, and *Geographical Names of New Brunswick* (304
pages) in 1975.

In 1973, I was appointed executive secretary of the Canadian Permanent Committee on Geographical Names, a
position I held until 1987. In that position, I worked with
the committee's secretariat, and with the personnel of the
federal, provincial, and territorial members of the committee in the development of national toponymic prin-
ciples and procedures.

In the spring of 1983, the chairman of the committee,
Jean-Paul Drolet, who was also a director of the Royal
Canadian Geographical Society, proposed to the publisher
and general manager of *Canadian Geographic* that a place-
names column be considered for the magazine. Fortui-
tously, the publisher was then Keith Fraser, and he greeted
the suggestion with enthusiasm.

The magazine's editor, Ross Smith, invited me to submit
a few sample columns. Subsequently, the first column, entitled 'Acronyms ... Such as Kenora, Koocanusa, and
Snafu Creek,' appeared in the December '83/January '84
issue of the magazine. By November/December '93, sixty-
one columns had been published on a variety of toponymic
topics, from names pronunciation and spelling to names
for royalty and governors general, and to prominent names
in the news, like Meech Lake.

The present editor of *Canadian Geographic*, Ian Darragh, and his capable editorial staff have provided considerable encouragement to continue writing the column
for the magazine. Studies of Canadian names transferred
from South Africa, of Ontario's Mississippi River, and of
Basque names in Eastern Canada are among the articles
that will appear in it during 1994.

Acknowledgments

I wish to thank Jean-Paul Drolet, chairman of the Canadian Permanent Committee on Geographical Names from 1964 to 1988, who proposed the idea of a column on place names in *Canadian Geographic* in the spring of 1983. As a member of the board of directors of the Royal Canadian Geographical Society, he took the idea to Keith Fraser, then executive director of the Society, and publisher of the Society's *Canadian Geographic*. I express my gratitude to Keith, who had been the executive secretary of the names committee in the 1960s. He picked up the idea of a names column enthusiastically, and turned it over to the recently appointed editor of the magazine, Ross Smith. For the next six years, Ross nurtured the column by suggesting suitable ideas to write about, and by deftly trimming awkward sentences and excessive wording. His successor, Ian Darragh, and the managing editor of the magazine, Eric Harris, have continued to encourage the writing of the articles. Finally, I thank my successor as executive secretary of the names committee, Helen Kerfoot, for her continuing advice on policies and practices relating to naming in Canada, and on particular topics for the names column.

Naming Canada:
Essays on Place Names
from
Canadian Geographic

Introduction

Naming Canada comprises the sixty-one 'Place Names' columns first published in *Canadian Geographic* from December '83/January '84 to November/December '93. Several corrections and changes have been made to reflect information provided by the magazine's readers. Some new details, dropped from the original articles because of space limitations or having come to light since publication in the magazine, have been added to some of the essays.

The idea for bringing the columns together in a single volume was initiated by Bill Harnum, vice-president of scholarly publishing at the University of Toronto Press. The initial arrangement of the essays into particular themes was undertaken by Laura Macleod. Subsequently, Gerry Hallowell and Beverley Beetham Endersby completed the editing of the texts for publication.

The essays are grouped into eight broad themes.

1 / *Looking at Canada's Places from the Atlantic to the Pacific, and to the Arctic.* The article on the origin of the name Canada, and the amusing alternatives proposed for the name of the new nation in 1867, was the thirty-seventh article published in the magazine, but it is the obvious lead-off essay in this collection. The article about the suppression of the title 'Dominion' was a natural second essay. The remaining five articles of the group deal with the highest points in each of the provinces and territories, Canada's national parks, my favourite twenty-four names

from coast to coast, Canada's federal electoral ridings, and the farthest points on the compass.

The declaration in the farthest-points article that there was an unnamed point farther north than Cape Columbia persuaded the Department of National Defence's Mapping and Charting Establishment to undertake precise measurements. The point was found to be 242 metres farther north than the designated most northerly site of Cape Columbia. The Canadian Permanent Committee on Geographical Names decided in 1992 to shift Cape Columbia to the point. The article on the federal electoral districts encouraged the staff of Elections Canada to set up an advisory committee for the selection of names of the new 301 ridings based on the 1991 census, and I was invited to serve on the committee. The article on the highest points in each jurisdiction guided sexagenarian climbers Clifford and Ruth Holtz of Oshawa, Ont., in their ascents in 1990 of each of the eleven highest points in the country – Québec and Newfoundland share the same highest elevation, but with different names. And one of the points of the Y-shaped summit may be nearly a metre higher in Newfoundland.

2 / *Scrutinizing Political Issues and Language Problems.* Ten of the essays concern a number of language issues and a variety of political problems involving names. In French, words like 'Québécois' and 'Acadien' are called *gentilés,* but no suitable English word for them has evolved. *Gentilés* are widely used all across Canada, from Haligonian to Winnipegger and on to Vancouverite. Suggestions on what I believed were the accepted pronunciations of several names aroused a couple of readers, who forcefully pointed out my errors. Although Canada does not have too many confusing sound-alikes and look-alikes, there are bothersome ones like St. John's/Saint John, Kenora/Canora, two major Churchill Rivers, and too many places called Windsor. The misspelling of place names

is quite common for places like St. Catharines and Edmundston, and it doesn't help when there is more than one official spelling, such as Timiskaming/Témiscamingue, and Okanagan north of the 49th parallel, Okanogan south of it. In another essay, actual mistakes, such as Cedoux evolving from Ledoux, and Barry's Bay from Byers Bay, are examined. Several names are acronyms, that is, created from parts of two or more words. Among them are Arvida, Estevan, and Tarfu Creek. The handling of the possessive apostrophe in names has had a mixed history over the past hundred years, with places like St. John's preferring it, and Smiths Falls ignoring it. Political correctness forced the change of Berlin to Kitchener, and the dropping of Mount Stalin, but name purifiers have been unable to divest Swastika of its 'good luck' identity. Sensitivity resulted in the banishment of Belly River and Foul Bay, but Crotch Lake and Bastard Township have survived attack. When former prime minister John Diefenbaker requested background material in 1976 relating to the public clamour to change Mount Eisenhower back to Castle Mountain, I assumed he would rise in the House of Commons to condemn the action taken in 1946 by Mackenzie King to assign a foreigner's name to one of Canada's most impressive mountains. However, he roundly condemned any attempt to sully the honour of the Supreme Commander of the Second World War forces, and Liberal minister Alistair Gillespie, who was responsible for the names committee, fully agreed with him. But three years later, during Joe Clark's brief government in 1979, we got our Castle Mountain back.

3 / *Receiving Names from Overseas and Exporting Names Abroad.* Great numbers of Canada's names first saw the light of day in foreign lands. Eight essays concern the transfer of names from abroad, and a ninth in this group of articles is about Canada's export of names to other countries. Athens, London, and Paris recall great world cap-

itals. Canaan, Goshen, and Damascus owe their existence
to biblical references. Zealandia and Australia Gulch are
among many names drawn from Canada's Commonwealth
partners down under. Portugal and Spain were leaders
among early explorers, so it is not surprising to find names
like Bonavista and Juan de Fuca Strait on our east and
west coasts. Hard-fought victories in the Crimean Peninsula by British and French forces introduced names like
Alma, Inkerman, and Canrobert to Canada's toponymic
fabric. First World War battles and victories in northern
France and in Belgium provided more than 125 names for
Canadian places and mountains, examples being Vimy
Ridge, St-Quentin, and Messines. Names reflecting
heaven, peace, and harmony are widely affixed to Canadian places, from Paradise in Newfoundland to Utopia
in Ontario, and Sointula in British Columbia. Canadian
names like Toronto and Ontario have been transferred to
other countries, especially the United States and Australia,
and even names like Québec have been given to places
in Britain and France.

4 / *Revealing Special Characteristics of Place Names and
Generic Terms*. Seven essays are devoted to special characteristics of Canadian place names and to generic terminology. The lead-off article reveals that Calgary has the
largest population of any incorporated 'city' in Canada,
and Greenwood, B.C., has the least population. In terms
of area, Timmins is Canada's largest, with Vanier, Ont.
(the home of the Royal Canadian Geographical Society,
publisher of *Canadian Geographic*), the smallest. The wide
use of 'butte' for a flat-topped hill and the frequent occurrence of 'coulee' for a steep-sided valley are legacies
of the French voyageurs and explorers who first investigated the resources of Western Canada. In Eastern Canada,
there is a fascinating variety of terminology in names like
Pinchgut Tickle, Pocomoonshine Deadwater, MacLean
Barachois, Mersereau Bogan, Pickards Padou, Framboise

Intervale, and Meetinghouse Rips.

Christmas is a joyous time, so it is not surprising to find names like St. Nicholas Peak; Tiny Tim Lake, and Yule Rock celebrating that season. Names like Lovers Cove, Heart's Delight, and Bow and Arrow Shoal inspired the writing of the essay on features with a theme relating to the playfulness and romance associated with Valentine's Day. In a contrasting theme, there are hundreds of names dedicated to Satan and his traditional homes of hell and Hades. Ominous examples include Backside of Hell Cove, Devils Elbow Rapids, and Ogre Mountain. The final essay of this series concerns the much misunderstood term 'haha' that occurs in several names in Eastern Canada, the best example being the village of Saint-Louis-du-Ha! Ha! Even though the term means 'an unexpected barrier,' the vast majority of people will probably continue to believe it was introduced in names for comic relief.

5 / *Adopting Names of Native Origin and Acknowledging Names Used by Indigenous Peoples.* Names of native origin are distinguishing marks of a country. The first of six essays draws attention to the strength and rustic beauty of names like Athabasca, Muskoka, and Keremeos. The second explores the trend to acknowledge the names actually used by the native residents of places like Iqaluit, the largest settlement in what is to become Nunavut, and Kuujjuaq in Northern Quebec, formerly Frobisher Bay and Fort Chimo, respectively. The next four essays celebrate individual names with native roots: Miramichi, Saskatoon, Medicine Hat, and Canso. To me, all four add an extra patina of beauty to the regions in which they are located. The last article of the series explores names like Moose Jaw, Moosonee, and Moose Bath Pond, which owe their origins to the word *moos*, from the description by Algonquian-speaking tribes of the browsing habits of the hulking animal occupying the Canadian wilderness from coast to coast.

6 / *Examining the Names of Particular Places.* The six essays in this next grouping are primarily about names of single places, with the first one about Cupids, Nfld., where the oldest British colony in present-day Canada was established in 1610. Acadia is the mystical home of a quarter-million people, who proudly proclaim their common heritage, but the name's roots are uncertain, and the area both historically and currently constituting Acadia widely differs among Acadians. Montréal is the most vibrant city in Canada, but the roots of its name from the adjacent 223-metre Mont Royal have been long disputed. The next article traces the roots of a name on every Canadian's lips in the late 1980s – Meech Lake, and examines the dual names of the next lake to the northwest, known as Harrington Lake in English, Lac Mousseau in French. The story of the origin of Flin Flon seems more fanciful than real, but it's an expressive name for a mining city set among Manitoba's rugged rocks. Robert Service's ballad of the cremation of Sam McGee on the shores of the Yukon's Lake Laberge, and correspondence with the man it is named for, Michel Lebarge himself, provide an interesting tale of naming in Canada's Yukon.

7 / *Observing Selected Names in Particular Regions.* Six of the essays deal with several names in particular regions. The lead-off article examines the incredible 4¾-year voyage of George Vancouver to Canada's west coast in the late 1700s, and the naming of features from the Strait of Georgia to Alaska's Cook Inlet. During the same period, Alexander Mackenzie undertook two arduous journeys, one to the mouth of the country's longest river, subsequently named for him by John Franklin, the second to the shores of the Pacific. Eleven geographical features honour Mackenzie's prodigious accomplishments. Calgary provides the focus for an essay about features associated with the 1988 Winter Olympics held there. The Thousand Islands comprise some 1,149 identifiable pieces of rock and

land surrounded by the waters of the upper St. Lawrence River, but only 367 in both Ontario and New York have official names. Downriver at Cornwall, the construction of huge dams in the 1950s resulted in the inundation of 8,000 hectares of land, the relocation of eight villages, and the creation of two new towns, Long Sault and Ingleside. The naming of the historic passes on the Great Divide of the Rocky Mountains is the subject of the last article of this series of essays.

8 / *Commemorating Prominent Individuals and Honouring Certain Family Names.* The final nine essays concern features named for noted individuals, or for particular surnames. There are 218 features with the name Fraser in Canada, the most famous being British Columbia's Fraser River. George Dawson, a brilliant scientist and scholar who overcame physical adversity, named many features himself, and in his honour, at least 25 features were named for him. No single individual has had more features – more than 300 – named for her in Canada than Queen Victoria, beginning with the capital cities of both British Columbia and Saskatchewan. The queen's eldest son, the Prince of Wales, had several features named for him during his visit to Canada in 1860. When his eldest son, also the Prince of Wales, visited Canada in 1919, a number of features were named in his honour. In 1979, the museum of native artifacts in Yellowknife was named for the present Prince of Wales. The nineteenth governor general, Georges Vanier, was a respected statesman for whom several features, including cities in Ontario and Quebec, were named. The naming of a mountain for Roland Michener and a lake for Jules Léger, Canada's twentieth and twenty-first governors general, reflects the great respect these public servants had among their countrymen. The most honoured Canadian in the naming of places is Sir Wilfrid Laurier, with at least 37 geographical features as well as a number of public institutions having

been named for him. President John F. Kennedy had a mountain named for him in 1964, and the following year it was climbed by is brother Robert. The final essay is about features across the country named Smith, the commonest surname in several countries in the world. The inspiration to write this article came to me during the summer of 1984, when, while visiting the editor of *Canadian Geographic*, Ross Smith, I thoughtlessly observed that consideration had once been given to changing the magical name Medicine Hat to the dull and uninspiring Smithville.

Here's to all those Smiths, Frasers, Poiriers, Macdonalds, Cartiers, Mercredis, Englebrechts, and millions of other Canadians of many races and cultures who have made this great land such a memorable experience, toponymically speaking. Thanks for *Naming Canada*.

Looking at Canada's Places from the Atlantic to the Pacific, and to the Arctic

Canada: A Native Name from the Land

'That's the way to Canada,' Jacques Cartier's young aboriginal companions, Taignoagny and Domagaya, shouted as the explorer neared Anticosti Island on the St. Lawrence River on 17 August 1535. Cartier turned his ship up the 'grande rivière de Hochelaga,' also called 'rivière de Canada,' and by 7 September was within 100 kilometres of Stadacona (site of present-day Québec City) in Huron chief Donnacona's territory, called Canada.

Donnacona, of an Iroquoian-speaking tribe, was the father of Cartier's two native friends, having allowed his sons to accompany the explorer to France the previous year. He and Cartier had met near what is now the town of Gaspé. Cartier later learned that Canada extended another 50 kilometres beyond Stadacona (the limits today would be Baie-Saint-Paul on the east, Portneuf on the west, and the south shore of the St. Lawrence River).

In his report of the 1535–6 voyage, Cartier appended a list of the local Iroquoian-language words. He noted that *kanata* meant 'town,' interpreted subsequently as meaning a cluster of dwellings, with the lands ruled by Donnacona being a series of towns. André Thevet, a contemporary French explorer, wrote that the name meant 'land.'

The words for town or village in various Iroquoian languages are similar. The Mohawks use *nekantaa*, the Onondagas *ganataje*, and the Senecas *iennekanandaa*.

So the origin and meaning of 'Canada' would appear to be beyond dispute. However, that has not prevented a proliferation of other stories, some of tenuous credibility.

It may have been Father Louis Hennepin who first observed the similarity of the Spanish *aca nada* ('here nothing') to Canada. He reported in 1698 that early Spanish explorers were disappointed in not finding gold and other riches in Canada, and frequently made that derisive declaration. It is said that natives picked up the phrase and passed it to Cartier as the name of their country. The historian Charlevoix mentioned it as an old tradition in his history of New France, published in 1744.

Some writers give the credit to the Portuguese, who also are said to have exclaimed in disgust *cà nada* ('here nothing').

In the 1880s, Marshall Elliott, an American writer, was convinced that a Spanish or Portuguese origin was correct and did much to cast doubt on the name's native provenance.

In 1760, Thomas Jefferys, a British map maker, published a geography in which he suggested the name was derived from a native language and that it meant 'mouth of the country,' an allusion to the mouth of the St. Lawrence River.

A writer in an issue of *Nova Scotia Magazine* of 1779 offered that a Frenchman called Cane had attempted to found a colony but failed, leaving only his name for the territory.

The most outrageous suggestion came from a writer in the *Kingston Gazette* in 1811. He said the origin could be traced to the first French settlers demanding a 'can a day' of spruce beer from the intendant, the colonial administrator.

In 1861, Rev. B. Davies, an English philologist, put forward an Oriental origin, noting the similarity of the name Canada with Canara or Carnata in the south of India. Such speculation was not based on a thread of historical or linguistic evidence.

Other suggestions have included the Latin word *candida*, the Sanskrit *kanada*, and the Spanish *cañada*, all with no more evidence than the mere coincidence of similar syllables.

The Dictionary of Canadianisms (1967) states that the etymology of Canada is by no means clearly established, which imparts a measure of respect to the many fanciful suggestions that have been proposed to discredit the information from Jacques Cartier in the sixteenth century.

Writers of this century, such as Francis Parkman (*Pioneers of New France*, 1905), Mark Orkin (*Speaking Canadian English*, 1970), and William B. Hamilton (*The Macmillan Book of Canadian Place Names*, 1978), have concluded that the weight of opinion favours the native source as reported by Cartier.

Maps made in France soon after Cartier's return in 1536 assigned the name Canada to a vast territory north of Anticosti Island. An exception was a map made for Nicolas Vallard in 1547, where the name is inscribed in the area of the present city of Québec.

Pierre Desceliers, an eminent cartographer near Dieppe, produced several maps of eastern North America in the mid-1500s. His 1550 map shows the name Canada four times. Near the head of the Saguenay it is written in large letters once, and in smaller letters twice. It is shown again on the south shore of the St. Lawrence River opposite the mouth of the Saguenay. Why the repetition? Perhaps he was told that the small lettering did not give sufficient prominence to Donnacona's territory, and was persuaded to inscribe the name in larger letters.

For more than two centuries, from the 1550s to the late

1700s, Canada was used as a popular alternative to New France, at least to that part bordering on the shores of the 'grande rivière de Canada,' the St. Lawrence. It was not until 1791 that it was given official status when the Constitutional Act created the two jurisdictions of Upper Canada and Lower Canada. The Act of Union in 1841 amalgamated the two regions into a single province of Canada, divided into Canada East and Canada West. But Upper Canada and Lower Canada remained in common use, even in debates in the Legislative Assembly of Canada.

In the 1860s, when union with the Atlantic provinces was in the offing, proposals for a suitable name for the confederation included not only Canada, but more than thirty others. Among those most frequently repeated were Tuponia or Tupona (an acronym for the United Provinces of North America) and Efisga (England, France, Ireland, Scotland, Germany, aboriginal). Other suggestions included Acadia, Albertland, Albertoria, Albionara, Albona, Alexandrina, Aquilonia, Borealia, Britannica, Cabotia, Canadensia, Colonia, Hochelaga, Laurentia, Mesopelagia, Niagarentia, New Albion, Norland, Superior, Transatlantica, Transylvania, Ursalia, Vesperia, Victorialand, and Victorialia.

When Thomas D'Arcy McGee addressed the Legislative Assembly on 9 February 1865 on the subject of the proposed union, he noted such suggestions as Tuponia and Hochelaga, and remarked whimsically: 'Now I would ask any Hon. Member of the House how he would feel if he woke up some fine morning and found himself, instead of a Canadian, a Tuponian or Hochelagander?'

When the British North America Act was declared on 1 July 1867, it announced that Canada would be the name of the new dominion. *The Canadian Encyclopedia* (1988) notes: 'the name Canada reveals strength, generates pride and reflects much of the land's rugged character and its resourceful people.'

How Canada Lost Its 'Dominion'

When many of us were growing up, we spoke about living in the Dominion of Canada, heard the word *Dominion* almost daily in the news and in references to our nation, and proudly celebrated Dominion Day every First of July. When the prime minister and premiers met, it was called a Dominion-provincial conference. In school we learned about the indomitable Dominion Land Surveyors who carved up the West, and on the classroom wall there was a distorted Mercator map of the world with a huge, bright pink land mass labelled in bold letters DOMINION OF CANADA. But we rarely hear or see Dominion any more. Why?

I did not notice the erosion of the word from our political lexicon until it was officially dropped from the name of the 1 July holiday in October 1982. About that time, I was asked by the United Nations to confirm the official long and short names of our country. I assumed the long title was Dominion of Canada, and the short was simply Canada. I was wrong. External Affairs declared that Canada alone was official as both the long and the short name.

Then early in 1990, an article on Canada's future in *Maclean's* magazine said that Canada 'is not, in any official usage, a kingdom, a commonwealth, republic or federation, much less a union. Nor is it anymore, in common government parlance, a dominion.' This set me off on an odyssey to discover when we had officially ceased to be the Dominion of Canada. To my surprise, I found the title has not been officially dropped; it has only been suppressed, with *federal*, *national*, and *central* substituted as adjectives, and *Canada*, *nation*, and *country* used to replace the noun.

At one time, Canada's public servants included the Dominion Fire Commissioner, Dominion Stone Carver (Parliament Buildings sculptor), Dominion Archivist, Dominion Astronomer, Dominion Statistician, and Dominion Cerealist. None of those titles can be found in the Government of Canada telephone directory today. But a few others remain: the Dominion Hydrographer, the Dominion Geodesist, and the Dominion Carillonneur. The only title in French with *Dominion* still retained is that of *Carillonneur du Dominion*.

Historians trace the origin of the title Dominion of Canada in the constitution to Sir Samuel Leonard Tilley, one of the Fathers of Confederation, from New Brunswick. While assembled at the London Conference in December 1866, the delegates from the provinces of Canada, New Brunswick, and Nova Scotia were pondering what to call the proposed federation. Kingdom of Canada had been considered but was judged pretentious and possibly offensive to Americans. Besides, Queen Victoria did not like it.

One morning, Tilley reached for his bible on awakening and read: 'He shall have dominion also from sea unto sea, and from the river unto the ends of the earth.' The appropriateness of the word struck him at once. Here was a term to fulfil the hopes of creating a great nation from the Atlantic to the Pacific, and from the mighty St. Lawrence to the vast northern reaches. The other delegates later agreed, and Lord Carnarvon, the colonial secretary and chairman of the conference, persuaded the Queen and the British prime minister, Lord Derby, to accept the title Dominion of Canada.

On 29 March 1867, the British North America Act received royal assent, and a new word appeared in the world's political vocabulary. The act stated that 'the Provinces of Canada, Nova Scotia, and New Brunswick shall form and be One Dominion under the Name of Canada; and on and after that Day those Three Provinces shall form and be One Dominion under that Name accordingly.'

When the Canadian constitution was patriated in 1982, the entire British North America Act was incorporated into it as the Constitution Act, 1867. So the word *Dominion* continues to be a part of the official title of this country (although its *legal* name is strictly Canada).

Until the Second World War, Canadian politicians, historians, and writers comfortably spoke and wrote about the Dominion. But during and immediately after the war, considerable tensions over Québec's relationship to Ottawa developed between Premier Maurice Duplessis and Prime Minister Mackenzie King. With the appointment of Louis St. Laurent as minister of external affairs in 1946, and his becoming prime minister two years later, the tensions were eased by quietly dropping references to the Dominion, viewed by Duplessis as an oppressive word implying Québec's subservience to the government in Ottawa.

By the 1960s, many titles of agencies in Ottawa were stripped of the word *Dominion*. The Dominion Bureau of Statistics became Statistics Canada; Dominion experimental farms became research stations. As early as 1948, the magazine *Saturday Night* referred to 'federal ministers' and 'national capital,' using *Dominion* only in relation to official functions. And by 1951, *Queen's Quarterly* was writing of 'federal-provincial conferences.'

From the 1940s to the 1970s, various private members' bills to change Dominion Day to Canada Day were 'talked out' in the House of Commons. Regardless, almost all references in the media and by the federal government after 1972 were to Canada Day.

Then, in May 1980, Hal Herbert, Liberal MP for Vaudreuil, introduced a private member's bill to replace Dominion Day with Canada Day. Many MPs expected nothing would come of it, but on 9 July 1982, the bill was given second reading and referred to the Committee of the Whole House. Although a quorum was not in the House, the call for third reading was made immediately.

When no objections were heard, the bill was carried and the House adjourned.

The bill was then sent to the Senate, where a vigorous debate took place in October. Although a stout defence of Dominion Day was advanced by Senator Eugene Forsey and the Monarchist League of Canada, the Senate, aware of a Gallup poll indicating 70 per cent of Canadians favoured the change, approved the bill without a recorded vote.

On 1 July 1989, Michael Valpy, a *Globe and Mail* columnist, assailed Canadian parliamentarians as 'vandals' and 'milquetoast stewards,' but it seems that most Canadians are content with our national holiday being called Canada Day.

Across the land, however, remnants of Canada's title still flourish: Dominion Square in Montréal; the town of Dominion, N.S.; the village of Dominion City, Man.; New Dominion, P.E.I.; Dominionville, Ont.; and several creeks, rivers, lakes, and mountains called Dominion. The southwestern Ontario town of Ridgetown is served by the *Ridgetown Dominion* weekly newspaper, and many businesses, from Dominion Cellulose Ltd. to Toronto-Dominion Bank, still proudly celebrate the historic title of our country.

Canada: The North, South, East, and West of It

The most easterly land of Canada – indeed of North America – is Cape Spear, which juts into the Atlantic at a longitude of 50°37′W.

Not long after the voyage of the Portuguese explorer João Fernandes in 1498 (partly in company with John Cabot), the names *Cauo de la spera* and *Riuo de la spera* appeared on some maps published between 1505 and 1508. These Portuguese names refer to the idea of 'waiting.' The area of the cape and the small bay on its northwest side were an important rendezvous for the Grand Banks fishery in the early 1500s.

In the 1540s, the name of the point was rendered on maps in French as *Cap d'Espoir* (meaning 'cape of hope'), and later as *Cap d'Espérance*. This was rendered into English as Cape Spear and that became the established form on British Admiralty charts.

The second Portuguese name, *Riuo de la spera*, became Cape Bay on early English charts, but was changed to Spear Bay in the 1700s. In 1981, the name Cape Bay was restored; Spear Bay Brook has remained for a small stream flowing into the bay.

The most southerly land feature of Canada is Middle Island in Lake Erie at latitude 41°41'N. (So much for thinking of Canada as entirely north of the 49th parallel!) Middle Island is at the same latitude as the Klamath Mountains of northern California; Great Salt Lake, Utah; Des Moines, Iowa; and Chicago, Ill.

Middle Island itself lies in the middle of the Lake Erie shipping channel, almost halfway between Pelee Island (Ont.) on the north, and Kelleys Island (Ohio) on the south.

Pelee Island is our most southerly occupied land. The name of the island is derived from nearby Point Pelee, itself named by the French because its east side was found to be devoid of trees, and thus *pelée* ('bare' or 'peeled').

Father Pierre Charlevoix, who took a journey along the shore of Lake Erie in 1721, noted in his journal, published in Paris in 1744, that Point Pelee was 'well enough wooded on the west side, but on the east side it has a sandy soil with only small red cedars of inconsiderable quantity.'

On looking at some maps of Canada, some people may conclude that the country's most westerly point is Frederick Island, the farthest west of the Queen Charlotte Islands. The longitude of this island is 133°11′W, but it is nearly eight degrees east of the Yukon–Alaska boundary at 141°. The southern point of this boundary is Mount St. Elias; its northern mainland limit is Demarcation Point.

Mount St. Elias was first noted on 16 July 1741 by the Danish-born explorer Vitus Bering during a voyage of discovery on behalf of the Russian government. On St. Elias Day, four days later, he named Cape St. Elias on Kayak Island in present-day Alaska. Subsequently, map makers assigned the cape's name to the mountain sighted but left unnamed by Bering, and to the highest range of mountains in Canada.

Demarcation Point, the most northwesterly point of Canada, was mentioned by Sir John Franklin in his *Narrative* of 1828. He noted it as having been so named 'from its being situated in longitude 141°W, the boundary between the British and Russian dominions on the northern coast of Canada.'

The name of the most northerly point in Canada has been debated for a number of years.

During his expedition to northern Ellesmere Island in 1875–6, Sir George Nares applied the name Cape Columbia (from the poetic name of the United States) to the most northerly extension of land at 83°06′N. At the same time he named an eastern extension of the same body of land Cape Aldrich for his first lieutenant, Pelham Aldrich, who had established that the vicinity of the capes was the most northerly land of the Arctic Archipelago.

In 1911, the Geographic Board published several decisions on names. Its approval of Cape Columbia includes the statement: 'Name given by Nares, as it is the most northerly point of North America.'

Moira Dunbar and Keith Greenaway, in their *Arctic Canada from the Air* (1956), stated without qualification that

Cape Aldrich is the northernmost point. They based this judgment on their interpretation of air photos.

In his *North of Latitude Eighty* (1974), Geoffrey Hattersley-Smith also asserted that Cape Aldrich is the most northern point by a few hundred metres, but noted that 'Aldrich himself accorded the distinction to Cape Columbia.' In the 1950s and 1960s, Dr. Hattersley-Smith raised with the names authority many questions about various names of northern Ellesmere Island, but he did not draw attention to any problems relating to the most northerly named point. In 1967, geographer Jim Lotz suggested naming the end of the whole 15-kilometre-wide body of land, including the two named capes, as 'Centennial Promontory.' No action was taken on this proposal.

The most recent representation on topographical maps of the area of Cape Columbia is the 1970 edition of the 1:500,000 scale map. It and the 1967 edition of the 1:250,000 scale map reveal a small point extending farther north than the points identified as Cape Columbia and Cape Aldrich.

When this article appeared in the Feb./Mar. 1987 issue of *Canadian Geographic,* it contained my suggestion that Cape Columbia could continue to be recognized as the most northerly land of Canada, but that the most northerly point of the cape be given a uniquely Canadian name.

In the summer of 1987, the Mapping and Charting Establishment of the Department of National Defence surveyed the area of Cape Columbia and determined that the small point was indeed the most northerly piece of land, being 242 metres north of the site identified as Cape Columbia.

In 1992, the Canadian Permanent Committee on Geographical Names decided that the small point, at the latitude of 83°06'41.35", would henceforth be known as Cape Columbia.

High Points Across the Land

The highest mountain in Canada is in the St. Elias Mountains in the Yukon. At 5,959 metres, Mount Logan is second only to Mount McKinley (6,194 metres) in Alaska as the highest elevation in North America.

In 1890, I.C. Russell of the U.S. Geological Survey, while undertaking a survey in the St. Elias Mountains, named Mount Logan for Sir William Edmond Logan (1798–1875). Born in Montréal and educated in Scotland, Logan founded the Geological Survey of Canada in 1842.

The St. Elias Mountains were named in the late 1800s after Mount St. Elias, a name in turn derived from Cape St. Elias in Alaska, named by the Danish explorer Vitus Bering on St. Elias Day in 1741. Mount St. Elias is on the western boundary of Canada and, at 5,489 metres, is our second-highest mountain. In fact, the next sixteen highest mountains in Canada are all in the St. Elias Mountains, all but one entirely in the Yukon. Fairweather Mountain (at 4,663 metres, the eighth-highest in Canada) straddles the B.C.–Alaska boundary. It was named by Capt. James Cook during his historic voyage along the west coast in 1778.

The highest mountain entirely within British Columbia is Mount Waddington (4,016 metres) in the Coast Mountains. It was named in 1918 by the Geographic Board of Canada for Alfred Waddington, who from 1858 to 1872 promoted the dream of a transcontinental route to the Pacific via Bute Inlet, the head of which is 60 kilometres south of the mountain.

Alberta's highest mountain is Mount Columbia (3,747 metres) located on the boundary with British Columbia in the Rocky Mountains. It received its name in 1899 from the Columbia River, itself named in 1792 by Capt. Robert Gray, an American, for his vessel, the *Columbia*. But Mount Columbia is not the highest peak in the Rockies;

that claim belongs to British Columbia's Mount Robson, whose elevation is 3,954 metres, but still only twentieth-highest in Canada. The origin of the Robson name is uncertain. One story is that it may have been named for Colin Robertson (1783-1842), a Hudson's Bay Company trader.

The highest point in Saskatchewan is an officially unnamed elevation in the Cypress Hills, which rises to 1,392 metres near the Alberta border. (The Cypress Hills rise even higher, to 1,465 metres, farther west in Alberta.) Early French voyageurs identified the jackpine as a *cyprès*, and this was rendered as 'Cypress' on the map of the Palliser report of 1857-60.

The highest crest in Manitoba is Baldy Mountain, at 832 metres. It is located in Duck Mountain Provincial Park, 60 kilometres northwest of Dauphin.

The highest peak in the Northwest Territories is officially unnamed, although referred to as 'Mount Nirvana' in the alpine literature. Called that in 1965 by William J. Buckingham, a mountain climber, it rises to 2,773 metres. The mountain is in the Ragged Range, southwest of the South Nahanni River. The range was named in 1960 by Hugh S. Bostock for the characteristic ruggedness of its summits. At an elevation of 2,764 metres, Mount Sir James MacBrien, 30 kilometres to the north of Mount Nirvana, is usually given the honour of being the highest in the Northwest Territories, but it is short by 9 metres. A native of Port Perry, Ont., MacBrien (1878-1938) was a distinguished soldier and commissioner of the RCMP, 1931-8. The highest point in the Arctic Archipelago is Barbeau Peak, named in 1969 for the distinguished anthropologist and folklorist Marius Barbeau (1883-1969).

The highest spot in Ontario, 95 kilometres north of Sudbury, was determined only in 1972 when Ishpatina Ridge, with an elevation of 693 metres, was found to be 28 metres higher than Ogidaki Mountain. The latter, near Sault Ste. Marie, was declared in 1966 to be the highest elevation.

Before that, Tip Top Mountain near Lake Superior, at 640 metres, was considered the highest. In the Ojibwa language, *Ishpatina* means 'high hill.'

The highest summit in Québec, at 1,652 metres, is Mont d'Iberville in the Torngat Mountains. This name was given in 1971 by the Commission de toponymie du Québec for Pierre Le Moyne d'Iberville (1661–1706), who led many ruthless expeditions in North America, including a destructive rampage in St. John's and the Avalon Peninsula of Newfoundland in 1696–7. In 1981, the Newfoundland Geographical Names Board ascertained that the peak so named was on the Québec–Labrador boundary, and decided that a name more suitable to that region's history should be assigned to the peak. The board gave it the name Mount Caubvik in honour of one of the five Inuit who accompanied George Cartwright, a trader on the Labrador coast, to England in 1772. So it is no coincidence that the heights of the highest points in Québec and Newfoundland are identical: they are the same feature, but with two quite different names.

On the island of Newfoundland, the highest elevation, at 814 metres, is an unnamed peak in the Lewis Hills in the Long Range Mountains. The summit is 40 kilometres southwest of Corner Brook, and only 6 kilometres from the Gulf of St. Lawrence.

The highest land in Nova Scotia is White Hill, a treeless peak with an elevation of 532 metres on the North Barren of the Cape Breton Highlands, 17 kilometres west of Ingonish.

Prince Edward Island's highest elevation is only 142 metres above sea level, and is located in Lot 67, Queens County. The community on the hill is rather oddly named, being composed of two words suggesting a place lower than its surroundings: Glen Valley.

In 1899, W.F. Ganong determined New Brunswick's highest elevation (820 metres) and named it Mount Carleton for Thomas Carleton (1736–1817), the first lieutenant-governor of New Brunswick. In 1969, a warden from a private fishing lodge drove me to the base (465 metres) of the mountain, and told me it would take 2½ hours to walk to the top. After 1¾ hours, I had reached its summit, and spent another hour viewing the grand vistas. Later, I asked the warden why he had not told me I could easily reach the top in less than two hours. In his reply, he revealed his respect for the mountain and his perceptive judgment of my nature: 'I wanted you to enjoy the climb without worrying how far it was to the top.'

How Our National Parks Got Their Names

The names of Canada's national parks reflect a variety of origins.

Some derive from a dominant local community (Banff, Revelstoke) or a physical feature (Riding Mountain, Gros Morne). Others come from a leading characteristic within the park's area (Glacier) or purpose (Wood Buffalo), while some convey a general description (Pacific Rim, Cape Breton Highlands).

Canada's aboriginal languages contributed a number of park names (Kouchibouguac, Kluane), with one of them, Auyuittuq, being the only park name specially created to identify a park.

Rocky Mountains Park was the name given 100 years ago to the first reserve set aside in Alberta for the education and enjoyment of the nation. Subsequently the park area was enlarged, until 1930 when it was renamed Banff, an identification it had had informally for several years. Banff is the name of a Scottish town and county, and was given in either 1883 or 1884 to a CPR station a little east of the present townsite, established in 1886 by George Stewart, the park's first superintendent. Although Banff is closely linked to Lord Strathcona and Lord Mount Stephen, it is not certain if either influenced its choice as a station name; the latter was born in Banffshire.

Jasper, created in 1907, took its name from Jasper House, a North West Company trading post founded in the early 1800s. The post had been named for Jasper Hawes, who ran the post in 1817.

The name Yoho, given to a river, a mountain, a station, and a pass, as well as the park, is usually equated with the Cree for 'wonder' or 'excitement.'

The name Kootenay – the park embraces the headwaters of the Kootenay River – may have been given by Blackfoot Indians to describe the 'people of the water' in the language of the Kootenay Indians. The 'ay' spelling was fixed in 1864 by Frederick Seymour, first governor of British Columbia, to differentiate it from Kootenai, the form used in the United States.

Mount Revelstoke – the park encloses some spectacular topography of the Selkirk Mountains – was named in 1914 for the city of the same name; the latter had been named in 1886 for Lord Revelstoke, head of a British banking house that had provided some of the financing for CPR construction. Glacier, also in the Selkirks, was created in 1886 and contains more than 100 glaciers.

Waterton Lakes, on the Alberta–Montana border, dates from 1895. The lakes were named in 1858 by Thomas Blakiston for a noted British naturalist, Charles Waterton. The three lakes are joined by narrows called Dardanelles and Bosporus.

Wood Buffalo is Canada's largest park. It was established in 1922 to protect a small herd of wood buffalo and to provide a reserve for a larger herd of plains buffalo transferred from Wainwright, Alta.

Saskatchewan's Prince Albert National Park is north of the city of Prince Albert, which was named for the consort of Queen Victoria. Grasslands in southern Saskatchewan represents one of Canada's major ecosystems.

Riding Mountain, which occupies the rugged landscape west of Lake Manitoba, was created in 1930 and takes its name from the park's highest elevation. Riding Mountain probably derives its name from Indian pack trails used by the early explorers.

The names of two parks in southern Ontario (St. Lawrence Islands, Georgian Bay Islands) merely indicate their locations. Pelee is named for a prominent point extending into Lake Erie; the French word *pelée* means 'bald' or 'denuded', a description given to the point in the early 1700s.

Pukaskwa, Ontario's newest national park, is located on the north shore of Lake Superior in the area of the Pukaskwa River. The name's origin is uncertain, with 'fish cleaning place' being the most plausible. There is also a story that the name recalls an Indian's killing and burning of his wife. The name is pronounced 'PUK-a-saw.'

Québec has three national parks. La Mauricie is on the west side of Rivière St-Maurice, a name given in the eighteenth century for the Sieur de la Fontaine, Maurice Poulin. The river had been named 'Rivière de Fouez' in 1535 by Jacques Cartier for a French family named Foix; it was also known as the 'Rivière des Trois-Rivières.' Forillon embraces the most easterly part of the Gaspé Peninsula. The name is said to relate to the practice of fishermen using fires to attract fish or to alert ships to dangers in navigation.

The latest Québec park, Mingan Archipelago, consists of a cluster of small islands on the north shore of the St. Lawrence, 160 kilometres east of Sept-Îles. The name Mingan was long thought to be the Montagnais word for 'wolf'; more recently, the preferred derivation is that it comes from a Breton word to describe the islands' topography, 'rounded stone.'

New Brunswick has two national parks. Fundy is on the north shore of the Bay of Fundy. The name is likely a corruption of 'fendu,' from the French name for Cape Split at the entrance to Minas Basin. Kouchibouguac, near Richibucto, was created in 1971. Taken from the Kouchibouguac River, the name derives from the Micmac expression *Pijeboogwek*, 'river of the long tideway.'

Cape Breton Highlands, the older of Nova Scotia's two national parks, takes its name from the most northerly part of Cape Breton Island. Cape Breton may have been named in the early 1500s for the fishermen from Britanny. Kejimkujik was created in 1964. Its largest lake, Kejimkujik Lake, has a Micmac name of uncertain origin. Nova Scotians pronounce it 'KEJ-im-KOO-jik,' 'KEJ-ma-KOOJ,' and 'KEJ-a-ma-KOO-jee.'

Terra Nova in Newfoundland takes its name from a river and a lake, both derived from the Latin for 'new land.' Gros Morne is north of Corner Brook in the Long Range Mountains. Gros Morne, from the French for 'great height,' is the highest point in the park, rising to 806 metres.

Kluane in the Yukon is on the east flank of the spectacular St. Elias Mountains, which are interspersed with impressive icefields and glaciers. The name, pronounced 'KLOO-aw-nee,' means 'whitefish place' in Tlingit. The new Northern Yukon park name simply indicates its location.

Nahanni is a corridor along 300 kilometres of the South Nahanni River, a wild and turbulent tributary of the Liard River in the Northwest Territories. Nahanni in Athapaskan means 'people of the west.'

Auyuittuq was established as a park on Baffin Island in 1972. Its Inuit name means 'place that does not melt' in reference to its most prominent feature, the Penny Ice Cap.

A Medley of Favourite Names

Do you remember this sonorous phrase of the 1950s and 1960s: 'Jack Pickersgill, the honourable member for Bonavista–Twillingate'? The two place names spoken together are quite melodious, and conjure up pleasant images.

The town of Bonavista is located at Cape Bonavista, 130 kilometres northwest of St. John's, Nfld. The name of the cape is one of Canada's oldest, possibly having been given in 1500 by the Portuguese explorer Gaspar Corte-Real for Boa Vista, one of the islands of Cape Verde off Africa's west coast. The town of Twillingate, situated on South Twillingate Island in Notre Dame Bay, is 140 kilometres northwest of Bonavista. It was named by French fishermen for Pointe de Toulinguet, at the entrance to the harbour of Brest, in Brittany, France.

Today Twillingate is joined to Gander in the name of a federal riding, while Bonavista is part of the riding of Bonavista–Trinity–Conception.

These pleasant, musical names have inspired me to select my two favourite place names from each province and territory.

Two names in Nova Scotia that I particularly like are Antigonish and Pubnico. Antigonish, the home of St. Francis Xavier University, takes its name from the Micmac phrase *Nalegitkoonech*. Its meaning may refer to the way two rivers enter Antigonish Harbour parallel and close together. The usual translation, 'where branches are torn off,' probably refers to the site of the town, and to an entirely different Micmac phrase.

Pubnico, 35 kilometres southeast of Yarmouth, is at the head of Pubnico Harbour. The 15-kilometre-long harbour has several communities on each side having Pubnico as part of their names. Among these are Lower West Pubnico, Middle West Pubnico, West Pubnico, Upper West Pubnico, Lower East Pubnico, Centre East Pubnico, Middle East Pubnico, and East Pubnico. The name comes from the Micmac *Pogomkook*, meaning 'dry sandy place.'

Rustico is my favourite in Prince Edward Island. It forms part of the names of several farming and fishing communities on the shores of Rustico Bay. Named for René Rassicot, who came from Normandy in 1724, Rustico became the local form by 1774.

I also like Strathgartney, the name of a provincial park 17 kilometres west of Charlottetown. In 1846, Robert Bruce Stewart selected the name for his homestead, naming it after a valley in Perthshire, Scotland.

Among my favourites in New Brunswick is Nackawic, a village at the mouth of Nackawic Stream. The name is derived from the Maliseet *Nelgwaweegek*, suggesting 'straight water,' because of the way the stream entered the St. John River before the river was dammed.

Kouchibouguac is a little village on the north bank of the Kouchibouguac River, 40 kilometres southeast of Chatham. In 1971, Kouchibouguac National Park was created along the seashore from Kouchibouguac Bay to Richibucto Harbour. The name means 'river of the long tideway' in Micmac.

Sorel, where the Richelieu flows into the St. Lawrence northeast of Montréal, is my favourite Québec place name. The site was granted in 1672 to Pierre de Saurel, a captain of the Carignan-Salières Regiment. Called Sorel before 1787, it was renamed William Henry for Prince William Henry, future King William IV, who visited the place that year. The name Sorel was restored in 1860, and by 1906 archivist Pierre-Georges Roy reported that William Henry was totally forgotten.

My other Québec choice is the town of Maniwaki, located on the Gatineau, 125 kilometres north of Ottawa.

The name, derived from the Algonquin for 'Mary's land,' was given in 1849 by the Oblates of Mary Immaculate.

Ontario's Muskoka evokes images of summer cottages, boat trips among the islands, and rambles in the woods. Lake Muskoka got its name from an Ojibwa chief called Misquuckkey, who signed two treaties surrendering the Muskoka area to Britain in 1815.

I like both the name Cobalt and the indomitable spirit of the people of this Northern Ontario town. Silver was discovered there in 1903. Dr. Willet Miller, the provincial geologist, went to the site in 1904 and chose the new railway station's name from traces of the mineral cobalt found near the station.

During my childhood, I read the name Wawanesa on a calendar in my grandfather's house and imagined the home of the national insurance company would be a great city on the Prairies. In fact, the village, 35 kilometres southeast of Brandon, Man., has never been the metropolis I envisioned, and now has fewer than 500 people. The name probably means 'whippoorwill' in Algonquin; the bird is mentioned in Longfellow's poem *Hiawatha* as *Wawonaissa*.

Minnedosa, a town 45 kilometres north of Brandon, is a mellifluous name created in the 1880s by a miller named J.S. Armitage. He derived it from the Siouan words for 'swift water,' in reference to the fast-flowing Little Saskatchewan River. The river, which flows through the town to the Assiniboine River, was officially called Minnedosa River in 1928, but the preferred local name, Little Saskatchewan River, was restored in 1980.

Assiniboia, 90 kilometres south of Moose Jaw, is one of my favourite Saskatchewan names. Formerly called Leeville for the first postmaster, Hubbard Lee, the town was renamed in 1913 for the former District of Assiniboia, part of the North-West Territories from 1882 to 1905. The district was named for the Assiniboine River, itself given for the Siouan tribe whose name in Ojibwa means 'one who cooks with (hot) stones.'

The centre of Saskatchewan's potash industry is Esterhazy, a town of 3,000 south of Yorkton. The name honours Court Paul Esterhazy, a Hungarian who, while living in New York in the 1880s, resolved to help his fellow countrymen working in desperate conditions in the Pennsylvania coal mines. He bought land north of the Qu'Appelle Valley and persuaded many of the miners to move there. Later they were joined by farm families who came to Canada from Hungary.

Pincher Creek is one of my favourite names in Alberta because it reflects the spirit of the wild west. The town of Pincher Creek, with a population of 3,650, is located on a tributary of the Oldman River, 85 kilometres west of Lethbridge. Its name recalls the loss of a pair of pinchers (an older form of 'pincers') in the 1860s by a prospecting party. Another story is that some of the prospectors were murdered by Indians. When the remaining members of the party came across the grisly site, they found the pinchers of one of their murdered friends near the creek.

Between Edmonton and Red Deer is the attractive town of Lacombe, with a population of 5,600. The name recalls the missionary Albert Lacombe (1827–1916), who ministered to the Indians and the Métis from Winnipeg to Lesser Slave Lake during the last half of the nineteenth century. In the 1880s, Father Lacombe, who was partly of native origin, helped the CPR reach an amicable settlement with Chief Crowfoot for the construction of the railway across Blackfoot lands in southern Alberta.

One of my favourite British Columbia names is Kitwanga, a village in the Skeena River valley between Terrace and Hazelton. I find its lilting syllables, 'KIT-wawn-GAH,' especially pleasant. The name is derived from a Gitksan phrase meaning 'people of the place of rabbits.'

Keremeos, a village of 700 about 40 kilometres southwest of Penticton, is another name I find appealing to the ear.

It was derived in 1887 from an Okanagan Indian phrase, possibly meaning land 'cut across in the middle' or 'a flat cut through by water' in reference to the Similkameen River crossing the flat lands near the village.

No name sings more about the Yukon and the gold rush days than Klondike. The name, from *Thron-duick*, meaning 'hammer water' in an Athapaskan dialect, relates to the practice of putting stakes in the river to catch salmon. Ironically, the fishing was so poor in the summer of 1896 that George Carmack and his party abandoned their stakes to prospect in one of the Klondike's tributaries, the legendary Bonanza Creek, and the stampede was on.

Whitehorse has a certain beauty and strength in its name. It is said that the first miners travelling down the Yukon River in 1880-1 thought the rapids at the site of the present city looked like the manes of white horses. The builders of the White Pass and Yukon Route first called the townsite Closeleigh in 1899, but reverted in 1900 to the name that had already become widely known throughout the world. In the early 1950s, Whitehorse replaced Dawson City as the territorial capital.

Another territorial capital, 1,000 kilometres to the east, has another of my favourite names. Gold was discovered on the north shore of Great Slave Lake in 1934. The community that sprang up at the site was named Yellowknife, derived from the name of a band of Athapaskans who made tools from yellow copper. Yellowknife, with a population of almost 15,000, has been the capital of the Northwest Territories since 1967.

Nanisivik is a small mining community on Baffin Island. It was developed in 1974 by Nanisivik Mines to extract lead, zinc, silver, and cadmium. In Inuktitut, the name means 'place where people find things.'

So there you have my twenty-four favourites. Half are names of native origin, revealing my preference for names derived from the languages of the first peoples of Canada.

There are no -ville, -town, -burg, or saint names among my selections. Although some are names transferred from other parts of the world, none is derived from places in England or the United States.

Riding Names: Some Gratifying, Some Grating

In my previous essay, I wrote that Bonavista–Twillingate used to be a favourite name of mine for a federal electoral district, and that Twillingate is now preserved in the name of Gander–Twillingate. Wrong. This was a riding name prior to the redistribution that came into effect in July 1988. The new riding is called Gander–Grand Falls.

The 1988 redistribution provided for 295 federal ridings, up from 282 in the previous Parliament. Of these, 107 were new riding names, while 188 were the names of the redistribution as they existed in July 1988. The next redistribution, based on the 1991 census, will result in 301 ridings, and many new names.

The creation of boundaries and the selection of names for each electoral district are the responsibility of commissions appointed in each province and territory following each decennial census. When a new district corresponds generally to a riding at the time the reports are tabled in the House of Commons, a sitting member's riding name may be changed or restored by a private member's bill. Following an election, a change in a riding name can also be made through a private member's bill.

After redistribution based on the 1971 census, more than forty name changes were accepted by the House of Commons. After the 1988 redistribution, there were eighteen changes to the new riding names to June 1993. The commission in Québec had recommended Chapleau for the area of the former district of Gatineau, but the sitting member successfully appealed in the summer of 1988 to have it renamed Gatineau–La Lièvre. In New Brunswick, the commission suggested Chaleur in place of Gloucester, in order to reflect the francophone majority and to commemorate the name given by Jacques Cartier in 1534. However, Gloucester, in continuous use since 1867, was retained after an appeal by the sitting member. Subsequently, in June 1990, it was changed to Acadie-Bathurst. In 1989, the riding of Restigouche was changed to Restigouche-Chaleur.

Among the most attractive riding names are single place names that clearly identify the specific area of the country. Examples are Athabasca, Peterborough, Kamloops, Wetaskiwin, Gaspé, Burlington, and Yukon. Also pleasing are riding names comprising two names that produce a musical cadence. Among these are Brome-Missisquoi, Rimouski-Témiscouata, Cariboo-Chilcotin, Regina-Wascana, Winnipeg-Transcona, Edmonton-Strathcona, Fundy-Royal and Timmins-Chapleau. But as more place names are added to a riding name, it becomes rather cumbersome, as in the case of Wellington-Grey-Dufferin-Simcoe and Swift Current-Maple Creek-Assiniboia.

St. John's East and St. John's West have been in use since 1949, but as several communities in the former are *west* of the latter, new names such as St. John's-Torbay and Avalon-Placentia might now be better choices. In the previous redistribution, Humber-Port au Port-St. Barbe was an awkward title. Its successor is equally awkward: Humber-St. Barbe-Baie Verte.

Prince Edward Island has four ridings, each with a single name chosen from a prominent physical feature. Although the single name has its appeal, each is rather vague as to the geographical area to which it refers. For example, Charlottetown would be more explicit than the current name of Hillsborough.

Only one riding name in Nova Scotia has been changed from the last House of Commons - Dartmouth-East Halifax becoming Dartmouth. Several of the province's eleven riding names are either vague or inappropriate. And some – Central Nova and South West Nova – are rather bland. Pictou–Musquodoboit would be an interesting alternative for the first, Yarmouth–Digby–Annapolis for the second. Two riding names are really misleading: the Cape Breton Highlands are for the most part not in the riding of Cape Breton Highlands–Canso but in Cape Breton–The Sydneys; and the main section of the Annapolis Valley is in South West Nova, not in Annapolis Valley–Hants.

In New Brunswick, Fredericton has been substituted for York–Sunbury, Miramichi for Northumberland–Miramichi, and Beauséjour for Westmorland–Kent. The province's commission believed that parts of the previous names could be confused with riding names in Ontario. That was also the reason for suggesting Chaleur in place of Gloucester. Beauséjour, derived from the name of a French fort built in 1750, destroyed by the British in 1755 and restored as a national historic park in 1926, is a pleasant name for this riding which takes in a large area to the north and east of Moncton, including the university town of Sackville on the Isthmus of Chignecto.

The commission in Québec has shown sensitivity for traditional names, with twenty-two of the original sixty-five names of 1867 still in use. Among the more pleasing to the ear are Bellechasse, Charlevoix, Portneuf, Richmond–Wolfe, Shefford, and Terrebonne.

The commission tried to restore the boundary of Québec-Est to include the heart of the old city, with Québec-Ouest to the west of it. But opposition persuaded the commission to maintain Langelier, in use only since 1966, in the downtown area, and to continue the use of Québec-Est to the *west* of the city centre. In 1990, Langelier became Québec (French) and Quebec (English). For the two, Québec-Limoilou and L'Ancienne-Lorette-Vanier might be suitable alternatives. Lachine-Pointe-Claire might be preferable to Lachine-Lac-Saint-Louis. Sainte-

Foy-Sillery would be more explicit than Louis-Hébert. As Montréal-Nord is the only municipality comprising Bourassa, the municipal name might be a better choice.

Some Ontario ridings have pleasant single names, such as Waterloo, Kent, and St. Catharines, but these also serve as components of other riding names. For Welland-St. Catharines-Thorold, Welland-Thorold should suffice.

Ontario has two unwieldy riding names. Hastings-Frontenac-Lennox and Addington, formed from parts of these three counties, is quite a mouthful. For it, Napanee-Bancroft might be a suitable alternative. For the ungainly Wellington-Grey-Dufferin-Simcoe, an innovative choice might be Ontario Highlands, the word *highlands* being widely used to describe this highest part of southern Ontario.

Wellington is also a component of the names of other ridings: Guelph-Wellington and Perth-Wellington-Waterloo. For the latter, perhaps Stratford-Listowel might be a pleasing alternative.

Simcoe North could well be named Huronia, which has strong historical associations with the Midland and Orillia areas, and is used as a regional name in weather reports. Quinte would be an apt substitute for Prince Edward-Hastings. There is a riding in Ontario called simply Ontario. Although it has a long electoral association with the area northeast of Toronto, the riding might be more suitably called Whitby-Pickering. The area of the new riding of Ottawa South would be understood better if the name Ottawa-Alta Vista were used, since the neighbourhood traditionally known as Ottawa South is actually in the riding of Ottawa Centre.

Brandon-Souris and Lisgar-Marquette are two of my favourite riding names in Manitoba. Unfortunately, four of the province's electoral districts have directional names, with two of them, Winnipeg North Centre and Winnipeg South Centre, being unwieldy and unimaginative. These names date back to 1924, but the choice of Assiniboine, Fort Garry, or Kildonan for these ridings would better reflect the rich history of the Red River Valley.

The fourteen electoral districts of Saskatchewan were completely reorganized in 1988, with only three names of the previous redistribution being kept. The commissioners avoided directional words, choosing instead such excellent names as Regina–Qu'Appelle, Regina–Lumsden, Saskatoon–Dundurn, and Saskatoon–Humboldt. The commissioners gave no reason in their report for selecting Saskatoon–Clark's Crossing. The choice of this former railway-siding name is mystifying; Saskatoon–Warman would more clearly identify the area of the electoral district. Mackenzie, used since Saskatchewan became a province in 1905, is a name more closely associated with the present Northwest Territories. Melfort–Nipawin might be better for this riding in east-central Saskatchewan. Mackenzie could then be considered for the present Western Arctic, which is somewhat of a misnomer for a riding almost entirely south of the Arctic Circle.

There are some colourful names in Alberta outside the two main cities. Crowfoot, from the name of the legendary Indian chief, and Wild Rose, from the provincial flower, are imaginative, although neither is especially identified with its respective area. Wild Rose, in the rural area north of Calgary, was first named Kneehill by the Alberta commission, but when it was pointed out that this is the name of a district municipality mostly in the adjacent riding of Crowfoot, the commissioners chose Wild Rose instead.

Eleven of Alberta's twenty-six electoral divisions have directional components in their names. The commission claimed that geographical directions are more easily recognized by the public, but Calgary–Glenmore (from Glenmore Reservoir and Glenmore Trail) might be just as effective as Calgary Southwest, and Calgary–Blackfoot (from

Blackfoot Trail) as well understood as Calgary Southeast. It is pleasing that Edmonton–Strathcona was kept. Perhaps better alternatives could be found for Edmonton Northwest, Edmonton Southeast, and Edmonton Southwest.

British Columbia has some of the most evocative riding names, such as Vancouver–Quadra, Nanaimo–Cowichan, Comox–Alberni, and Esquimalt–Juan de Fuca. Kelowna might be an excellent substitute for Okanagan Centre. The addition of Merritt to Okanagan–Similkameen–Merritt is awkward. For Fraser Valley East, perhaps Chilliwack–Abbotsford might be a suitable title, and for Fraser Valley West, perhaps Langley–Matsqui.

In 1988, one riding name in Québec was given both English and French forms: Mount Royal and Mont-Royal, which are statutory forms of the city's name. In 1990, four more Québec ridings were assigned bilingual names. Otherwise, forms like Témiscamingue, Trois-Rivières, and Bonaventure–Îles-de-la-Madeleine are respected in English. Elsewhere almost all the official French names of ridings with directional words are translated, such as Edmonton-Nord-Ouest, York-Sud–Weston, Kootenay-Ouest–Revelstoke. However, Southwest Nova and Central Nova are not translated. Some names are awkward hybrids, such as Cap-Breton Highlands–Canso, St. John's-Ouest, and Fraser Valley-Ouest. Adding accents to some names (e.g., Nanaïmo, Végréville, Malpèque) goes against the official forms of these names. Saanich–Gulf Islands is an excellent name, but interpreters should not have to burden their listeners with Saanich–Les Îles-du-Golfe. Mysteriously, names with *river* (e.g., Peace River, Beaver River, Rouge River) have been saved from translation. In 1993, the Ontario riding of Timiskaming became Timiskaming–French River, in both English and French.

Twillingate may be gone from the name of a federal

riding, but we still have such distinctively Canadian names as Skeena, Medicine Hat, Nunatsiaq, Nickel Belt, Hochelaga-Maisonneuve, and Bonavista–Trinity–Conception.

Scrutinizing Political Issues and Language Problems

Of Hatters and Capers, Townies and Trifluviens, and Other Monikers People Call Themselves

Haligonian, Montrealer, Torontonian, Winnipegger, Calgarian, Vancouverite. These are abbreviated ways of referring to the residents of places, but there does not appear to be a distinct term in English to describe such words. Some dictionaries offer *gentilitial* and *ethnonym*; they are rarely used. Some writers have used *ethnic* and *dominym*, but these are not very helpful in explaining the concept of people living in particular locations. I have suggested *patrial*, without success, as well as *nopitacs* (names of people in towns and cities), but these have not been received with much enthusiasm either.

Francophones use the word *gentilé* to describe such words as Parisien, Montréalais, and Gaspésien. The Commission de toponymie du Québec has ruled on the correct *gentilés* for most municipalities in the province; these terms are listed in their masculine and feminine forms in the government's municipal directory, *Répertoire des municipalités du Québec*.

Since the English language does not appear to have a specific word to describe the residents of a geographically defined place, I will use the word *gentilé* (pronounced 'JAWN-tee-LAY').

All the provinces and the Yukon have distinctive *gentilés* in English. Only the Northwest Territories does not lend itself to a *gentilé*. Some, such as Newfoundlander and Albertan, possess a very strong sense of historical and cultural identity.

The *gentilé* for a person from the province of Québec – Québécois – is spelled both Quebecer and Quebecker in English. The term Québécois in English usually implies a Quebecer whose language and culture are distinctively French Canadian.

In Québec, a few *gentilés* have been endorsed in English, such as Shawvillite, but most follow the rules of the French language; for example, Ayer's-Cliffois. Several are derived from Latin roots, such as Trifluvien (Trois-Rivières) and Fidéen (Sainte-Foy). A few reflect the place's history, with Havre-Saint-Pierre having Cayen from its Acadian roots, and Sainte-Élisabeth having Bayollais, from the full name of St. Elizabeth of Bayolle.

There are five different ways to form a *gentilé* in English; the final syllable of the source name usually provides a clue as to whether it should take *n*, *ian*, *onian*, *ite*, or *er*. Names ending in *a* and *ia* add an *n*: thus we have Oshawan, Mississaugan, Kelownan, and Victorian. An exception is a resident of Kenora, dubbed a Kenoraite by Mark Orkin in *Speaking Canadian English*, published in 1970, and confirmed in 1989 by the editor of the *Daily Miner and News*.

The *onian* suffix is almost always used by places ending in *ton*, resulting in Monctonian, Frederictonian, Edmontonian, and Hamiltonian. A number of other places, with no apparent relationship in their final syllable, also have the *onian* ending, such as Haligonian (Halifax), Amherstonian, Galtonian, Woodstonian, Saskatonian, and Pictonian, the last for both Pictou, N.S., and Picton, Ont. While Orkin gives Bellevonian for Belleville, the editor of the city's newspaper, *The Intelligencer*, stated in 1989 that he prefers the term Bellevillian.

In the United States, names ending in *town* usually form their *gentilé* by using *tonian*, but the preference in Canada may be to add *er*, as in Charlottetowner.

Names ending in consonants and silent vowels form their *gentilé* in one of three ways: by adding *ian*, *ite*, or *er*. Usually names with *ville* drop the *e* and add *ian*, but sometimes such names also end in *ite*, especially if residents suspect that an outsider may invert the *a* and the *i* and refer to someone from Brockville as a 'Brockvillain.'

At one time, names with *ian* were likely more numerous in Canada than those with *ite*, but *gentilés* with the latter seem to be growing in popularity. Vancouver residents were once known as Vancouverians, but Vancouverite is now universally used. Among Canadian *gentilés* with the *ian* ending are Stratfordian, Fort Erian, Bathurstian, Yarmouthian, Sudburian, Kamloopsian, and Calgarian. People in Peterborough are called Peterburians. The residents of the capital of Newfoundland have been referred to as St. Johnsians, but they are really better known as 'townies,' as opposed to 'baymen,' who live in outport communities.

Names with *ite* include Sydneyite, Granbyite, Cornwallite, Guelphite, St. Catharinite, Brandonite, Thompsonite, and Banffite, but these forms are rarely used. Orkin adds Barrie-ite, Sooite, and Nanaimoite, but they are not common.

Among names with the suffix *er* are: Saint Johner, Lunenburger, Summersider, Londoner, Winnipegger, Flin Floner, Medicine Hatter (often simply Hatter), and Yellowknifer.

Some places may not have a *gentilé* at all, especially those with two or more words, like Niagara Falls, North Bay, and Thunder Bay, although some people have told me that Niagara Fallsian, North Bayite, and Thunder Bayite have been used by the media. Residents of Thunder Bay may be more familiar with Lakeheader.

Sometimes the residents of several adjacent communities use a common *gentilé*. The people living on the island of Montréal between Dorval and Sainte-Anne-de-Bellevue are collectively called West Islanders. Residents from Port Hawkesbury to Glace Bay in Nova Scotia, and all the villages and crossroad communities in the region, are proud to be called Cape Bretoners or Capers. Labradorian is a badge of honour for the long-time residents of Newfoundland living on the mainland side of the Strait of Belle Isle. The people of Prince Edward Island are known simply as Islanders, sometimes as Spud Islanders. A Gulf Islander is someone who has settled into the bucolic life on one of the islands in the Strait of Georgia between mainland British Columbia and Vancouver Island.

A *gentilé* that does not seem to fit any pattern is Moose Javian, although it may be related to Shavian, used in referring to the literature and ideas of George Bernard Shaw. I have also seen the form Moosichapishanisippian, given in jest by a former Reginan.

Many people are not above composing humorous *gentilés* for various places, among them being Niagara Felons, Fort Erings, Smithereens, and Terracites (for Smithers and Terrace, towns in northwestern British Columbia), and Bragg Crickets (for Bragg Creek, a community near Calgary).

There appears to be a large number of places, with populations exceeding 10,000, that do not possess a *gentilé* in English. They include Corner Brook, Nfld.; Truro, N.S.; North Battleford, Sask.; Grande Prairie, Alta.; Prince Rupert, B.C.; and Whitehorse in the Yukon.

Pronouncing Names as the Locals Do

Queries are often received by names offices as to the correct pronunciation of certain place names. Other than suggesting the range of suitable pronunciations, names authorities invariably avoid making pronouncements on pronunciation.

Some names permit a range of pronunciation. While there may be a general preference for three pronounced syllables for Toronto ('t-RAHN-to'), to call it 'TRAWN-to' is not considered entirely wrong. Fredericton is called 'FRE-drick-tun' and 'FRE-dik-tun,' and Calgary is pronounced both as 'KAL-ga-ree' and 'KAL-gree,' with the first in each instance appearing to be more correct and the latter somewhat sloppy diction.

Sometimes, the same name is pronounced differently in separate parts of Canada. Dalhousie University in Halifax and Dalhousie, N.B., are usually pronounced 'dal-HOW-zee,' but the street in Ottawa and the township in Lanark County, Ont., are heard as 'dal-HOO-zee,' and Port Dalhousie in St. Catharines comes out as 'port-da-LOO-zee.'

In Prince Edward Island it is 'SOO-ree' for the village of Souris, but the same name in Manitoba is 'SOO-ris.' In Nova Scotia, Greenwich is pronounced 'GREE-nich,' in New Brunswick it is 'GREEN-wich,' and in Prince Edward Island, 'GREN-ich.' The various Elgins in Canada are usually pronounced with a hard 'g,' but Elginburg near Kingston, possibly influenced by American pronunciation, is usually called 'el-JIN-berg.' St. John's, Nfld., is generally pronounced 'sint-JAHNZ,' but Saint John, N.B., comes out with equal emphasis on both syllables: 'SAYNT-JAWN.'

Some names have had distinctly separate developments in terms of spelling and pronunciation, with the spelling form appearing to be unlike the pronounced form. Such a name is Magaguadavic River in New Brunswick, which was fixed in its spelling at the end of the eighteenth century, but has long been pronounced as 'ma-ga-DAY-vee.' The pronunciation of the nearby Digdeguash River ('DIG-gi-dee-WASH') is reflected in the spelling of another New Brunswick name: Diggity Stream.

There is the classic case of Bay d'Espoir in Newfoundland, which has long been ironically known as 'BAY-dis-PAYR.' Such a pronunciation, however, reflects seventeenth-century French speech. Etobicoke, the name of the city on the west side of Toronto, may come out of a stranger's lips as 'ee-TO-bee-KOKE,' but locally the form 'e-TO-bee-KO' is preferred. The name of the largely rural city of Nanticoke, on Lake Erie near Simcoe, is pronounced 'NAN-te-KOKE.' Stouffville, near Toronto, is called 'STO-vul,' not 'STOOF-vil.' Gleichen in Alberta is pronounced 'GLEE-shun,' although the CPR financier for whom it was named, Count Albert Gleichen, pronounced his name 'GLAYK-kun.'

There are some names whose pronunciations seem to be designed to separate the local residents from outsiders. An example is Newfoundland, which is locally pronounced 'NYOO-fin-LAND,' not 'noo-FOWND-land.'

A pronunciation that certainly distinguishes a westerner from an easterner is the mouthing of Saskatchewan. A native barely enounces the first, third and fourth syllables, saying 'sis-SKATCH-eh-win,' while an easterner is inclined to stretch it out to 'sas-SKA-choo-wahn.'

Another interesting example is North Gower, a village south of Ottawa. Residents rhyme it with 'door,' not 'power.' Antigonish in Nova Scotia is 'an-ti-ga-NISH' not 'an-TIG-a-nish.' Maugerville east of Fredericton is called 'MAY-jer-vil' not 'MAW-ger-vil.' One can never be too certain about the letter 'g' in names. Margaree in Nova Scotia has a hard 'g' but Langenburg in Saskatchewan has a soft 'g' in the middle and a hard 'g' at the end.

Many names of French origin, or native names that have come into English via French, have acquired some unusual pronunciations. Examples are Rencontre, Nfld. ('ROWN-kown-ter'); Pouce Coupe, B.C. ('poos-KOO-pee'/'poos-KOO-pay'); Quesnel, B.C. ('kwe-NEL'); Des Joachims, Que. ('de-SWI-shah'); Bienfait, Sask. ('BEEN-FAYT'); Quirpon, Nfld. ('KAR-poon'); and L'Ardoise, N.S. ('LORD-WAYZ').

In this sampling there are no doubt some perceived errors in the suggested pronunciations. As well, some unusual names have been omitted because of uncertainty about local preferences. In this group are Trepassey and Aquaforte, Nfld.; Gabarus and Necum Teuch, N.S.; Apohaqui, N.B.; Breadalbane, P.E.I.; Nicabong and Kazabazua, Qué.; Caesarea, Wanapitei, and Schreiber, Ont.; Melita, Man.; Wauchope, Sask.; Provost, Alta.; Ucluelet, Tsawwassen, and Skidegate, B.C.; Rancheria, Y.T.; and Aklavik, N.W.T.

As with personal names, we all like to pronounce places as they are spoken by the local population. The stranger is usually forgiven, but announcers on radio and television are expected to know the local preferences.

Sorting Out the Sound-alikes and Look-alikes

Do you, like many of us, sometimes get confused by the look-alike, sound-alike cities of St. John's and Saint John? Do you know which one is the capital of Newfoundland? Do you wish they had more distinctive names so you would have no doubt which is which?

St. John's, the chief city and capital of the province of Newfoundland, traditionally takes its name from the discovery of its harbour by John Cabot on the feast of St. John the Baptist, 24 June 1497. The first reference to the name of the harbour, *R de Sam joham*, is on a map produced by Pedro and Jorge Reinel in 1519. The earliest mention of the city's name in its present form is in a letter written in 1527 by John Rut, who led an English expedition to North America that year. With a name having 460 years of continuous use, St. John's could hardly be expected to surrender it for another.

The St. John River in New Brunswick was named

Rivière saincte-Jean by Sieur de Monts and Samuel de Champlain on 24 June 1604. The city that developed at the river's mouth in one of Canada's most scenic settings – albeit often fogbound – was known as Menagoueche ('little peninsula') by the Micmacs and Maliseets, and also as Ouigoudi ('village') by the Maliseets. On the arrival of the Loyalists in 1783, two names came into use: Parr Town (for John Parr, governor of Nova Scotia) and Carleton (for Sir Guy Carleton, then commander-in-chief of British forces in North America, not for his brother, Thomas Carleton, first lieutenant-governor of New Brunswick). Two years later, Ward Chipman, a distinguished lawyer and politician, proposed the name Saint John for the first incorporated city in what is now Canada, and for the county extending along the Bay of Fundy shore.

In English, St. John's and Saint John receive some distinction in their spellings, the Newfoundland city having an apostrophe *s*, and the New Brunswick city always having its *saint* spelled in full. There is also a small distinction in their pronunciation: 'sint-JAHNZ' for the one; and, with equal emphasis on the two syllables, 'SAYNT JAWN' for the other. The unofficial French form, Saint-Jean, is often used for both, but it is not authorized for federal maps and documents.

The city of Saint-Jean-sur-Richelieu, 40 kilometres southeast of Montréal, is the site of the well-known Collège militaire de Saint-Jean. Once known in English as St. Johns, this form was officially dropped in 1962.

No doubt many people groaned in 1965 when Premier Joseph Smallwood of Newfoundland announced that Hamilton River in Labrador would be renamed Churchill River for Winston Churchill, ignoring the fact that Canada already had another major river by the same name. The latter, which drains much of northern Saskatchewan and Manitoba, had been named in the late 1600s for John Churchill, Duke of Marlborough, a governor of the Hudson's Bay Company. An effort to have the name Hamilton River restored, while maintaining the widely known Churchill Falls, did not gain support.

About 1985, I read a report that a person from Toronto was going to Sackville, N.S., to give a lecture. My first reaction was that this was an error for the home of the well-known liberal arts institution, Mount Allison University, in Sackville, N.B. However, the unincorporated, loosely connected community from Lower Sackville through Middle Sackville to Upper Sackville, some 20 kilometres north of Halifax, was actually meant. The unofficial name, Sackville, has been gaining acceptance for this whole complex of some 25,000 people. While Nova Scotians may have no difficulty distinguishing their place from the little town of 5,500 people just over the border in the neighbouring province, the same name for two towns in the Maritimes will surely be confusing for other Canadians.

One of the most duplicated names in Canada is Windsor. As well as the city in southwestern Ontario, there are incorporated towns of Windsor in Québec and Nova Scotia, and an unincorporated community in New Brunswick. In Newfoundland, the town of Grand Falls–Windsor has a population of 14,700.

In 1973, the Ontario town of Durham in Grey County fought unsuccessfully to prevent the use of the same name for the new Regional Municipality of Durham, which embraces the county of Durham and parts of the counties of Ontario and Northumberland east of Toronto. Ontario has several other towns and villages whose names are duplicated by counties elsewhere in the province: Dundas, Simcoe, Perth, Prescott, Hastings, and Wellington.

The discrepancy of having the original community of Pickering, Ont., within the municipal boundaries of the town of Ajax and not those of the town of Pickering was partly resolved in 1987 by having it renamed Pickering

Village. In 1975, the old community of Caledon, 50 kilometres northwest of Toronto, was renamed Caledon Village to distinguish it from the town of Caledon. The same may be necessary to differentiate the small community of Nanticoke within the boundaries of Canada's biggest rural city, also called Nanticoke, which fronts on Lake Erie south of Brantford.

There are some confusing duplications in Western Canada too, starting with the largest city on the west coast, Vancouver. In 1886, it was incorporated as a city, duplicating not only the name of the biggest island on the coast, but also the name of a city in the state of Washington.

Other confusing community names in the west include: Hudson Bay in Saskatchewan; Dawson Creek in British Columbia and Dawson City in the Yukon; Sidney in British Columbia, often spelled the same as Sydney, N.S.; Cochrane in both Alberta and Ontario; and Fort Saskatchewan, an Alberta town 25 kilometres northeast of Edmonton.

Although duplicated names will always be with us (Québec – city and province; Kenora, Ont., and Canora, Sask.; Chatham and Newcastle in both Ontario and New Brunswick), there are really not too many confusing look-alikes in Canada. Fortunately, for populated places with similar names, the correct postal code can usually prevent mail from going to the wrong look-alike.

Standard Spelling Eliminates Confusion ... Usually

Almost every place name in Canada has a single correct form, but some, like St. Catharines and Edmundston, are commonly misspelled. Some names of features crossing provincial boundaries (Timiskaming/Témiscamingue) or international boundaries (Kootenay/Kootenai) have variant spellings in the different jurisdictions. And a few names are spelled differently by postal or rail authorities.

One of the most frequently misspelled place names is St. Catharines, Ont. When I saw this spelling on a railway station sign in the 1950s, I assumed it was a mistake. Surely, I thought, there is only one proper way to spell St. Catherines. This assumption was reinforced by a sign pointing to St. Catherine's Cathedral.

The confusion about St. Catharines is compounded by a dispute over the origin of the name. The usually accepted story is that it refers to the first wife of Robert Hamilton, Catharine Askins Robertson, who died in 1796. A reference the same year to a church at 'St. Catherines' led Catharine Welland Merritt to claim in 1926 that the honour belonged to Catherine Butler, wife of the leader of Butler's Rangers. In doing so she chose to ignore an 1875 biography of her own grandfather, William Hamilton Merritt, which stated that the community was formally named in 1809 for the wife of Robert Hamilton, a prominent public official in the Niagara Peninsula in the late 1700s and early 1800s.

Another suggestion made in the 1920s that the name was given in honour of Catharine Prendergast, who married William Hamilton Merritt in 1815, has no substantiation. All that may be said is that both 'Catherine' and 'Catharine' were names commonly given to girls in the late 1700s, a time when Empress Catherine the Great of Russia (1729–96) held court on the world stage.

Another name frequently misspelled is Edmundston, N.B., named in 1851 for Sir Edmund Walker Head, lieutenant-governor of New Brunswick from 1848 to 1854. Numerous references – maps, CN express slips, road signs, and advertising items – refer to 'Edmunston.'

During a test for a professional position with Energy, Mines and Resources in 1976, nine applicants were asked to locate Edmundston on a map; seven of them wrote 'Edmunston.' The omission of the 'd' may be partially explained by its phonetic weakness in a series of four consonants.

The proper spelling of Athabasca is difficult to pin

down. Strong cartographic, documentary, and local practice in the 1800s favoured Athabasca, the form adopted
in 1882 for one of the four new districts of the North-
West Territories. In 1902, the Geographic Board of Canada
changed the name of the district, lake, and river to Athabaska, in keeping with international rules of nomenclature
requiring a hard 'c' to be spelled with a 'k.'

After Alberta was established as a province in 1905,
usage there favoured Athabasca, especially for the town
120 kilometres north of Edmonton. But when the Geographic Board of Canada was asked by postal officials in
1912 to review its decision, it reaffirmed the 'k' spelling
it had made ten years earlier.

The sinking of H.M.C.S. *Athabaskan* during the Second
World War, with great loss of life, reinforced the spelling
'Athabaska.' In 1947, however, the newly formed Geographic Board of Alberta adopted the form Athabasca and
urged the federal board to concur. On receiving the agreement of Saskatchewan, in which more than half of Lake
Athabasca is located, the Geographic Board of Canada
agreed to Athabasca in 1948 for the river, lake, town, falls,
mountain, and glacier, and several other minor features
in Alberta.

Confusion about the spelling continues today, although
prominence in the news of the Athabasca tar sands has
encouraged acceptance of the 'c' form.

On the north side of the Fraser River, 50 kilometres east
of Vancouver, is the community of Whonnock, a name
derived from the humpback salmon. In 1939, the Geographic Board respelled it Whonock, after the name of a local
Indian reserve. Railway and postal officials also opted for
the one 'n' form, even though predominant local use had
been Whonnock for a hundred years. After a concerted
campaign in the 1960s, the extra 'n' was restored in 1969.

Also in the Fraser Valley, 40 kilometres farther east, the

city of Chilliwack and the surrounding township of Chilliwhack were spelled differently for many years. But after a poll in 1979, the two were united into the District Municipality of Chilliwack on 1 January 1980. The name is from a Salish tribe; its meaning is uncertain.

In the late 1860s, Governor Frederick Seymour of British Columbia decided that one means of distinguishing American and British territories was to create different spellings for names of some prominent rivers. He decreed that the names Okanagan, Kootenay, and Yahk should be used in British Columbia to contrast with their spelling south of the border: Okanogan, Kootenai, and Yaak. These distinctions remain.

The spelling of 'Temiskaming' has caused much confusion, especially since this is *not* one of the three official forms of that name. Temiskaming was formerly part of the name of the Ontario Northland Railway (Temiskaming and Northern Ontario Railway). This spelling is also commonly used in the names of businesses in New Liskeard, Haileybury, and Cobalt.

The territorial district and federal electoral district in Ontario are spelled Timiskaming. The county and the federal electoral district in Québec are Témiscamingue. The lake's name is officially Timiskaming in Ontario and Témiscamingue in Québec. Adding to the confusion, the Québec town on the Ottawa River, 60 kilometres northeast of North Bay, is Témiscaming. So much for ensuring standard spelling for names with the same origin!

In 1982, the New Brunswick government legislated a change in the spelling of the town of Shippegan to Shippagan, but made no correction to several other names with Shippegan: the territorial parish, bay, park, beach, channel, and harbour. Canada Post spelled the name Shippegan from 1850 to 1852, 1862 to 1900, and 1955 to 1982, when it adopted Shippagan. The post office was Ship-

pigan from 1852 to 1862 and 1900 to 1955, a common form
of the name for associated features in the 1800s, and the
form still used by Canadian National. Confusing, isn't it?

Who's to Blame for Mistake Names?

Mistakes happen – and are sometimes corrected. It would
have been the Meach Lake Accord if Québec's Commission
de toponymie had not repaired a century-old error in 1982.
The lake got its name from pioneer settler Asa Meech,
but it was misspelled Meach on an 1870 map and it took
years (and appeals from Meech's descendants) to get it
changed.

There are countless such tales of Canadian place names
altered through spelling mistakes, bad handwriting, faulty
translation, or confusion between sound-alike words.
Often these alterations become commonly used and then
prove very difficult to correct. Indeed, until about 1970,
names authorities were reluctant to correct past errors at
all, citing long usage in public documents, land descriptions, and maps. In recent years, however, serious requests
to correct the spellings of names have been greeted with
more sympathy, as in the case of Meech Lake.

In 1765, Monckton Township was established at The
Bend on the Petitcodiac River in New Brunswick, and
named for British general Robert Monckton (1726–82),
who was lieutenant-governor of Nova Scotia from 1755
to 1759, and James Wolfe's second-in-command at the capture of Québec in 1759. The following year, when New
Brunswick's townships were redesignated parishes, the 'k'
was accidentally dropped. As a village grew at the 'Hub
of the Maritimes,' it became known as Moncton, which
was incorporated as a town in 1855, and a city in 1890.
In March 1930, the city council passed a motion to rename
the city Monckton, but fierce opposition ensued, and the
motion was quickly rescinded in April.

During the early 1600s, a small river in Nova Scotia's Annapolis Valley was named for Louis Hébert, the apothecary who accompanied Pierre du Gua de Monts to Port Royal, and Samuel de Champlain to Québec. When the Loyalists arrived in the late 1700s, they anglicized the name to Bear River. And that, to this day, is the name of the river, and a village of 900, nestled in a picturesque and surprisingly rugged setting, 12 kilometres inland from Digby.

Bury Head, near Alberton, P.E.I., was Barry Head on a 1770 plan and Berry Head on charts and maps from 1845 to 1966, when it was respelled to recall the site of an early graveyard. Some long-entrenched mistakes, on the other hand, are unlikely ever to be changed. Carleton Place, Ont., was named in 1830 for Carlton Place, a street in Glasgow, with its erroneous spelling probably influenced by nearby Carleton County. Aquaforte, Nfld., was initially Aguafuerte, but mapmaker Robert Robinson changed the Portuguese original on a 1669 map and the change stuck. And Geary, N.B. (pronounced 'GA-ree'), was settled about 1810 by Loyalists who called their settlement New Niagara for the Ontario peninsula where they had lived for a few years. Adopting the last two syllables of the contemporary pronunciation, 'NY-a-GA-ree,' they shortened the name to New Gary, and then to Geary.

Some incorrect names have been accepted without complaint. Around the turn of the century Joseph Chowaniec moved from Ledoux, Minn., and settled north of Weyburn, Sask. When his neighbours accepted his proposal in 1905 to name their new post office Ledoux, Chowaniec submitted it to the Post Office Department in Ottawa. A clerk misread his writing, however, and put Cedoux on the date stamp. It is Cedoux, Sask., to this day.

Cedoux is just one of many place names misspelled by government clerks and surveyors. On the Canadian National line, 30 kilometres northeast of Calgary, is the community of Kathyrn, named after Kathryn McKay, whose father donated the town site in 1911. The letters *r* and *y* were transposed on a sign in 1913, and the Post Office Department continued the erroneous – but by then adopted – form in 1919. As if to complete a circle, two Alberta place-names books published in the 1970s and the 1980 *Canada Gazetteer Atlas* all missed the long-established spelling of the community, referring to Kathryn rather than Kathyrn.

Philip and Helen Akrigg, authors of *British Columbia Place Names* (1986), have their summer home at Celista, B.C., on Shuswap Lake, northeast of Kamloops. In their book, they note that in 1908 postal authorities suggested Celesta, the name of a creek 35 kilometres to the northeast near the head of Seymour Arm, as the name for a post office. But an error in handwriting resulted in Celista. It became the name of the community, and was later adopted for the names of the creek and nearby Celista Mountain.

One of the main tributaries of the Ottawa River is the Madawaska River, which rises in Algonquin Park and joins the Ottawa River at Arnprior. Its name derives from the Matouoüescarini, a tribe encountered by Champlain in 1613, and it was called the Mataouachita on a 1703 map by Guillaume Delisle, and Mataouaschie in Sir David W. Smith's *Topographical Description of Upper Canada* in 1799. If the river's name had evolved solely from its rendering in early cartographic and documentary sources, its spelling might have become more like Matawashita. But its present spelling may have been influenced by New Brunswick's unrelated Madawaska River, which means 'land of the porcupine' in Maliseet. As early as 1725, engineer Gaspard Chaussegros de Léry spelled the Ontario river Matouasca, almost the exact spelling, Madouasca, used for the New Brunswick river on Delisle's 1703 map. In Alexander Sherriff's 1831 report of the lands between the Ottawa River and Georgian Bay, map maker William Henderson rendered the name Madaouaska. The present spelling was settled in surveyors' reports in the 1840s and on Thomas Devine's *Government Map of Canada* in 1861.

Two places in Ontario's Madawaska Valley have curious 'mistake' names. Camel Chute, at the head of Centennial Lake, 70 kilometres upriver from Arnprior, is called after a local sawmill owner named Campbell (a name sometimes pronounced 'KAM'l' in Eastern Ontario). When surveyor Duncan McDonell visited in 1846 he wrote Campbells Chute in his notes. When another surveyor, John Haslett, visited the next year, he first wrote Camels Chute in his diary but corrected it the following day to Campbells Chute. In 1890, the post office at the site was named Dubreuil, but difficulty with its spelling and pronunciation led local settlers in 1903 to ask for a name change – to Camel Chute. The MP for Renfrew South, Aaron A. Wright, mildly objected to the misspelling, but thought his protest of no consequence, 'since Camel Chute is shorter, it might be better to spell it that way, particularly since they have petitioned for it.'

Fifty-five kilometres farther up the Madawaska River from Camel Chute, on Kamaniskeg Lake, is the village of Barry's Bay. For a century and a half, local residents, historians, and names experts have puzzled over who the Barry was who left his name on the bay. In my *Geographical Names of Renfrew County* (1967), I mentioned the early name of 'Barry's Camp on the Bay.' And in the second edition (1989), a number of other claims were offered: Barry was a foreman for McLachlin Brothers, an Arnprior-based lumber company; he was a hunter or trapper; there wasn't a Barry at all but a field of blueberries!

But then, in 1992, I found in the Archives of Ontario the misfiled microfilm of surveyor John Haslett's diary of his 1847 survey east from Kamaniskeg Lake and back again. Going east, he crossed 'Barry's Bay'; returning west, he crossed the Madawaska at lumberman William Byers's hay farm. As there were no settlers in the area before the late 1850s, I have concluded that Haslett wrote Barry's Bay when he should have written Byers's Bay, and the error was continued on maps and in survey records thereafter. It may be sheer coincidence, but even today Barry's Bay is often pronounced as though it were Byers Bay.

Acronyms ... Such as Kenora, Koocanusa, and Snafu Creek

Acronyms are words formed from one or more first letters of other words. Many do not reveal that they are not original words in their own right, such as Fiat, Sabena, and snafu.

Place-name specialists have been more lenient in their interpretation of 'acronym,' allowing names compounded from any parts of other words to qualify; for example, Mantario, a village in Saskatchewan, from Manitoba and Ontario.

Acronyms as place names are rare in Eastern Canada, but they have attained full flower in the Prairie provinces. There are at least fifty-six in Alberta, fifty-one in Saskatchewan, and thirty in Manitoba. Few are known beyond their own neighbourhood, and many have disappeared altogether, though the names persist in the old records.

Perhaps the best known of Canada's acronyms is Kenora, a town of some 10,000 inhabitants in northwestern Ontario.

In the late 1800s, the area on the north side of the Lake of the Woods was known as Rat Portage. In 1880, the postal designation Keewatin was chosen to replace that of Rat Portage, and in 1886 another post office between present Keewatin and Kenora was named Norman for a son of a manager of the M & O Lumber Co. In 1904, a proposal was made to unite Keewatin, Norman, and the eastern part of Rat Portage into a single municipality known as Kenora. The name Kenora was adopted, but Keewatin remained a separate incorporated town.

Quetico Provincial Park is between Kenora and Thunder Bay. Some sources indicate that the name Quetico is derived from Quebec Timber Company, but other suggested origins from French and native languages leave the correct meaning in doubt.

Another well-known acronym is Arvida, once a town in its own right, but since 1975 a neighbourhood of Jonquière in the Saguenay–Lac St-Jean region of Québec. Arvida was established in 1926 by the Aluminum Co. of Canada, and named for its president, Arthur Vining Davis.

Batawa, 7 kilometres north of Trenton, Ont., is derived from the Bata Shoe Company, plus an ending common to many Ontario names, such as Ottawa. Nolalu, 45 kilometres southwest of Thunder Bay, Ont., is named for the Northern Land and Lumber Company. Noranda, part of the Québec city Rouyn–Noranda, is a contraction of North Canada.

When the Libby Dam was built in the state of Montana in 1967, a huge reservoir resulted, backing up the Kootenay (Montana's Kootenai) River into British Columbia. People and municipal authorities on the Canadian side favoured Lac Morigeau (after a pioneer). The preference of Montana residents, Koocanusa Lake, was determined to be the overwhelming favourite. In 1968, the United States and Canadian authorities approved Koocanusa, an acronym formed from Kootenay, Canada, and U.S.A.

Estevan, a city of some 9,000 people in southern Saskatchewan, derives its name from parts of the names of George Stephen and William Van Horne, the first two presidents of the CPR. North of Yorkton, Sask., is the town of Canora, named in 1905 from the first and second letters of Canadian Northern Railway.

Among Alberta places deriving their names from other

words are: Cadomin (Canadian Dominion Mine), Marwayne (W.C. Marfleet and Wainfleet, England), and Westlock (two settlers, Westgate and Lockhart).

Two of Manitoba's better-known acronyms are Transcona (Transcontinental Railway and Strathcona) and Sherridon (Sherritt and Gordon).

The names Snafu Creek and Tarfu Creek in the Yukon are derived from acronyms of Second World War vintage. The first means, 'Situation normal, all fouled up'; the second, either 'That's always really fouled up' or 'Things are really fouled up.'

Use of acronyms as place names has been generally out of favour since the late 1960s. Provincial and territorial names authorities have usually rejected the cute and casual proposals submitted to them, preferring instead names having local or historical significance.

Avoid the Apostrophe ... But Not Always

The name Hudson's Bay has a long history, dating from the ill-fated voyage into this great body of water by Henry Hudson in 1610, and the establishment of the Governor and Company of Adventurers of England in 1670.

In 1900, the Geographic Board of Canada published the following decisions: 'Hudson bay and strait; inland sea and passage communicating with the Atlantic (not Hudson's).' Canadian maps and charts then began using the name Hudson Bay. Subsequently, the Hudson Bay Railway was built to Churchill, Man., the Hudson Bay Mining and Smelting Company was opened in Flin Flon, Man., and the town of Hudson Bay (pop. 2,400) was established in Saskatchewan, east of Prince Albert.

The board's decision was in keeping with one of its basic rules adopted in 1898, which stated that the possessive form of names should be avoided whenever it could be done without destroying the euphony of a name or changing its descriptive application. The rule added that, if the possessive were retained, the apostrophe should be dropped.

This rule had universal application in the English-speaking world, having been adopted in the 1890s by names authorities in Britain and the United States (while respecting well-established names with the apostrophe), and later in this century by Australia and New Zealand. But in the 1970s, the rule was amended in Canada to permit the apostrophe where it was well established and in current use.

There are several names in Canada with the apostrophe. Examples are St. John's in Newfoundland, St. Mary's District Municipality in Nova Scotia, Campbell's Bay in Québec, and Lion's Head in Ontario. These forms are in keeping with the principle of geographical naming that names established in the statutes by other authorities must be accepted without change.

In the first half of this century, the Geographic Board severely restricted the use of the possessive 's,' even when local communities had long used it – such as Reed's Point, Moore's Hill, and so on.

Occasionally, in its zeal to trim the 's' from names, the board erroneously modified some personal names ending in 's.' In Lanark County, Ont., the board imposed Wood Lake, Nichol Lake, and Bower Lake even though these were derived from the family names Woods, Nichols, and Bowers. Corrected forms were entered into the official records in the 1960s.

The practice of omitting the apostrophe from supposed possessive names varies from community to community. The town of Smiths Falls, Ont., was established in the statutes in 1882 with the apostrophe, but that spelling was ignored locally. The Ontario Municipal Board noted the discrepancy in 1968, and required the Ontario legislature to pass an act recognizing the form Smiths Falls before allowing the issuing of debentures. The town of St. Marys, Ont., similarly did not use the apostrophe, although recorded in the statutes, so it was also changed to its current form in 1968. Subsequently, the town authorities persuaded the St. Mary's Cement Company, whose trucks are seen throughout the province, to omit the apostrophe from its name.

The Geographic Board did not accept the statutory name Lion's Head, Ont., in 1913, but substituted Lionhead. The form Lion's Head, widely used for local services and the post office, was restored in 1940. Nearby is the local community of Colpoy's Bay. The adjacent bay (on the Georgian Bay side of the Bruce Peninsula) was named about 1820 for Sir Edward Colpoys, but the local residents, unaware that the terminal 's' is not possessive, use an apostrophe. The name Barry's Bay, Ont., is used by the residents, but the post office is Barrys Bay. The name Burk's Falls, Ont., is also used widely, although it is ignored by the postal authorities and the weekly newspaper, the *Burks Falls–Powassan Almaguin News*.

The apostrophe is rarely used in official names in western and northern Canada. Some writers refer to Gibson's Landing, a charming community on Howe Sound northwest of Vancouver, where the popular TV show *The Beachcombers* was based, but the village has long been known as simply Gibsons. The municipality of Hudson's Hope in northeastern British Columbia was established in 1965, but the post office, opened in 1913, remains Hudsons Hope.

The Lions Gate Bridge and the village of Lions Bay both derive their names from 'The Lions,' distinctive peaks that look down on Vancouver. Some writers incorrectly add an apostrophe either before or after the 's' in such names.

Names like Kingsport, Kingscourt, and Kingston do not

require the apostrophe, although they are composed of two or more fused words, with the prefix suggesting a possessive characteristic. The same approach should be followed with names such as Kings Point, Kings Lake, and Kings Head since, as proper names of features in the public domain, they no longer have any possessive connotation. It follows that names like McLarens Landing, Fiddlers Elbow, and Haydens Corners also do not require apostrophes.

In dealing with names ending in 's' with the possessive apostrophe, it is wise to avoid autocratic rulings. If residents insist on using St. Kyran's, Heart's Content, Colpoy's Bay, and Ayer's Cliff, names authorities should be flexible enough to grant them their wish.

When Names Become Politically Incorrect

Pride and fond memories of homelands and heroic leaders across the sea have influenced many place names in Canada. London, Ont., New Glasgow, N.S., New Denmark, N.B., and Labrador's Churchill River are just a few of the hundreds of examples. However, several name changes took place after Canadians fought wars against countries where some of our names originated, or when foreign heroes were subsequently judged monstrous.

Of the three international powers Canada has been at war with in this century – Germany, Italy, and Japan – only Germany has been the source of a large number of Canadian place names. By the beginning of the First World War, there were some thirty names of probable German origin in southwestern Ontario between Stratford and Guelph – the largest concentration of German settlement in Canada. Only three of these were changed during wartime. In 1941, a small community between Guelph and Waterloo, originally called New Germany, was renamed

Maryhill after the Blessed Virgin Mary and the hill on which St. Boniface Church was located. Two years later, German Mills – 6 kilometres south of downtown Kitchener – was changed to Parkway.

The most significant change in the area occurred during the First World War, when the city of Berlin – now Kitchener – was forced to choose a name more in tune with the ideals of freedom, democracy, and service to the British Empire.

Berlin was named about 1833, and by 1911 it was the ninth-largest city in Ontario, with 70 per cent of its population having German roots. But by 1916, the name Berlin had become untenable, observed co-authors John English and Kenneth McLaughlin in *Kitchener: An Illustrated History*. Berlin's city council and business leaders feared the patriotism of its residents would be judged suspect, and worried about the loss of business. In February 1916, the council appealed to the Ontario legislature for permission to change the name, but it was told to hold a plebiscite first. On 19 May, 3,057 Berliners cast their ballot, with approval for a name change winning by only eighty-one votes. But the change to Kitchener was not made without considerable resentment and acrimony, especially in the German parts of the city.

The selection of a new name was not easy. From thousands of submissions, the choice was reduced to six, all of which were rejected by council because of widespread criticism. Council also defeated a subsequent proposal to amalgamate with Waterloo, and instead drew up another list of six names: Adanac, Benton, Brock, Corona, Keowana, and Kitchener. The last was in honour of Lord Horatio Kitchener, a British military hero who drowned on 5 June 1916. Only 892 residents voted, with Kitchener receiving the most votes, 346, followed closely by Brock with 335. The remaining four received only 48, with 163 voters spoiling their ballots by writing in either Berlin or Waterloo. Considering the turnout too low to justify a change, opponents gathered twice as many signatures in opposition. Regardless, council changed Berlin to Kitchener on 1 September 1916.

Not all efforts to change names have succeeded. In one case, a place name with Nazi overtones – Swastika, Ont. – was successfully protected from assault by toponymic purifiers. The town was named in 1906 by Bill and Jim Dusty, who discovered the first gold in Northern Ontario while exploring for silver on behalf of investors in Tavistock, Ont. A cross on a charm worn by a woman from Tavistock inspired Bill Dusty to name the mine Swastika, meaning 'good luck' in Sanskrit. Both the village and railway station adopted the name.

But during the Second World War, the swastika – the official emblem of the Nazis – came to symbolize misery and the annihilation of millions. Consequently, Ontario's Minister of Highways announced in 1940 that Swastika would be changed to Winston in honour of the British prime minister, Winston Churchill. In defiance, residents of Swastika tore down the new sign, replacing it with another that read: 'To Hell with Hitler. We had the swastika first.' As John Wroe reported in *Saturday Night* magazine in 1986, 'the government never got its wish and, as the war receded in memory, the controversy diminished.' Since then, occasional efforts by outsiders to get rid of the name have been fiercely resisted by the residents of Swastika, now part of the town of Kirkland Lake.

In 1936, a Canadian Pacific station across the Fraser River from Hope, B.C., was named Petain in honour of Marshal Henri Philippe Pétain, a distinguished French military leader during the First World War. Four years later, when the free world learned that Pétain had collaborated with Nazi Germany, Canadian Pacific changed that station name to Odlum for Maj. Gen. Victor Odlum, then a widely respected Canadian diplomat. But Mount

Pétain in the Canadian Rockies and two lakes and a township in Québec remain as honours to the French military genius.

Military and political leaders who fought with the Allied powers during the Second World War have also had their names affixed to geographical features in Canada. Among those honoured was Marshal Joseph Stalin, whose name was given to a mountain in north-central British Columbia and a township 50 kilometres southwest of Sudbury. But in 1985, names scholar Jaroslav Rudnyckyj and members of the Ukrainian Canadian Committee urged federal and provincial politicians and names boards to expunge the name Stalin – a person they deemed to be one of history's most notorious criminals – from Canadian maps. In the Ontario legislature, the cause was taken up by MLA Yuri Shymko, whose private member's bill to substitute Hansen Township for Stalin Township was unanimously passed on 6 November 1986. The new name honours Rick Hansen, who gained international attention during his Man in Motion wheelchair tour to promote research into spinal cord injuries and other physical disabilities.

In April 1987, the British Columbia government followed Ontario's lead, changing Mount Stalin to Mount Peck in honour of Don Peck, a widely respected trapper, guide, and outfitter who lived at Trutch, B.C., on the Alaska Highway, from 1949 to 1963. But the change was not universally endorsed. The Vancouver Historical Society protested the rewriting of an important part of Canadian history. And one Fort Nelson resident wrote to several newspapers to say that Stalin had been honoured because he stood steadfast in defeating the German foe, and that to eliminate his name from our maps was no better than the Stalinesque purges impugned by the free world.

Some names now gracing our cities, towns, mountains,

and rivers may well be judged politically incorrect in the years to come, and vigorous efforts may yet be made to replace them with names considered more appropriate to Canada's vision of peace, tolerance, and freedom. However, since I am not a revisionist at heart, I hope such demands for change will be rare.

Hot and Bothered by 'Disgusting' Names

Place names derived from words deemed coarse or unspeakable have frequently aroused sensitivity, offence, and even hostility. Over the years new names and masked substitutes have been used to banish names found vulgar or suggestive.

In 1924, almost 200 property owners in Victoria asked city council to change the name Foul Bay to Gonzales Bay, after a nearby point named in 1790 for the first mate of a Spanish sloop. The change was opposed by Post No. 3 of the Native Daughters of British Columbia, among others, but the matter was raised again ten years later by Henri Parizeau, long-time director of the Canadian Hydrographic Service on the west coast. He claimed that 'it would be in the interests of the public in general, that this most objectionable name around the coast of Victoria, should be changed to a more respectable and decent name.' It was a sentiment shared by the Foul Bay Community Association, which noted that the name was 'a constant source of offence to residents and of ridicule by non-residents and tourists,' as well as an obstacle to residential development. Finally, in November 1934, with endorsements from the councils of Victoria and Oak Bay and provincial authorities, the Geographic Board of Canada authorized the change. However, the boundary street between the two municipalities is still Foul Bay Road.

Two names of native origin on Vancouver Island, Kokshittle Arm and Kowshet Cove, were also changed in 1934, to Kashutl Inlet and Cullite Cove. George G. Aiken, provincial member of the Geographic Board, assumed a high moral tone in support of the changes. 'We do not wish,' he wrote, 'to have the daughters of our present and future citizens feel embarrassment in naming the locations of their homes. We cannot, as a Board, in this democratic country, ignore these objections of the citizenry when these objections are founded on good taste and reason.'

In 1959, a family of Finnish extraction named Suni advised the Ontario Department of Municipal Affairs that the word *paska* ('shallow' in Cree), as in the name Paska Township, was a vulgar word for excrement in Finnish. Municipal Affairs advised the Department of Natural Resources of the offending names Paska Lake and Paska Creek, and Canadian National Railways of the embarrassingly named Paska siding. As there was a large Finnish population in Northern Ontario, especially in Thunder Bay, 250 kilometres to the southwest, the township, the siding, and the two natural features were renamed – after the Suni family.

Other examples of undesirable names changed include, in Newfoundland, Distress becoming St. Bride's, Famish Gut switching to Fairhaven, Scilly Cove opting for Winterton, and Turk's Gut changing to Marysvale. In Alberta, Meighen (pronounced 'mean') was changed to Viking. And in New Brunswick, Pisarinco became Lorneville.

A century ago, Sipweske was a growing village near Brandon, Man. Its name, derived from a Cree word, had unwelcome overtones of intemperance to some. According to Penny Ham in her *Place Names of Manitoba* (1980), Wawanesa ('whippoorwill'), adapted from Wawonaissa in Longfellow's *Hiawatha*, was then introduced. The village of 482 is the headquarters of the Wawanesa Mutual Insurance Company.

Crotch Lake is a reservoir on Ontario's Mississippi

River, 110 kilometres southwest of Ottawa. In 1848, land surveyor John Harper gave it the euphemism Cross Lake, and this was endorsed by the Geographic Board in 1941. I made a field survey of the area in 1965, and found the original name was universally preferred. It was subsequently reaffirmed by the Canadian Permanent Committee on Geographical Names.

In 1910, the Lethbridge Board of Trade declared, 'We are certainly very much disgusted with the present name and wish to make a change of some kind.'

The object of the board's disgust was the name of the river on whose banks the city of Lethbridge, Alta., was situated. It was the Belly River, and Lethbridge citizens were convinced that their thriving young city deserved to be set on a river whose name did not engender discomfort and embarrassment. (In those days 'belly' was a word avoided in polite company.) They had campaigned since 1886, but it took almost thirty years to secure a more distinguished appellation.

Alberta's Belly River rises some 20 kilometres south of the 49th parallel in Montana and flows north to join the Oldman River 18 kilometres upstream from Lethbridge. It was given its name during a survey in 1858 by Thomas Blakiston, a member of the Palliser Expedition, and the name first appeared on a map in 1865.

Blakiston derived the name from the Blackfoot *Mokowanis*, meaning 'big bellies,' referring to the local Atsina Indians and equivalent to the name Gros Ventre used by French explorers and voyageurs. Blakiston applied the name Belly to the whole river from its source to its confluence with the Bow River, where the two rivers become the South Saskatchewan River, 90 kilometres northeast of present-day Lethbridge.

Thus when the city of Lethbridge was laid out near a series of rich coal deposits in 1885, it found itself on the east bank of the Belly River.

Just one year later, Minister of the Interior Thomas White visited Lethbridge, and residents asked him to get the name changed. No action was taken, and in 1900, *Lethbridge News* publisher E.T. Saunders – who had earlier found the name historic and euphonious – urged a change, too. He wrote about the discomfort of strangers and the blushing embarrassment of ladies. To get around the problem, he suggested that the St. Mary River, a tributary of the Belly upriver from Lethbridge, be designated the main watercourse, with the Belly as a branch of it. That way, Lethbridge would sit beside the St. Mary.

Six years later (and still no action), Saunders again appealed to the authorities. He claimed the name Belly made Lethbridge appear to be a crude frontier settlement, and this time suggested extending the name South Saskatchewan River to some point upriver from Lethbridge.

In 1910, the Lethbridge Board of Trade wrote a letter to the Department of the Interior proposing the name Alberta River for the entire watercourse, including the present Oldman and South Saskatchewan rivers. The Geographic Board rejected the proposal, stating the new name had no authority based on usage, and noting in any case that the Bow was the principal tributary of the South Saskatchewan. The Board of Trade asked for other alternatives to Belly, but the Geographic Board responded by urging it to canvass local residents for their own alternatives.

The matter languished until 1913, when the Board of Trade again asked the Department of the Interior to replace Belly River with Alberta River, 'a name citizens could call attention to with pride.' But the Geographic Board told the Board of Trade to obtain the views of local authorities and then seek the endorsement of the provincial government. In 1915, the Board of Trade asked Premier Arthur Sifton to approve Alberta River, but Sifton said he preferred Lethbridge River. This new proposal was sent to the Geographic Board, which declined to accept

it. Geologist and Geographic Board member Donaldson
Dowling pointed out that the Oldman River carried con-
siderably more water than the Belly at their confluence,
and suggested carrying the name Oldman River to its juncture with the Bow. This would make the Belly the Oldman's tributary and put Lethbridge on the Oldman. It was
the compromise the Geographic Board approved in August 1915, and thus after many years of appeals, Lethbridge
finally got rid of its Belly River.

Fortunately, the purging of place names has become
quite rare in recent times. People are sometimes astonished
to encounter Bastard Township in Ontario's Leeds
County, but in 1796, when the township was surveyed and
named, Bastard was a respectable surname in England,
and John Pollexfen Bastard was a member of Parliament.
The names of both Bastard Township and adjoining Kitley
Township are derived from the Bastard family seat in
Devonshire.

In 1966, I asked Reeve Gerald Cross of the Township
of Bastard and South Burgess if thought had ever been
given to changing the name. He replied that the question
had been raised with the Department of Municipal Affairs
in Toronto, but when told it would cost $1,200, the council
decided such funds should be spent on more important
matters.

Castle Mountain and Its Thirty-five-Year Eisenhower Hiatus

On 17 August 1858, Dr. James Hector, a naturalist-
geologist with the Palliser Expedition, was exploring the
Bow River valley upstream from present-day Banff. Beside
Vermilion Pass (which now leads to Windermere, B.C.),
he noted a majestic 11-kilometre-long mountain. It reminded him of the great crenellated castles of Britain, and

he promptly named it Castle Mountain.

(Two days later, Thomas Blakiston, another naturalist with the same expedition, assigned the name Castle Mountain to a feature west of present Pincher Creek, which is about 250 kilometres southeast of Banff. However, it was renamed Windsor Mountain in 1915.)

On 9 January 1946, the day before the visit to Ottawa by Gen. Dwight Eisenhower, then Supreme Commander of the Allied Forces in Europe, Prime Minister Mackenzie King, acting on a suggestion from his friend Leonard Brockington, instructed the Geographic Board of Canada to rename Castle Mountain in honour of the illustrious general. Apparently the prime minister had learned that the general had been presented with a castle in Scotland, and Mr. King regarded the presentation of this Canadian 'castle' as a gift of much greater magnitude and significance.

In Alberta, the provincial government was astonished by the arbitrary name change, and proceeded to establish its own names board to make sure that all naming in Alberta henceforth would receive provincial approval. The Alpine Club of Canada called the renaming a sacrilege; and editorials noted that there were many unnamed mountains in the Rockies to which the general's name could have been given.

In the early 1970s, efforts were begun to restore the name Castle Mountain and to assign Eisenhower to another feature. Freeman Keyte, a scientist who was living in Calgary at the time, took the crusade to the Geographic Board of Alberta, members of Parliament, and the Canadian Permanent Committee on Geographical Names. The editor of *The Crag and Canyon* in Banff raised the issue with the provincial minister of culture, and subsequently newspapers in Calgary and Edmonton published many letters urging reinstatement of the name Castle Mountain. The letter writers claimed that the original name embodied the country's ruggedness and independence. The publisher of the *Edmonton Journal*, however, expressed his opposition to the reinstatement.

In February 1975, the Historical Society of Alberta passed a resolution calling for restoration of the name Castle Mountain, and suggested that Eisenhower Peak be given to its most prominent tower. This was endorsed by the Alberta Historic Sites Board, the new provincial names authority.

Because the mountain is in Banff National Park, the matter was referred to Parks Canada, then part of the Department of Indian and Northern Affairs. The name change was approved, but no announcement was to be made until after the United States bicentennial celebrations in 1976. However, the news became known in April 1976 to the *Edmonton Journal*, whose publisher repeated his opposition.

In May 1976, the issue was raised in the House of Commons by former prime minister John Diefenbaker, then an opposition MP. He was strongly opposed to changing the name back to Castle Mountain. Alistair Gillespie, the minister responsible, assured the House that the name Mount Eisenhower would stay. And so it did ... for another three years.

However, immediately after the election of the Conservative government of Joe Clark in May 1979, the Alberta Historic Sites Board took up the issue again. Freeman Keyte, then residing in the Ottawa area, pursued the matter tenaciously with Mr. Clark's office, with the minister responsible for Parks Canada, John Fraser, and with the provincial minister of culture, Mary J. LeMessurier.

Although federal endorsement of the change back to Castle Mountain was finally given in October, Alberta's concurrence was not received until the morning of Thursday, 13 December. On the evening of the same day, Mr. Clark's government was defeated in a non-confidence vote in the House.

This landmark federal-provincial decision restored Castle Mountain, and assigned Eisenhower Peak to its prominent eastern elevation. It also confirmed the name Castle Junction for the intersection of Highways 1A and 93.

In the years since the reinstatement of Castle Mountain, the only reaction received by the committee's names secretariat has been that of enthusiasm and pleasure.

Receiving Names from Overseas and Exporting Names Abroad

Touring the Middle East without Leaving Canada

The Gulf crisis of 1990–1 focused the world's attention on the city of Baghdad, capital of Iraq since 1921. This ancient city of Mesopotamia lies in the fertile valley of the Tigris, only 40 kilometres east of the Euphrates River.

It is one of many historic Middle East cities, regions, mountains, and rivers reflected in Canada's place names. In the late 1880s, the name Bagdad (without the 'h') was given by the Central Railway of New Brunswick to a flag-stop 35 kilometres northwest of Sussex. Although Canadian Pacific abandoned the line in the 1960s, Bagdad remains the name of the small community.

Another ancient city of the Tigris Valley recalled in Canada is Nineveh, once the capital of the Assyrian Empire. Its intricate streets, squares, and a magnificent palace were unearthed by British archaeologists between 1820 and 1851. The farming community of Nineveh, 25 kilometres northwest of Bridgewater, N.S., was settled in the 1840s. There is another locality by the same name on Cape Breton Island, 23 kilometres southwest of Baddeck.

Tales of the mysterious Middle East and stories from the Bible are likely the source of some 140 place names in Canada. About 75 of these occur in Southern Ontario, in an arc from Chatham in the west through Barrie and Newmarket to Belleville in the east. There are clusters of such names in a 40-kilometre radius around both Belleville and Lindsay. Québec, New Brunswick, and Nova Scotia have about a dozen each, with concentrations northeast of Granby, Qué., and around Sussex, N.B. In all of Western Canada, there are only about 15 Middle East names. Only one appears to have been given in the two territories: Ophir Creek in the Yukon.

The giving of Middle East place names in Canada appears to be a nineteenth-century phenomenon. Most were chosen between 1820 and 1885 when much of the naming took place in the Maritimes, Southern Québec, and Southern Ontario. Many towns and villages in Northern Ontario and the West were founded after 1885, when few turned to the Bible or Arabic tales for inspiration.

Many names from the Middle East were given to rural communities or crossroads where Protestant congregations established meeting-houses. When a school, post office, or railway flagstop was established, the leaders of each community encouraged the use of their church name.

The original Garden of Eden, thought to have been in the Middle East near the headwaters of the Euphrates, has also influenced Canadian place names. About 30 kilometres southwest of Antigonish, N.S., are Garden of Eden and Eden Lake. There is also a place called Eden 35 kilometres northeast of Port Hawkesbury, N.S. In Ontario, there is a Garden of Eden 10 kilometres north of Renfrew, an Eden south of Tillsonburg, and an Eden Grove northwest of Walkerton. Eden Mills is east of Guelph, and Edenvale is northwest of Barrie. There is one Eden in Manitoba, 15 kilometres north of Neepawa. In Saskatchewan, the village of Edenwold, 35 kilometres northeast of Regina, was a German settlement when it was named in 1890. Kaleden, B.C., was the winning name in a 1909 contest: a minister combined the Greek word for 'beautiful' with the name of the biblical garden of paradise.

Egypt and Lebanon are also among Canada's place names. Nova Scotia has a place called Egypt Road, and Québec has a place called Égypte. In Ontario, Egypt is just south of Lake Simcoe, Little Egypt is northeast of Goderich, and Lebanon is 35 kilometres northwest of Waterloo. The regions of Ophir and Sheba, in the southern part of the Arabian Peninsula, are both reflected in the names of townships in Northern Ontario. Ophir is also a community 50 kilometres east of Sault Ste. Marie. Sheba was once a Canadian Pacific flagstop northwest of Thunder Bay.

Cairo and Damascus also turn up in Canada. In 1852, a post office called Sutherland's was opened 40 kilometres northeast of Chatham, Ont. In 1896, it was changed to Cario, and respelled Cairo the following year. There is also a Cairo Township in Northern Ontario. Damascus, 30 kilometres west of Orangeville, Ont., dates back to 1872. Another Damascus, 28 kilometres northeast of Saint John, N.B., was named by a surveyor in jest because the tortuous road leading to it reminded him of Paul's conversion on the way to the original Damascus.

The biblical story of Moses leading the Israelites from the Land of Goshen (near the present mouth of the Nile) to the promised Land of Canaan prompted many early settlers to name their communities after one or the other. In the early 1800s, a traveller baptised two places south of Renfrew, Ont., Goshen and Canaan when he was denied food in the first, but was offered nourishment in the latter. Both names were adopted by their respective communities, but ironically only Goshen survived.

There are two places called Goshen in New Brunswick – one 25 kilometres northwest of Sussex, and the other 25 kilometres east of Sussex. To avoid confusion, the latter used the name Sheba for its postal address, but the community remained Goshen. The Canaan River in New

Brunswick spawned several community names: New Canaan, Canaan Road, Canaan Station, and Canaan Rapids.

Nova Scotia has two places called Goshen. One is 65 kilometres northwest of Halifax. The other, 27 kilometres south of Antigonish, was so named because twice a year two members of the community were sent to Halifax for supplies, much like the sons of Jacob went to Goshen in Egypt to buy corn. There are also three places called Canaan in Nova Scotia, and another called New Canaan.

Before he died, Moses viewed the promised land from atop Mount Pisgah, a height of Mount Nebo east of Jericho and the River Jordan. Mount Pisgah, 13 kilometres northeast of Sussex, N.B., offers an excellent view of lush fields in the valleys below. Mont Nebo, 75 kilometres west of Prince Albert, Sask., was at one time a Canadian National flagstop.

Mount Hebron, Mount Hermon, and Mount Carmel are also prominently mentioned in biblical stories. Hebron in Labrador was established by Moravian missionaries in 1829. In New Brunswick, Mount Hebron is 10 kilometres north of Sussex. In Ontario, New Hermon is 20 kilometres east of Bancroft. Mount Carmel occurs as a place name five times in Ontario, and is the name of an Acadian community in western Prince Edward Island.

Mount Zion was the fabled city of David on the eastern ridge of Jerusalem. New Brunswick has New Zion and Zionville, and Ontario has six places called Zion, as well as Zion Hill and Zion Line.

Jerusalem itself was widely known as Salem. This name occurs six times in Ontario; there is also a Salem Corners southwest of Lindsay. Salem, New Salem, and Salem Road can all be found in Nova Scotia.

Among prominent places of the Holy Land mentioned in the Old and New testaments are Bethany, Bethel, Bethesda, Siloam, Galilee, Jordan, and Ebenezer. All of these are reflected in Canadian place names, especially in Ontario. The places where Jesus was born and raised are not commemorated in English-speaking Canada, but both occur in Québec: Bethléem is 50 kilometres east of Sherbrooke, and Nazareth is a neighbourhood of Rimouski.

The community of New Sarepta, 40 kilometres southeast of Edmonton, was named in 1905 after Sarepta, now known as As Sarafand in present-day Lebanon. Sardis, a community in the District Municipality of Chilliwack, B.C., was named in 1888 for the site of one of the seven churches of Asia, in the western part of present-day Turkey. There is a Troy 25 kilometres west of Hamilton, Ont., another 25 kilometres east of Chatham, Ont., and yet another 10 kilometres northwest of Port Hawkesbury, N.S.

The Plain of Sharon is a fertile region on the Mediterranean coast north of present-day Tel Aviv. The reference in the Song of Solomon ('I am the rose of Sharon ... ') inspired David Willson in 1831 to name the Children of Peace community of Sharon, 5 kilometres north of Newmarket, Ont. At the north end of the Plain of Sharon is Caesarea. It is also the name of a community 25 kilometres southwest of Lindsay, Ont. Its name is of dual origin, since the place was settled by the Caesar family in 1836.

The biblical stories and classic tales of the Middle East and the Holy Land reinforced the resilience and perseverance of Canada's nineteenth-century pioneers. Today, the names add variety to the toponymic fabric of Canada, especially in Ontario, New Brunswick, and Nova Scotia.

Capitalizing on Foreign Capitals

The map of Canada shows a sprinkling of place names derived from world capitals, reflecting the strong attachment many settlers felt towards their homelands. Most, predictably, are named for capitals in northern Europe and the British Isles. A national capital possesses a measure of prestige and an aura of strength and longevity, but the history of these Canadian namesakes is not always based on such stalwart qualities.

For example, the town of Paris, Ont., 10 kilometres west of Brantford, was not named for the grand French city of *savoir-vivre*. Rather, this Paris derived its name from the development, in 1829, of local gypsum deposits that were used to make plaster of Paris and fertilizer.

The community of Warsaw, Ont., with a population of 230, situated 20 kilometres northeast of Peterborough, was named by Thomas Choate in 1841 after his birthplace, Warsaw, N.Y., which was itself named for the Polish capital.

One might conclude that the village of Hague, 50 kilometres north of Saskatoon, was named for the Netherlands' seat of government, The Hague, but it was really named for J.H. Hague, a railway engineer who later ran a hotel in Vancouver.

The majority of capital-city namesakes in Canada, however, were legitimately named for foreign capitals. Athens, Ont., an attractive village of 960 people, 20 kilometres west of Brockville, was named in 1888 to honour the great city of Greece and its respect for education. The village, which then went by the mundane name of Farmersville, had three schools, including a teacher's training school.

The city of London, Ont., on the Thames River, takes its name from the surrounding London Township, itself named for Great Britain's capital in 1798. In 1791, Lt.-Gov. John Graves Simcoe wanted to locate the capital of Upper Canada at the Thames River site, then known as The Forks. He called it Georgina, for the reigning monarch. York (now Toronto) was subsequently chosen as the capital of Upper Canada and, in 1825, Georgina and The Forks were replaced by London when a post office was opened and the seat of government for London District was moved there. It was moved from Vittoria, a small community near the town of Simcoe, 70 kilometres east of London.

A few communities in Canada were named for capital cities that were prominent in the news. In the early 1870s, Belgium made headlines when Britain secured its neutrality during the Franco-Prussian War. In 1871, Brussels, the anglicized version of Belgium's capital, was chosen to replace the community name Ainleyville and the postal name Dingle, 85 kilometres north of London.

Belgium's capital also turns up in its French form, 85 kilometres southeast of Brandon, Man. A settlement of Belgians, Bruxelles was named in 1892 by Catholic archbishop Alexandre Taché.

In 1854, the Crimean War and Russia in general were popular topics of discussion. In that year Springfield, Ont., changed its name to Moscow, commemorating the retreat of Napoleon from the Russian capital in 1812. Moscow, with a population of 65, is located 30 kilometres northwest of Kingston.

But capitals in the news were not always looked upon favourably. During the First World War, tensions arose over the loyalty of the predominantly German residents of Berlin, Ont. The name had been chosen for a post office in 1833 by the early settlers. Berlin was settled first by Mennonite families from Pennsylvania in 1807, later by Pennsylvania 'Dutch' families (of German stock) and, after 1830, by German immigrants. In 1916, amid much rancour, a vote was taken to change the name. Among six choices, Kitchener was the most popular. It commemorates Lord Kitchener, the hero of Khartoum who drowned that year.

Khartoum, the capital of Sudan, also spawned another Canadian place name. Khartum, Ont., a locality in Renfrew County, was named in 1909 to commemorate Ottawa Valley rivermen who joined the Nile expedition in the 1880s.

A Canadian traveller can arrange an extensive tour of European capital cities without having to take along a passport. Amsterdam is 55 kilometres north of Yorkton, Sask. It was homesteaded about 1912 by settlers from the Netherlands, and was named for that country's administrative centre.

Stockholm is a village of 390 people, 60 kilometres south of Yorkton. The colony of New Stockholm was settled by Swedes in the 1880s. When the Canadian Pacific Railway arrived there in 1903, the name Stockholm was proposed for a station and post office.

The community of Copenhagen, with a population of 200, is 20 kilometres southeast of St. Thomas, Ont. Recalling the capital of Denmark, it had a post office from 1870 to 1914. Vienna, a village of 480 people, 35 kilometres southeast of St. Thomas, was named in 1836 by Capt. Samuel Edison (the inventor's grandfather) for the Austrian city where one of his ancestors was born.

Dublin is the name of a community of 255 people, 30 kilometres northwest of Stratford, Ont. Named Carronbrook in 1854, it was renamed Dublin in 1878 to honour settlers from Ireland. New Dublin is a small community of 60 people, 14 kilometres northwest of Brockville, Ont. Dublin Shore and West Dublin are seaside communities 18 kilometres southeast of Bridgewater, N.S. An Irish settlement was located in that part of Lunenburg County in the 1760s and was named New Dublin Township.

Other modified capital namesakes include New London, a rural community 38 kilometres northwest of Charlottetown, P.E.I. New London was established as a port in 1773 on Grenville Bay, which became known as New London Bay by the mid-1830s. A former farming community 25 kilometres northeast of Edmonton had a post office called New Lunnon from 1876 to 1907. This spelling reflects a Cockney pronunciation of London. The neighbouring town of Gibbons has preserved the name in Lunnon Drive.

Cairo, Ont., Bagdad, N.B., and Damascus, Ont., are Canadian communities representing Middle East capitals. Manilla, a community of 450 people, 20 kilometres west of Lindsay, Ont., replaced Mariposa in 1857 as the postal name. It is named for Manila, the capital of the Philippines. Delhi, 15 kilometres west of Simcoe, was laid out in 1828 as Fredericksburg, but when that name was found to be in use elsewhere, the township name Middleton was given to the post office in 1831. The name was changed to Delhi (pronounced 'DEL-HYE') in 1853, in honour of the then-capital of India, but the name Fredericksburg remained in general use even after the second change.

Settlers may have had great expectations for their new towns, hoping they would one day deserve their proud, capital names. But with the exception of London and Paris, none of the namesakes has reached a population of more than 1,000. Some, such as Reykjavik, Man., Riga, Sask., and New Kiew, Alta., are now nothing more than wind-blown fields. Then again, these founders of capital communities may not have been attempting to build great cities; perhaps they were simply seeking a fond reminder of their former homes or a curious footnote in place-name geography.

Anzac to Zealandia: Names from Down Under

In another essay, I referred to Canadian place names found in New South Wales, Australia, including *Toronto* and *Canada Bay*. That prompted several readers from down under to send me more examples: *Labrador* in Queensland; *Canadian Bay* and *Sherbrooke* in Victoria; and *Quebec, Alberta, Calgary, Toronto, Vancouver, Ottawa,* and *Ontario* avenues in Clapham, near Adelaide, South Australia. Their interest has inspired me to pursue this southern link further, by researching names from the South Seas that are found in Canada.

Before his luckless third voyage to Canada's Arctic, Sir John Franklin served as governor of Van Diemen's Land – later renamed to Tasmania – from 1836 to 1843. Franklin disappeared in 1845 along with his entire expedition to the Northwest Passage. At the request of Franklin's wife, Lady Jane, a group of islands on the west side of the Boothia Peninsula was named the Tasmania Group in 1859, in honour of Sir John's service in Tasmania. In 1910, they were designated Tasmania Islands.

Lighter emotions inspired other names. In 1858, a group of settlers set sail from Charlottetown, P.E.I., to begin a new life in New Zealand. At the same time, another group from Charlottetown moved east to the area of Souris, P.E.I., to take up farming. They called their settlement New Zealand – a light-hearted reference to the first group's destination – and it later became the name of their post office from 1879 to 1914.

In 1871, residents needed a name for the new post office at Davis Corners, west of Perth, Ont. The postal inspector proposed Zealand, in honour of the South Seas country, shortening the name for postal efficiency. Although the office was closed in 1915, the rural community is still known as Zealand.

New railways frequently generated new place names. In 1905, the Canadian Northern Railway picked the name Ranfurly for a village 145 kilometres east of Edmonton. It was named for the Fifth Earl of Ranfurly, who had just completed a four-year term as governor of New Zealand. But CNR officials were thwarted when they chose the name Brock for a station on another line, 95 kilometres southwest of Saskatoon. The new settlers insisted on choosing their own name, and from several submissions they picked Thomas Englebrecht's suggestion of Zealandia. Englebrecht had emigrated from New Zealand on the S.S. *Zealandia* around 1907, and became one of the area's first settlers from abroad.

Australian Hugh McRoberts established Richmond Farm south of Vancouver in 1861. One of his daughters suggested that name after a favourite place in Australia (possibly the town of Richmond, near Sydney), according to Philip and Helen Akrigg in their *British Columbia Place Names* (1986). Richmond was subsequently chosen for the district municipality embracing Lulu Island, which is now a city of 125,000.

During the First World War, the Australian and New Zealand Army Corps (ANZAC) fought with distinction at Gallipoli, Turkey, and on the Western Front in Belgium and France. During that war, a tributary of the Parsnip River, north of Prince George, B.C., was named Anzac River in their honour. When the British Columbia Railway was built in 1967 from Prince George to Dawson Creek, a sixty-nine-car siding was built near the mouth of the river and called Anzac. Also during the First World War, land surveyor Frank C. Swannell undertook extensive surveys in the Nechako and Bulkley valleys west of Prince George. He named Bennett Lake for an Australian assistant who had served overseas with the Anzac forces. When informed that the province already had a Bennett Lake, Swannell recommended the subsequent change to Anzac Lake. The name Anzac was also given to a station on the Canadian Pacific Railway line just south of Fort McMurray, Alta., in 1922.

The Second World War created new place-name links with the South Pacific. Commonwealth Lake in northern Manitoba was named to recognize the British Commonwealth Air Training Plan of 1939-45. The islands in the lake were called Beaver for Canada, Kiwi for New Zealand, Kangaroo for Australia, and Lion for Britain. These appellations were given in 1974 by Allen Roberts, a New Zealand–born pilot who trained in Manitoba and subsequently became the province's director of surveys.

Sir Robert Richard Torrens was an Adelaide lawyer and

state legislator who introduced the Torrens system of land titles in South Australia in 1858. In 1922, surveyor Richard W. Cautley named Mount Torrens, near Grande Cache, Alta., for him – sixteen years after Alberta adopted the Torrens system of transferring land ownership by registration and certificate, rather than by deed.

Australian prospectors travelled to the Yukon in the 1890s to probe the northern gravel bars for gold, even before the Klondike Gold Rush of 1896: they brought a wealth of place names from down under. There are now two streams in the Yukon named Ballarat Creek, which recall a gold rush at Ballarat, in central Victoria, in the 1850s.

A tributary of Indian River, south of Dawson City, was named Australia Creek sometime between 1891 and 1894. A small tributary of that creek, called Melba Creek, is likely named after Dame Nellie Melba, a world-famous operatic soprano at the turn of the century and a native of Melbourne.

A tributary of the Klondike River, east of Dawson City, was also named Australia Creek in 1897. To avoid confusion with the creek named earlier, geologist W.H. Miller renamed it Aussie Creek in 1935. Australia Hill stands at the nearby confluence of the Klondike River and Hunker Creek.

Walhalla Creek, southeast of Dawson City, was named by a prospector who was believed to have worked the goldfields of Walhalla in Australia's state of Victoria, according to Robert C. Coutts in *Yukon: Places & Names* (1980). A few kilometres to the west is Australia Gulch.

Fiji may have been the birthplace of James Asasela, although Vilhjalmur Stefansson described him in *The Friendly Arctic* (1922) as a Samoan. 'Jim Fiji,' as he was commonly called, represented the Samoas in an exhibit of 'native races' at the 1893 Chicago World's Fair. On the way home he boarded a ship in San Francisco that he assumed was sailing towards the Hawaiian Islands, because he saw some Hawaiians on board. But the ship was a whaling vessel that spent the next three years in the Arctic. He returned to the Arctic in 1896 for another three-year stint, and thereafter remained in the North. Asasela sailed with Stefansson's Canadian Arctic Expedition to the Beaufort Sea from 1913 to 1917. He then became a trapper, and disappeared about 1930 while sealing in Amundsen Gulf. In his memory, the Inuit of Paulatuk renamed Little Booth Island, east of Cape Bathurst, Fiji Island; and named an anchorage on the south side of the island Jim Fiji Harbour.

Motorists travelling between Winnipeg and Brandon pass signs for Sidney and Melbourne, only 8 kilometres apart, and may speculate about an Australian connection. In fact, no direct connection exists, although both Melbournes are named for the same British prime minister. Sidney is named for Sidney Austin, a British journalist who travelled on the first westbound CPR train (besides, the Australian city is spelled 'Sydney'). But there is still an impressive exchange of names that celebrate the enduring links between Canada and its Commonwealth partners in the South Seas.

A Touch of Portuguese on the East Coast

Portuguese navigators of the fifteenth and sixteenth centuries were tireless in their search for new lands, fishing grounds, and trading opportunities. Colonies flying the Portuguese flag sprang up around the world.

The Portuguese presence in Canada is reflected mainly on Newfoundland's east and south coasts, where such names as Bonavista, Burgeo, Fogo, and Ferryland are found. Labrador too is derived from Portuguese, and so is Bras d'Or Lake in Cape Breton Island.

From 1480 to 1509, Portuguese navigators accompanied several English expeditions from Bristol. João Fernandes, a *lavrador* ('small landholder') of Terceira in the Azores, may have sailed in 1497 to the New World with John Cabot. In 1499, he was directed by King Manuel I of Portugal to search for new lands. The following summer he sighted Greenland, which was soon identified on maps as Tiera del Lavrador. Some sixty years later, map makers restored the Norse name to that island and assigned the name Labrador to the mainland to the southwest.

King Manuel gave a similar directive in 1501 to Gaspar Corte-Real who, with three ships, explored the coast of Labrador and the east coast of Newfoundland. The ship carrying Corte-Real disappeared while travelling separately, but the others returned to Portugal with information about the lands, the fishery, and the natives. When Miguel Corte-Real sailed in search of his brother in 1502, he suffered the same fate.

The voyages of the Corte-Reals, and of subsequent Portuguese explorers, resulted in several names that are still in use today, either in obscure Portuguese forms or in English translation.

Cape Race, the most southeasterly point of Newfoundland, occurs on the earliest maps as *capo raso*, a description of the flat cliffs observed there. It also may have been named for Cabo Raso at the mouth of the River Tagus, the last point that sailors would see on leaving Lisbon.

Following the Newfoundland coast northward, one reaches Renews, a name identifiable with the Portuguese word *ronhoso* ('scabby'); rocks there are encrusted with shells and seaweed. Fermeuse and Aquaforte appear on a 1519 map as *R fermoso* ('beautiful') and *R da aguea* ('freshwater'). Ferryland may be traced to *farelhão*, meaning 'steep rock' or 'reef.'

Cape Spear, the most easterly point in North America, is shown on a map of 1505–8 as *Cauo de la spera* ('place of waiting'). Perhaps one of the vessels of the Corte-Real expeditions waited here for Gaspar or Miguel.

St. John's is believed by some to have been discovered by John Cabot on 24 June 1497, St. John the Baptist's Day. On a 1519 map, the entrance to the harbour is called *R de Sam joham*. Cape St. Francis appears as *c d s francisco*. The Portuguese identified Conception Bay with several variations of *baia da conceição*, a name that honours Our Lady of the Immaculate Conception. Baccalieu Island, off the tip of Bay de Verde Peninsula, is shown on a 1505 map as *y dos bacalhas* ('codfish island').

Some writers believe that Gaspar Corte-Real first applied the name Trinity Bay (in Portuguese, of course) to that body of water. While there is no cartographic evidence to support this, it is known that subsequent Portuguese travellers called it *baia de santa ciria*. The English seem to have chosen Trinity Bay in the late 1500s. Catalina, at the outer end of the bay, may have its roots in the name *p de S Catarina*, shown on maps of the mid-1500s.

Cape Bonavista is said to have been the first place reached by John Cabot in 1497. The name itself is Portuguese, appearing on early maps as *C de boa vista*. Cape Freels, from *y do frey luis* ('island of Brother Luis'), is the main landmark at the north side of Bonavista Bay.

Fogo Island and Cape Fogo, off the northeast coast, derive their names from the Portuguese *y do fogo* ('island of fire').

The first point west of Cape Race is Cape Pine, which occurs on sixteenth-century charts as *c de pena*. Across St. Mary's Bay is Cape St. Mary's. The bay is shown on a 1537 map as *Sa maria*, and the cape, on a 1536 map, as *Cabo de Sancta Maria*.

The French islands of Saint-Pierre and Miquelon were known in the 1500s as *Arcepelleguo das honze mill virgeens,* named for St. Ursula and the 11,000 virgins murdered by the Huns in the fourth or fifth century. A corrupted form of *virgeens* appears to have been transferred over 100 kilometres to the northwest to the present town of Burgeo and to Burgeo Islands.

Other south-coast names with probable Portuguese roots include: Great Colinet Island - *colmat* (possibly *colina* - 'hill'); Red Island - *ilha roxa*; St. Lawrence - *baia de sa lourenço*; Lamaline - *le belim* (possibly *baleia* - 'whale'); Cape Chapeau Rouge - *c roxo*; Fortune Bay - *fortuna*; Penguin Islands - *isla de pitogoen*; and Cape Ray along with several adjacent features with the specific, Codroy - *c rei*. Cape St. George on Newfoundland's west coast may have begun as *c de S Jorge*.

João Alvares Fagundes, who sailed along the south coasts of Newfoundland and Nova Scotia about 1521, may have named Bras d'Or Lake to reinforce control of Portuguese discoveries near the boundary of Spanish exploration, set by the 1494 Treaty of Tordesillas. Bras d'Or is generally regarded as a corruption of 'labrador.' None of the other names from Fagundes's travels, including Cap Fagunda for present Cape Breton, survives.

Spanish Names Along Our West Coast

In 1596, an old sea captain called Juan de Fuca met Michael Lok, an English trader, in Venice, and told a fantastic tale of exploration and discovery along North America's northwest coast four years earlier. The mariner explained that he had been instructed by the Viceroy of Mexico to seek the fabled Straits of Anian, a water body believed to provide a convenient, practical sea passage between Europe and the Far East.

Nearly thirty years later, Lok's tale was recounted in *Purchas His Pilgrimes*, a world history by Rev. Samuel Purchas. Lok reported that the sea captain had claimed to have discovered, between the 47th and 48th parallels, a wide inlet leading into a broader sea with many islands, and that there was 'an exceeding high Pinacle, or spired Rocke, like a piller' at the entrance to the strait.

Some 150 years later, in 1778, when Capt. James Cook explored the same coast, he missed the entrance because bad weather forced him to sail north far from shore. Nine years later, Capt. Charles W. Barkley, an English fur trader, sailed by the entrance. Knowing about Lok's story, he decided the name of the old seaman should be commemorated. The latter had been born Apostolos Valerianos on the Greek island of Cephalonia, but in the service of the Spanish for some forty years he bore the name of Juan de Fuca. A year after Barkley's trip, Capt. John Meares entered and charted the strait. He partially retained Barkley's designation, giving it the name John de Fuca.

Thus Barkley and Meares made the Lok tale seem authentic, although many historians and explorers thereafter wondered whether de Fuca had only woven a clever tale, and that it was simply a matter of luck that the area's geography partially fitted Lok's interpretation. In 1792, Capt. George Vancouver used Straits of Juan de Fuca on his chart, although he questioned the tale's authenticity. Research by historians in Spanish and Mexican archives has failed to reveal any evidence of Juan de Fuca's voyage.

Capt. John Walbran, who knew the British Columbia coast intimately and who studied its geographical names thoroughly at the turn of this century, agreed with Barkley's decision, declaring that de Fuca 'was undoubtedly the discoverer of the strait which bears his name.' Walbran went on to declare that a spire at the entrance to the strait next to Tatooche Island in present-day Washington state fitted the description by Lok, and thus it received the name Fuca Pillar.

Curiously, the Geographic Board of Canada delayed until 1934 its approval of the name of the water body which forms Canada's boundary south of Victoria and

Vancouver Island, and then identified it as Juan de Fuca Strait. The United States board approved the style Strait of Juan de Fuca, so both forms occur on present-day maps and charts.

During his voyage of discovery, Capt. Vancouver became friends with the Spanish naval officer Juan Francisco de la Bodega y Quadra, and decided that the main island on the west coast should be called Quadra and Vancouver's Island. Ultimately the single name Vancouver Island came into use. In 1903, the Geographic Board of Canada named Quadra Island near Campbell River for the Spaniard.

There were several Spanish voyages along Canada's west coast from 1774 to 1792. Among the explorers honoured with names of geographical features are Gonzales López de Haro (Haro Strait), Alejandro Malaspina (Malaspina Strait), Jacinto Caamaño (Caamaño Sound), Dionisio Alcalá Galiano (Galiano Island), and Cayetano Valdés (Valdes Island). Cortes Island and Hernando Island recall the conqueror of Mexico, Hernando Cortés.

Other noted Spanish officers and administrators commemorated include Pedro Alberni (Alberni Inlet), Luis de Córdova (Cordova Bay), Manuel Antonio Flores (Flores Island), Juan Maria Lasqueti (Lasqueti Island), Felix de Texada (Texada Island), Vicente Tofino de San Miguel (Tofino Inlet), and Ciriaco Ceballos (Zeballos Inlet).

Many Spanish names have been superseded, among them Gran Canal de Nuestra Señora del Rosario la Marinera for the present Strait of Georgia, Río Florida Blanca for Fraser River, Entrada de Juan Pérez for Dixon Entrance, Puerto de Revillagigedo for Sooke Inlet, Rada de Valdés y Bazán for Royal Roads, and Bocas de Winthuysen for Nanaimo Harbour.

All told, Spanish exploration on Canada's west coast is recalled by about 100 names. These names, from Alberni to Juan de Fuca and Quadra, have provided us with a rich toponymic heritage.

Crimean Victories Commemorated Across Canada

In 1854, in support of Turkey, Britain and France declared war on Russia. An expedition, under the allied command of Lord Raglan and General Saint-Arnaud, was mounted from Varna (in present-day Bulgaria) to destroy the Russian naval base at Sevastopol.

After landing on the west coast of the Crimean Peninsula on 14 September 1854, the allied forces engaged the Russians in a bloody battle at Alma, and moved on to Sevastopol, where they wintered after costly engagements at Balaklava and Inkerman.

The war continued through 1855, with the allies destroying Kinburn, the Russian base at the mouth of the Dnieper, and the Russians taking Kars, in present-day eastern Turkey, after a heroic defence by the British general Fenwick Williams. In March 1856, Russia accepted the Treaty of Paris which, among other terms, gave formal recognition to the neutrality of the Black Sea.

The Crimean War has been commemorated in many place names across Canada.

News of the victory at Alma reached Canada in late October 1854 when the area of Rivière Saguenay near Lac Saint-Jean was being surveyed. The surveyors named an island in the river after the battle. The site ultimately became the city of Alma, which today has a population of 26,000. The territorial Alma Parish in New Brunswick was named in 1855 by a person who, on observing the site of the present village of Alma at the mouth of the Salmon River, was reminded of the heights above the Crimean battlefield of Alma. A community in Nova Scotia, another in Ontario, and possibly a third in Prince Edward Island were named Alma in honour of the victory in the Crimea.

The Battle of Balaklava was fought on 25 October 1854. The name Balaclava was given to communities in Renfrew and Grey counties in Ontario, and Balaklava was given to an island in Queen Charlotte Strait in British Columbia.

The Russian army was defeated at Inkerman on 5 November 1854. A territorial parish in New Brunswick, and a community in Dundas County, Ont., 40 kilometres southeast of Ottawa, were named for the victory.

The city of Sevastopol was finally captured in September 1855 after a siege of nearly a year. The name Sebastopol was given to a township in Renfrew County, Ont. Two defences of Sevastopol, Malakoff and Redan, are recalled in the names of two small communities in Ontario, one in Carleton County, the other in Leeds County. Malakoff, east of Moncton, N.B., was named by a surveyor to commemorate the battle.

Outside the Crimea itself, an engagement in 1855 at the mouth of the Dnieper River brought the name of the fortress called Kinburn into prominence. Kinburn, in Carleton County, Ont., became a post office at that time, and was named for the allied assault. Another Kinburn in Huron County, Ont., may have been named before 1855 for a place in Scotland.

The valiant defence of Kars by General Fenwick Williams occurred when the community of Wellington on the Rideau River applied for a post office. As the illustrious hero of Waterloo had been already commemorated elsewhere in Upper Canada, the name Kars was given to this little place 30 kilometres south of Ottawa. A territorial parish in New Brunswick and a township in Northern Ontario were also named Kars, and in 1888 Karsdale was given as a postal name in Nova Scotia.

General Williams, the great hero of Kars, was born in Annapolis Royal, N.S. He became commander-in-chief of British forces in North America in 1859, and from 1865 to 1867 was lieutenant-governor of Nova Scotia. He was honoured in Nova Scotia with the community names Port

Williams in Kings County and Fenwick in Cumberland County, as well as in Ontario's Niagara Peninsula with the community name Fenwick and with Fenwick Township beside Kars Township in Northern Ontario.

Also in Ontario: Varna, a community in Huron County, south of Goderich, recalls the Black Sea port where the allied forces gathered in 1854 for the expedition to the Crimea; Odessa, a community in Lennox and Addington County, is a reminder of an April 1854 bombardment of the prominent Black Sea port; and Kertch, a small place in Lambton County between London and Sarnia, commemorates an 1855 battle at the eastern end of the Crimea.

Brudenell Township in Renfrew County, Ont., Cardigan Strait in the Arctic, and Cardigan Rocks in Queen Charlotte Strait, B.C., recall James Brudenell, Seventh Earl of Cardigan, the leader of the famous charge of the Light Brigade at Balaklava.

Raglan Township in Renfrew County, Ont.; the community of Raglan in the city of Oshawa, Ont.; Raglan Range on Melville Island, N.W.T.; and Raglan Point on Balaklava Island in British Columbia were all given for James Henry Fitzroy Somerset, Lord Raglan, who died of cholera at the siege of Sevastopol in 1855.

Two other points of Balaklava Island were given names after officers: Nolan Point for Captain Edward Louis Nolan, who carried the order for the charge of the Light Brigade and was killed at the Battle of Balaklava; and Scarlett Point for Sir James York Scarlett, who led the charge of the Heavy Brigade at Balaklava. Adjoining Balaklava Island are Lucan Islands, which recall George Charles Bingham, Third Earl of Lucan, a commander of cavalry in the Crimean War. Lucan, a village 25 kilometres northwest of London, Ont., is also believed to have been named for him.

Griffith Township, adjacent to Sebastopol Township,

in Renfrew County, probably honours the leader of the Scots Greys at the Battle of Balaklava, Colonel Henry Darby Griffith.

Cathcart in Brant County, Ont., was named for Sir George Cathcart, who was killed at the Battle of Inkerman in 1854.

St. Arnaud Hills on Melville Island, N.W.T., recalls the commander-in-chief of the French army, Marshal Jacques A. Leroy de Saint-Arnaud, who became ill at the Battle of Balaklava and died at sea in 1854.

Canrobert, a Canadian Pacific railway point in Ange-Gardien, 16 kilometres southwest of Granby, Qué., and Canrobert Hills on Melville Island, N.W.T., were named for General François Certain Canrobert, who had succeeded Marshal Saint-Arnaud at the Battle of Balaklava.

The commander of the French fleet during the Crimean War was Admiral Ferdinand Alphonse Hamelin. He was honoured with the name Mount Hamelin on Melville Island, N.W.T. Hamelin's second in command, Admiral Bruat, is remembered in Mount Bruat, also on Melville Island.

Many thousands of soldiers died in the Crimea from untended wounds and disease. Into the horrible carnage came the indomitable founder of modern nursing, Florence Nightingale, who earned a reputation for her profound dedication to caring for the wounded and to improving sanitary conditions in field hospitals.

The community of Florence in Lambton County, Ont., was named for the Italian city in 1856, having been earlier called Zone Mills and Victoria. It may be more than coincidence in the naming of this place that the heroic 'lady with the lamp' gave the name Florence prominence. The village of Florenceville, the 'frozen french fries capital' in New Brunswick, received its name from the Angel of Crimea in 1855, having been earlier called Buttermilk Creek. About 1865, two adjacent elevations in the Coast Mountains of British Columbia were named Mount Florence and Mount Nightingale. The community of Nightingale, between Calgary and Drumheller, Alta., was named in 1911 in honour of the illustrious nurse.

Numerous streets and avenues commemorate the victories and officers of the Crimean War, among them being Raglan Street, the main street in Renfrew, Ont., and Alma Street in Vancouver.

Surprisingly, the most prominent name of the war, Crimea, was not applied to a Canadian feature. Nor was Yalta, the Crimean resort community made famous as the meeting place of the allied victors of the Second World War.

On the Western Front: Names from First World War Battles

Few European names are more honoured in Canada than Vimy. And rare is the city, town or village that does not have a First World War monument with Vimy proudly displayed among the French and Belgian names of places where fierce and bloody battles were fought and more than 60,000 Canadians and Newfoundlanders lost their lives. Across Canada, more than 125 mountain, lake, river, township, village, and street names are perpetual reminders of these places.

Near the France–Belgium border, 125 kilometres southwest of Brussels and 160 kilometres north of Paris, Canadian soldiers valiantly fought with the Western Allies against German forces. They took part in many battles during the four-year war, but it was their capture of Vimy Ridge in April 1917, with 3,598 Canadian lives lost, that hastened Canada's elevation to equal partnership among the nations of the world.

In Ontario, the military barracks at Kingston is named

Vimy; a locality 60 kilometres east of Timmins is called
Vimy Ridge; and Vimy Ridge Island is in Lake of Bays
near Huntsville, Ont. As well, thirty-five towns and cities
from St. John's, Nfld., to Duncan, B.C., have a street
named Vimy.

Several townships in Québec recall other Western Front
battle sites, including six near Val d'Or: Vimy, Denain,
Ypres, Cambrai, Lens, and Festubert. Many lakes and rivers
in the same part of the province also reflect the names
of engagements and skirmishes: Yser, Douai, Arras, Loos,
St-Pol, Flanders, Courcelette, Courtrai, Langemarck, Messines, Poperinghe, Farbus, Verdun, Somme, Givenchy,
Bruges, Armentières, and Amiens.

At Canadian Forces Base Valcartier, west of Québec City,
there are mountains named for Vimy, Mont Sorrel, and
Cambrai, and a river named after the Battle of the Somme,
where more than 24,000 Canadians lost their lives in the
summer and fall of 1916. The military post office on the
base is called Courcelette, honouring a victorious Canadian advance in September 1916.

Vimy is also the name of a hamlet 65 kilometres north
of Edmonton, and there is an imposing crest named Vimy
Ridge in Waterton Lakes National Park in southwestern
Alberta. The crest's steep northern flank is called Vimy
Peak.

In Wells Gray Provincial Park, north of Kamloops, B.C.,
a few features also recall the sites of battles – Vimy Lakes,
Vimy Ridge, and two creeks named Lys and Fleurbaix.

In the Canadian Rockies, Valenciennes River, Flanders
Mountain, Mons Peak, and Verdun Glacier recall battles
and actions on the Western Front.

During the First World War, the highlands 115 kilome-
tres east of Edmundston, N.B., were opened for settlement.
A French-speaking community there, which was called
Anderson Siding until 1920, changed its name to St-
Quentin to honour a battle that took place in 1918. St-

Quentin is now a village of 2,300, serving a large farming and logging region.

In 1915, H.G. Richards of Saskatchewan was killed during the Battle of Hooge in Belgium. In the 1950s, his brother proposed that a new customs post 140 kilometres south of Swift Current be named Hooge. Officials liked the spirit of Richards's idea but instead of Hooge they chose the name Monchy, a place near Hooge where a decisive battle in the breaking of the Hindenberg Line took place in 1918.

Messines, Qué., 100 kilometres north of Ottawa, was named in 1921, replacing the name Burbridge, which had been given for the federal deputy minister of justice who had prosecuted Louis Riel in 1885. Messines, Belgium, was the site of important offensives in 1917 and 1918.

Armentières, as in the marching song 'Mademoiselle from Armentières,' is a French town on the Belgian border where a number of engagements took place. It appears twice on the British Columbia coast: as the name of a channel on the west side of the Queen Charlotte Islands and as the name of a rock on the west side of Vancouver Island, 45 kilometres southwest of Port Alberni.

Flanders, Belgium, the scene of many First World War battles, is the name of a township in Northern Ontario, a railway siding 255 kilometres west of Thunder Bay, and a locality 25 kilometres east of Sherbrooke, Qué. The French form, Flandre, occurs as a township in Pontiac County, Qué., and is near Artois, a township named after a region in France.

Several townships across Northern Ontario also derive their names from the battles and engagements that took place along the Western Front. Among them are Verdun, Langemarck, Marne, Mons, Somme, and St. Julien.

One name almost always seen on First World War monuments is Passchendaele, the site of some of the war's worst slaughters. In 1931, the post office gave the name to its

Dominion No. 4 office on Cape Breton Island. In 1940, the office became Glace Bay Sub Office No. 3, but Passchendaele remains the name of a neighbourhood in Glace Bay, N.S.

Only one Western Front battle name appears north of the 60th parallel, and that is Somme Creek in the Yukon, about 260 kilometres northwest of Whitehorse.

Heavenly Places from Coast to Coast

Giving names suggesting perfection on earth, or greater beauty than actually exists, is as old as civilization. Witness the biblical naming of Canaan, the land of milk and honey; or the naming of Greenland by Eric the Red in the tenth century.

There are names from one end of Canada to the other that reveal this seeking for perfection, for a heaven on earth, for some sort of never-never land. Perhaps the people who assign such names hope that an ordinary, even ugly, place will seem more beautiful, and thus a better place to live. Others may give such names as an ironic twist, knowing that the place has few good qualities.

In about 1670, Nicolas Denys, the governor of Acadia, was delayed by inclement weather for a week at the mouth of a stream flowing into Northumberland Strait, 30 kilometres northeast of present-day Moncton. He did not consider his stay unpleasant and called the stream 'Rivière de Cocagne.' Cocagne River recalls the fabled 'Land of Cockagne,' which was described in a thirteenth-century English satire as a mythical land of good food and happy times.

As early as 1684, the French called a section of the Annapolis Valley 'Paradis terrestre.' Subsequently, when the English arrived in the 1760s, they gave the name Paradise Brook to a tributary of the Annapolis River. The adjoining communities of Paradise and West Paradise, 8 kilometres east of Bridgetown, have together about 575 people.

Although it is a region with extensive rocky landscapes and an often harsh climate, Newfoundland has more places called Paradise than any other province. The town of Paradise is 12 kilometres west of St. John's. There is another community with the same name about 50 kilometres north of Grand Falls–Windsor, and a third on the Labrador coast near Hopedale. Paradise River is a community about 200 kilometres east of Happy Valley–Goose Bay, Labrador. Thirteen physical features, such as Paradise Arm, Paradise Cove, and Paradise Sound, are similarly blessed.

Québec has more than fifty features named Paradis, but many may have been derived from personal names. Ontario has fifteen lakes, points, and other features named Paradise. The pleasantly named Cootes Paradise, a marsh in the Hamilton suburb of Dundas, was named in the late 1700s for Thomas Coote, a British officer and keen sportsman.

The village of Paradise Hill, with a population of 455, is located 45 kilometres northeast of Lloydminster, Sask. This is the only 'paradise' in Saskatchewan; Manitoba has none, but Alberta has five and British Columbia, twenty. In the Yukon, there is a Paradise Creek, named in 1903 for its attractive setting.

References to the biblical 'Garden of Eden' occur in several Canadian names. Garden of Eden and Eden Lake in Pictou County, N.S., were named in 1830 when the area was settled by William McDonald, nicknamed Adam. Mount Adam north of the lake was named for him. The contradictory Garden of Eden Barrens is located south of the lake.

Ontario has fifteen features with Eden, including Eden Mills, Edenvale, Glen Eden, and two places called Eden Grove. Manitoba has five communities with Eden, including Edenburg, 20 kilometres west of Emerson, and Eden, 15 kilometres north of Neepawa.

There are four places with Eden in Saskatchewan. However, one of them, Edenbridge, does not get its first element from the biblical garden, but from the Yiddish plural of 'Jew,' as the place was originally a Jewish settlement. Edenwold, a village 35 kilometres northeast of Regina, named in 1890 by Austrian settlers, combines the biblical Eden with the German *wald* meaning 'forest'; postal authorities misread the 'a.' Alberta has two features with Eden, a lake and an Indian reserve.

British Columbia has seven with Eden combinations. Eden Mountain on Vancouver Island is adjacent to mountains named for Cain and Abel. The village of Kaleden in the Okanagan Valley was named in 1909 by Walter Russell, selecting the first element from the Greek word meaning 'beautiful,' and the second from the biblical garden.

There are six features in the Northwest Territories with Eden, but only one, Eden Island, has any relation to the biblical garden, the others being personal names. The island in Frobisher Bay was named in 1960 in association with a hydrographic station called Eve located there.

In about 1783, a surveyor called Buffington drew up a survey plan near the mouth of the Magaguadavic River in present-day New Brunswick, and lots were granted. It was subsequently discovered that a large lake existed where many of the lots were shown on the plan. Either Capt. Peter Clinch or Lt.-Gov. Thomas Carleton is reported to have said that the possibility of acquiring the grants in the lake was comparable to that of achieving the perfection described in Sir Thomas More's *Utopia*, and therefore assigned it the name Lake Utopia.

Twelve kilometres west of Barrie, Ont., is the small community of Utopia, named in 1840s for More's fictional island. Utopia Lake, 40 kilometres north of Vancouver, was the site of the Utopia copper claim filed in 1908. Perhaps it was named because the lake is the utmost source of Britannia Creek and is nestled in a valley almost perfectly round.

Heaven occurs in four names in Ontario, including Blue Heaven Lake and Little Heaven Island, but is not an element in names elsewhere in Canada. There are three features with 'ciel' in Québec. More common are those with Valhalla, the Norse palace where the souls of slain heroes feast. Ontario has four Valhallas, including two called Valhalla Lake. Two communities, one in Manitoba and another in Alberta, are known by the name of Valhalla. In British Columbia, the word occurs in six names, including Valhalla Ranges, northwest of Nelson. Several other names in the ranges reflect a Norse theme. Valhalla Mountain on Baffin Island is near several other mountains named in association with Norse mythology.

Nirvana, a Sanskrit word suggesting a perfect state, occurs in two names in Canada. Lac Nirvana is in Québec's Parc de la Vérendrye. Nirvana Pass is in British Columbia's Pantheon Range, which has many features named for mythological gods.

Achieving harmony in any community is difficult, but Nova Scotia has three places with the word, including Harmony Mills in Queens County. Prince Edward Island has a place called New Harmony.

In 1901, a Finnish utopian community was established on Malcolm Island, between Vancouver Island and the mainland, and named Sointula (Finnish for 'harmony'). Although the colony was disbanded in 1905, today Sointula is a fishing village with a population of about 675.

And then there are the heavenly names given by real estate developers ...

Canadian Names Around the World

From Abilene and Buckingham to Valparaiso and Zurich, Canada has been a great importer of place names. Little known, however, is Canada's export of place names to other countries. Some of them, such as Inglewood, had been previously brought from the Old World to Canada. But most names carried to other countries – mainly to the United States and Australia – are genuine 'home-made' Canadian names. Some, like Canada and Québec, have even found their way back to the British Isles and France.

On the Island of Bute in Scotland, Canada Hill overlooks the mouth of the Firth of Clyde. From this vantage point, islanders used to watch vessels carrying friends and relatives to 'exile' across the Atlantic.

On the north side of Lincoln's Inn Fields, adjoining the Royal Courts of Justice in central London, is a footpath called Canada Walk. Canada Way in Hammersmith, 5 kilometres west of London's Marble Arch, is part of a 1930s housing development that includes Commonwealth Avenue and Australia Road.

On the Paramatta River in Sydney, Australia, is Canada Bay. This is where a party of French Canadians was exiled in 1839 after the aborted rebellions of 1837-8 in Lower Canada.

In the United States, Little Canada is a northern suburb of St. Paul, Minn. Settled in the 1840s by Benjamin Gervais and other French Canadians from Lower Canada, Little Canada became a township in 1858, a village in 1953, and a city in 1974. Today the suburb has a population of 8,000.

The names of Canada's two largest provinces are well represented in Europe and the United States. Ontario, a city of 100,000 people, located 55 kilometres east of Los Angeles, was founded in 1882 by George and William B. Chaffey, who were born in Brockville, Ont. Their success in developing irrigation projects for the citrus industry in San Bernardino County led to an invitation in 1887 to undertake similar work in Australia.

Ontario, Ore. (population 9,000), is situated on the west

side of the Snake River – the Columbia River's largest tributary – 65 kilometres northwest of Boise, Idaho. It was named in about 1883 by James W. Virtue for his native province. Although Virtue was one of the founders of the town, he actually settled 120 kilometres northwest of there in Baker, where he became the sheriff.

Québec is a popular designation for places and streets in France, England, the United States, and Mexico. Jean Poirier, the dean of Québec toponymy, has counted fifty-one 'Québec' streets and roads in France alone. In 1980, the City of Paris named Place du Québec in its Latin Quarter in honour of the close ties between France and Québec. In Acapulco, Mexico, the Plaza de Québec was inaugurated in 1983 as a sign of friendship between the citizens of Acapulco and the people of Québec.

Quebec is also a village 8 kilometres west of Durham in northern England. This authentic Canadian name first appeared as the name of a farm on a British topographical survey map in 1862. The mists of time have obscured the reason why the name was given.

Eighty kilometres southeast of Nashville, Tenn., is an unincorporated village called Quebeck. The unusual spelling was given in 1889 by J.S. Cooper, the town's founder, who constructed a sawmill there. The name was inspired by Cooper's travels in Québec, where he was impressed with the province's lumber industry.

Toronto may be the most common Canadian name transferred abroad. The best-known is Toronto, Ohio, a city of 7,000 on the Ohio River, 50 kilometres west of Pittsburgh. It was named in 1881 by Thomas M. Daniels in honour of the home city of W.F. Dunspaugh, the chief stockholder of the Great Western Fire Clay Company, then a principal industry in eastern Ohio.

In 1844, George W. Thorn, a native of Ontario's capital, founded the village of Toronto, Iowa, about 40 kilometres northwest of Davenport. There are a number of smaller American centres named Toronto, in Indiana, Kansas, Missouri, and Tennessee.

There is also a town called Toronto in New South Wales, Australia, 140 kilometres north of Sydney. According to the philatelic journal *The Canadian Connection*, it was named in 1888 to mark a visit that year by Ned Hanlan, the Ontario-born world sculling champion in 1880. The town is located on Lake Macquarie, Australia's largest permanent salt lake, which is noted for its water sports.

Montreal, Canada's second-largest metropolitan area, is the name of two small communities in Arkansas and Missouri. There is also a city of 900 called Montreal in Wisconsin; it is near the Montreal River, which forms part of the Wisconsin–Michigan boundary.

Incidentally, none of the places called Ottawa in the United States traces its origin back to Canada's capital. American cities such as Ottawa, Ill., and Ottawa, Kan., were named for the Ottawa Indians, who migrated from the area north of Lake Huron to the American Midwest.

Like ice hockey and Brantford's 'Great One,' Inglewood, Calif., is another Canadian export. Located 13 kilometres southwest of downtown Los Angeles, the city of 125,000 is the home of the Great Western Forum, where Wayne Gretzky practises his hockey wizardry. Inglewood owes its origin to a visit in 1887 by the sister-in-law of N.R. Vail, a developer. She lived in the little Ontario village and railway junction nestled in the Credit River valley, 20 kilometres northwest of Brampton. Inglewood, Ont., was named in 1885 by Thomas White, the local member of Parliament, after a place in England.

Except for a few street names in cities such as Atlanta, Orlando, and Los Angeles, it is difficult to find any of Western Canada's cities, towns, and villages repeated outside of Canada. An exception is Klondike, which occurs in several villages and townships throughout the United

States. At least one book, *Michigan Place Names*, claims the name recalls the gold rush that took place in the Klondike region of Alaska!

As I was completing research for this essay, an acquaintance told me that an ancestor of his wife, a Simcoe, Ont., farmer and preacher named Abraham Austin, built a Baptist church in 1884 at a crossroads 75 kilometres north of Birmingham, Ala. First called Austin City, it was renamed Simcoe that same year. The little village of three churches and several houses still exists. I wonder how many other Canadian names are dotted across the United States and in other countries of the world?

Revealing Special Characteristics of Place Names and Generic Terms

Cities: Source of Pride, Broken Dreams

Teeming millions grow
And the anxious world rolls on;
Brilliant cities tall and wide
Boast their numbers and their pride.

— from the sonnet 'Liberty'
by Archibald Lampman

For growing municipalities, the ultimate stamp of success is to achieve city status. Indeed, in the past many frontier communities added the title to their names to give the impression of stability and permanence.

The exception is the province of Québec. Since 1968, it has used the term *ville*, not *cité*, to designate urban centres, be they cities or towns. Montréal and Québec City (officially, Québec) were once known as *cités*, but there are now only two incorporated *cités* in the province: Côte-Saint-Luc and Dorval on the Island of Montréal.

Over the past eighty years, the number of incorporated cities in Canada has nearly doubled as a result of increasing urbanization. That number would be tripled if the 87 Québec *villes* with more than 10,000 people were included.

Most of Canada's 139 incorporated cities are in Ontario and British Columbia, with 51 and 39 cities, respectively. In 1911, there were 74, with British Columbia leading the way with 25, followed by Ontario with 19 and Québec with 10.

The most populous incorporated city in 1911 was Montréal with 470,500 inhabitants, followed by Toronto with 376,500. Although Toronto now is referred to as Canada's largest city, it is technically in second place, with a population of 635,395. (At 1,017,666, Montréal is Canada's largest urban municipality, but is *not* classed in Québec as a city.) The city with the largest population is Calgary, at 710,677. Calgary has, of course, absorbed almost all of its suburbs, while Metro Toronto has four other cities and a borough.

The city with the smallest population – 725 people – is Greenwood, B.C., located near the United States border east of the Okanagan Valley. In 1911, it had 778 people, but it was not the least populated then. That year, the city of Sandon in the West Kootenay had only 151 people, down from about 5,000 when it was incorporated in 1898. Sandon is now a ghost 'city.'

Founded in 1785, Saint John, N.B., has the distinction of being Canada's oldest city.

Timmins, Ont., covers the largest area of any Canadian city, embracing several urban centres and vast expanses of lakes, rivers, and unpopulated woodland over 3,000 square kilometres. The smallest city, with only 2.79 square kilometres, is Vanier, which is surrounded by the city of Ottawa and is home to the Royal Canadian Geographical Society.

No place with 'city' in its name is incorporated as such. Labrador City, Nfld., a town of 9,061 people, is the largest of these so-called cities. Others, such as King City, Ont., and Crystal City, Man., have maintained the title in their names with great pride and vigilance. The community of King City, 30 kilometres north of Toronto, had long been known by that name on registered plans, but postal authorities decided in 1841 that King would be enough. The Post Office Department rejected a change to King City in 1932, even though the Geographic Board of Canada authorized the change. Ontario incorporated King City as a police village in 1934. Finally, after persistent requests, the postal authorities accepted the change in 1953.

In the south end of Welland, Ont., is a little neighbourhood that proudly calls itself Dain City. Located where the Canadian National tracks cross an earlier route of the Welland Canal, it was officially called Air Line Junction in 1880 and Welland Junction in 1910. But in 1980, Dain City – named after a family that lived there during its early development – was recognized by the Ontario Geographic Names Board.

Places with the word *city* are rare in the Atlantic provinces. The only one other than Labrador City is Forest City in southwestern New Brunswick, a small community adjacent to Forest City, Me.

In Western Canada, many settlements included 'city' in their names with the expectation they would one day grow to live up to that title. Unfortunately, in many cases those dreams remained unfulfilled.

Dominion City, on the Roseau River, 80 kilometres south of Winnipeg, was first called Roseau. But when it was confused with Rosseau, Ont., Dominion was proposed in 1878 for a new railway station on the line linking Winnipeg to St. Paul, Minn. During the following two years of boom times, 'city' was attached to the name. Today, Dominion City has fewer than 400 people.

On the Little Saskatchewan River, 30 kilometres north of Brandon, Man., is a town of 406 people called Rapid City. The town was named in 1878 when an assembly of settlers rejected Saskatchewan City as being too long, and unanimously passed a resolution to append 'city' to a rough English translation of Saskatchewan.

Crystal City is a village of 437 people on Crystal Creek, 110 kilometres southeast of Brandon. It was named about 1883 by its founder, Thomas Greenway, premier of Manitoba from 1888 to 1900. Greenway was optimistic it would become a great city. The village still proudly advertises itself as the 'Friendly City of the South.'

Located 100 kilometres southeast of Prince Albert, Sask., is Star City, a town of 507 people. It was founded by Walter Starkey, who homesteaded there in 1900. He chose the first syllable of his last name and added 'city' in the hope it would become a prominent place.

In 1954, after the discovery of uranium north of Lake Athabasca, Uranium City, Sask., became a town and municipal district. In 1973, E.T. Russell – author of *What's in a Name* – optimistically described it as having passed its boom stage to become a stable community of 1,000 residents. But its municipal offices were closed down in 1985 after Eldorado shut down its mining and milling operations.

Bow City, officially called Eyremore until 1958, was established on the north bank of the Bow River in 1924, 120 kilometres northwest of Medicine Hat. It never really developed beyond a few houses, with its population varying between 10 and 20 over the past thirty years.

The West Kootenay region of British Columbia has seen many instant cities come and, with few exceptions, disappear over the past 100 years. At the turn of the century, between the head of Kootenay Lake and Upper Arrow Lake were places called Duncan City, Trout Lake City, Circle City, and Dawson City. Near the northern tip of Lower Arrow Lake there were Burton City, Cariboo City, and Mineral City. With the exception of Burton, with a population of 130, little evidence remains of any of them.

Slocan, 30 kilometres northwest of Nelson, was an incorporated city from 1901 to 1958, when it was reduced to the status of a village. However, its Canadian Pacific station has retained the name Slocan City.

Queen Charlotte, the unofficial capital of the Queen Charlotte Islands, was grandly named Queen Charlotte City in the 1880s; this has remained a second official name for the community of 280 people.

The Yukon has also been the home of many instant cities. Among those that lasted long enough to be recorded were Calico City, Canyon City, Caribou City, Conrad City, Klondike City, Lynx City, Silver City, and Wind City. The most noted of all was Dawson City, which existed as an incorporated city from 1902 to 1904. It is now an incorporated town still widely known as Dawson City.

Most of these 'cities' sprouted overnight along rail lines or in bustling mining camps. Unfortunately, more often than not, the title did not work as a talisman to protect them from disappearing, if not during a single season, at least after a generation.

Legacy of the Voyageurs on the Prairies

In the West, an isolated, often flat-topped elevation is called a butte, meaning 'small hill' in French. The word was likely first applied by French-speaking voyageurs, hunters, and trappers in the eighteenth century. It was one of several terms, such as prairie, meaning 'meadow,' and portage, meaning 'carrying place' that were absorbed into the English language.

Butte (pronounced 'byoot') occurs in the names of sixty-six physical features and five communities in the four western provinces and the two territories. Some are the most prominent feature for many kilometres around, examples being Lone Eagle Butte, north of Medicine Hat; Sarcee Butte, near Drumheller, Alta.; and Castle Butte, south of

Regina. Nahanni Butte, adjacent to the Liard River in the Northwest Territories, is not a true flat-topped erosional remnant, but is called a butte because it is isolated from other hills.

Some of the names reveal fascinating tales of the West. Massacre Butte, near the head of the Crowsnest River in Alberta, was the place where twelve members of the Fiske Expedition were killed in 1867 by Blood Indians led by Medicine Calf. The town of Picture Butte, 12 kilometres north of Lethbridge, is named for petroglyphs on a former butte, which was excavated and is now the site of a subdivision.

Frenchman Butte, beside the North Saskatchewan River, northeast of Lloydminister, Sask., recalls the tale of a *canadien*, possibly a voyageur from Fort Vermilion, who was killed there by Indians about 1800. Henry and Harry's Butte, near Shaunavon, Sask., is named after two half-brothers, Henry Thormeset and Harry Westvig, who home-steaded there.

The most common term for ravines and glacial spillways in the West is coulee (pronounced 'KOO-lee'), which oc-curs in 219 official names. The word comes from *couler*, meaning 'to flow' in French.

Coulees occur in areas where the topography has been extensively altered by glaciers, heavy rains, and melting snow. They are usually steep, extending back from a broad valley to the flat landscape above. A few, such as Chin Coulee and Etzikom Coulee in southern Alberta, are huge glacial troughs, often a kilometre or more wide, that cut across the short-grass prairie for some 50 kilometres.

Opinion is divided as to whether a coulee is a flowing water feature, a valley, or a combination of the two. Some descriptions in the toponymic records are contradictory. Philp Coulee, in Alberta, is described as 'a land feature (that) flows north from Montana into the Milk River.'

Coulees were best described by geologist Robert Bell in

1875: 'They are valleys or ravines with steep sides, often 100 feet or more in depth, which terminate or close sharply, often at both ends, forming a long trough-like depression; or one of the extremities of a coulee may open into the valley of a regular water course. The coulees sometimes run for miles and are either quite dry or hold ponds of bitter water, which evaporate in the summer and leave thin encrustations of snow-white alkaline salts.'

During the last quarter of the nineteenth century, the southern Prairie provinces were laid out in townships, ranges, and sections. The surveyors, accustomed to gullies and ravines back east, struggled with the unfamiliar term, often writing 'cullies' and 'coolies' in their reports.

Some coulee names have interesting origins. Etzikom Coulee takes its name from the Blackfoot expression for 'Crow Spring,' because the Crow Indian war parties used to obtain water in that coulee. Chin Coulee is a translation of the Blackfoot *mistoamo* ('beard') because the slopes looked like a bearded chin from a distance. Blackstrap Coulee in central Saskatchewan recalls a tale of a pioneer settler who spilled a crock of molasses on a bank of the coulee.

Although coulee occurs in names from the Red River Valley in Manitoba to the Peace River Valley in northeastern British Columbia, the densest concentration of named coulees is in the extensively eroded landscape surrounding the Cypress Hills of southwestern Saskatchewan and southeastern Alberta, and in the valleys of the South Saskatchewan, Oldman, and Belly rivers in southern Alberta. A marked characteristic of these hills and valleys is an annual water deficit for crop production. Various irrigation schemes have been implemented since the turn of the century to tap into the water collecting in the coulees, thus making them economically significant features in the landscape.

There are large areas of the Prairies with no named coulees at all, such as the Souris River Valley in southwestern Manitoba and southeastern Saskatchewan, and the North Saskatchewan River Valley of Alberta. Farmers and ranchers living there are likely to consider *coulee* a word out of a wild west novel, like gulch or canyon. The ravines and gullies in such areas usually contain flowing water during most of the year and, if they are given names, are usually called creeks.

All told, French-speaking explorers and map makers, and later, English-speaking travellers and homesteaders, used words like coulee and butte for unfamiliar landforms, and thus contributed to the rich toponymic tapestry of the Canadian West.

Of Tickles and Rips, Barachois and Bogans

Giving names to land and water features is a fundamental activity of mankind, creating a meeting-place of culture with topography and hydrography. The Atlantic provinces have a fascinating variety of terms describing land and water features.

How many of us are aware that the generic term for a named feature, be it a *lake, creek, hill,* or *bay,* has been imprinted on our minds since early life so that we readily use the same term when we encounter similar features during our travels? Each of us is familiar with about 40 terms, and the kinds of features they apply to. However, English speakers in Canada use nearly 500 different terms in official names for Canadian land, water, and permanent ice features.

Some terms, however, are used for quite different kinds of features. Take *gully,* for example. In central Canada most people consider a gully to be a small ravine or a cut on a hillside formed by a heavy rain. But in the Maritime provinces, the term, derived from the French *goulet* ('neck'), is usually applied to narrow salt-water channels joining water bodies behind sand bars with the sea. The best-known ones in New Brunswick are Tabusintac Gully and Big Tracadie Gully. In Newfoundland, which has more than 250 officially recognized names with gully or gullies, the term is applied to three different kinds of features: a small pond with adjacent wetlands (Tom Howes Gully, Tilleys Gullies); a flowing watercourse (Black Hummock Gully); and a coastal cove (Partridge Berry Gully).

Tickle occurs in nearly 250 approved names for water features along the coasts of Newfoundland and Labrador, and in 7 names in Nova Scotia. It is a narrow, treacherous salt-water channel, often characterized by hazardous tidal currents and rocks, both submerged and exposed. Among the many intriguing names in Newfoundland are Blind Mugford Tickle, Pinchgut Tickle, Headforemost Tickle, and Ingargarnekulluk Tickle.

Outside the Atlantic provinces, stretches of watercourses with no perceptible flow are usually unnamed in Canada. However, such features are frequently named in Newfoundland, Nova Scotia, and New Brunswick. The commonest word for a quiet stretch of water in Newfoundland is *steady*, approved in 71 names, including Elijaks Steady, Old Shop Steadies, and Rattling Brook Steadies. A similar feature in Nova Scotia is best known as a *stillwater*, where there are more than 175 with names like Black Rattle Stillwater, Corkum Stillwater, and Devils Funnel Stillwater. Nova Scotia also has 41 authorized names with *deadwater*, two being Coolan Deadwater and Barrio Deadwater. The most widely used term in New Brunswick for a smooth section of a river is *deadwater*, with nearly 60 names bearing the term. Pocomoonshine Deadwater, Pocowogamis Deadwater, and Semiwagan Deadwater are examples.

Barachois is used extensively for a coastal salt-water pond on the south and west coasts of Newfoundland, and along the Gulf of St. Lawrence shores of the three Maritime provinces and Québec. Originally applied by the Basques and the Acadian French to the gravel bar in front of the pond where fishing boats could be drawn up, the term was extended to the pond protected by the bar. Subsequently, it became an element in many other names.

In Newfoundland, the term *barachois* has not been standardized into a single spelling. The most frequent spelling there is *barasway*, as in Barasway de Cerf, Belleoram Barasway, L'Anse au Loup Barasway, Peltry Barasway, and 62 other approved names. As well, 29 names in Newfoundland use the form *barachois*, examples being Rocky Barachois Bight, Barachois Outside Pond, and Middle Barachois River. Just to be contrary, there is a locality on Hermitage Bay called Barachoix, with Barasway Harbour the name of the adjacent cove.

Nova Scotia has 34 *barachois* features, among them being Gabarus Barachois and MacLean Barachois. The term occurs eight times in New Brunswick and twice in Prince Edward Island. The community of Barachois-de-Malbaie on Québec's Gaspé Peninsula has a population of more than 500.

A backwater channel adjoining a river in northern New Brunswick is commonly known as a *bogan*. The term, derived from the Micmac and Maliseet languages, is given to 30 names, including Fanton Bogan and Mersereau Bogan. A synonymous term of Micmac and Maliseet origin is *padou*, which occurs in two names upriver from Fredericton – Pickards Padou and Sugar Island Padou. Both terms occur in the name Banks of Padou Bogan on the Tobique River and, with a variant spelling, in Drakes Perdue Bogan on the Southwest Miramichi River.

A low-lying, seasonally flooded section along a river where wild hay can be cut is often called *intervale*. Nova

Scotia has 16 named intervales (for example, Framboise Intervale) and New Brunswick has 12 (Meduxnekeag Intervale).

In Nova Scotia and New Brunswick, several flat, wet areas with low-growing vegetation are known as *heaths*. An example in Nova Scotia is Spinneys Heath; in New Brunswick, Dorsey Heath. A similar feature in Nova Scotia is also called a *savannah*, where Black Georges Savannah and Dumpling Savannah are found.

A common term for rapids on rivers in southwestern New Brunswick is *rips*. Winding Stairs Rips and Meetinghouse Rips are two such rapids. Some turbulent waters in Passamaquoddy Bay also have named rips.

Aboiteau, a French word for a one-way sluice, has been extended to Parrsboro Aboiteau, a pond in Nova Scotia. *Drook* and *droke* are sometimes used to describe a grove of trees in Newfoundland, but in names they apply to brackish watercourses there and in Nova Scotia.

Among other unusual generic terms occurring in the names within one or more of the Atlantic provinces are: *gulch* (a ravine), *thoroughfare* (a channel), *soi* (a salt-water cove), *thrum* (an exposed rock in the sea), *nub* (a small island), *tolt* (an isolated hill), *vault* (a ravine), *mocauque* (a cranberry barren), *runround* (a subsidiary river channel), *flowage* (a shallow pond), *gut* (a narrow salt-water channel), *blow-me-down* (a steep headland), *brandies* (submerged rocks), *cay* (an exposed rock in the sea), *dyke* (a small watercourse), *lead* (a channel), *mash* and *mish* (a marsh), and *oven* (a coastal cave).

Christmas Creek ... and Other Yuletide Honours

Christmas is a joyous time, a season for celebration and glad tidings. It is not surprising, therefore, that many of the words and expressions associated with Christmas should be applied to geographical features across Canada.

In the remote forests of central New Brunswick a turbulent brook goes by the name of North Pole Stream. It was called that by the lumbermen in the mid-1800s, either because it was the farthest north that they had cut trees or because it was especially cold when they ventured towards its head.

In 1964, Arthur F. Wightman, then the New Brunswick member on the Canadian Permanent Committee on Geographical Names, gave the name North Pole Mountain to a 210-metre height at the head of the stream, stating that he was naming it for the mythical home of Santa Claus. To an adjoining peak he gave the name Mount St. Nicholas. This, in turn, inspired him to name eight nearby peaks for St. Nick's trusty reindeer. To the right of Mount St. Nicholas (looking downstream), he named Mount Dasher, Mount Dancer, Mount Vixen, Mount Prancer, and Mount Comet; to the left, Mount Blitzen, Mount Donder, and Mount Cupid.

Wightman derived these names from the famous poem by Clement Moore, *A Visit from St. Nicholas*, better known by its opening lines: ''Twas the night before Christmas, when all through the house ... ' First published anonymously in 1823 in the Troy, N.Y., *Sentinel*, it was republished in *The Globe* of Toronto in 1854 under Moore's name. The version in *The Globe* refers to Dunder and Blixen, and turns Vixen into Nixen!

Continuing with this enchanting theme, Wightman proposed honouring the most famous reindeer of all, Rudolph of red-nosed fame. He was informed that such a name smacked of commercialism and did not have the sanction of long recognition in the literature of the Christmas season. So there is no Mount Rudolph in New Brunswick.

On the British Columbia–Alberta boundary, some 25

kilometres north of Kicking Horse Pass, is a towering mountain with the name St. Nicholas Peak. It was named in 1908 by A.O. Wheeler, a topographical surveyor, who was impressed with a resemblance to the profile of Santa Claus on one side of the mountain.

In the Yukon, two streams are called Christmas Creek. On the one that flows into Christmas Bay of Kluane Lake, Richard Fullerton and Rev. John Pringle, a Presbyterian minister, found and staked a claim on Christmas Day, 1903. On the other, a tributary of Matson Creek west of Dawson, gold was discovered on 25 December 1911.

British Columbia also has two streams named Christmas Creek, and one of them has Tiny Tim Lake near its headwaters. Christmas Hill and Christmas Point, and even Yule Rock and Yule Lake, are in the province too, but unfortunately none of the stories associated with them has been collected for the official records.

In Alberta, a tributary of the Athabasca River is called Christmas Creek, and Manitoba has three lakes called Christmas Lake. One of these is a translation of the Cree for Christmas, *Makosakeesekow*. Another was named in 1948 to honour Richard Edward Christmas, who was killed overseas during the Second World War while serving with the Royal Winnipeg Rifles.

On the Saskatchewan–Northwest Territories boundary is Santy Lake. It was not named for 'Santy' Claus, but for Flight Sgt. Samuel F. Santy of Moose Jaw, another casualty in the Second World War. Santa Lake in the Parry Sound district of Ontario was named for Pte. Ambrose Santa of Drayton, Ont., who was killed overseas in 1944.

In Ontario, there are two islands in lakes in Muskoka District called Christmas Island. Both were named in 1968: one had been given as a Christmas gift; the other is almost exactly halfway between the equator and the North Pole, home of Santa Claus. Santa's Village, a tourist attraction in Bracebridge, was named for the same reason. Another Christmas Island, near Kenora, was named in 1980 because the pine trees growing on it portrayed an image of the festive season.

Nova Scotia has two islands named Christmas as well, both in Bras d'Or Lake. The one near Eskasoni is known in Micmac as *Abadakwitcetc* ('a small portion set aside'). The other is 12 kilometres to the west; the community of Christmas Island is located nearby.

On the south coast of Newfoundland, at the mouth of La Poile Bay, is a prominent point called Christmas Head. Near the town of Grand Falls–Windsor is a body of water called Upper Christmas Pond, but the lake, formerly called Christmas Pond, upstream from Upper Christmas Pond, is officially Lewis Pond.

Québec has several features and places with the names Saint-Nicolas and Saint-Noël, with some of them no doubt associated with Christmas. Numerous lakes and other features in the province are called Noël. Near Joliette, northeast of Montréal, is the town of L'Épiphanie, which honours the Twelfth-night of Christmas, sometimes called Little Christmas. The municipality of Biencourt, east of Rivière-du-Loup, was formerly called La Nativité.

And what is Christmas without the traditional Christmas feast?

Begin the celebration with Pointe à Champagne (Qué.) in Committee Punch Bowl (Alta.), with a reading from Charles Dickens Point (N.W.T.). Seat your guests around Dinner Place Creek (Man.). On each plate serve generous slices of roast Turkey Point (Ont.), accompanied by baked Potato Creek (Yukon), boiled Carrot River (Sask.), and Peas Brook (N.S.), and, of course, large dollops of Cranberry Point (P.E.I.). After the main course offer steamed Pudding Burn (B.C.), flambéd with Brandy Brook (N.B.), and a piece of pie made with Bakeapple Bay (Nfld.). Complete the dinner with Coffee Creek (Ont.) and selections from Lac des Bonbons (Qué.).

Season's greetings!

Of Valentines and Other Matters of the Heart

On 14 February 1718, a French missionary celebrated the first mass in a new settlement on the west side of Rivière Richelieu, some 20 kilometres south of present-day Saint-Jean-sur-Richelieu, Qué. In honour of the occasion, the settlers were given permission to name the place Saint-Valentin.

Valentine's Day embodies a pleasant mix of mystical romance, playfulness, and innocent amorous entreaty, usually expressed through florid, gushy cards, flowers, and chocolates. Why is there a joyous but somewhat frivolous day dedicated to a saint? Why Valentine? Why the middle of February?

Valentine's Day has its roots in the ancient Roman fertility festival of Lupercalia, observed on 15 February, when the first urgings of spring touched all the senses. Legend has it that one, perhaps two, Christians by the name of Valentine were martyred in Rome about 14 February in the third century. The early church adroitly associated the name of the saint, or saints, with the pagan celebration to sanction the festive practices of its Christian believers.

Besides Saint-Valentin, there are twenty-four features – mostly islands, lakes, and hills – in Canada with *valentine* or *valentin*. Many were named because of their distinctive V shape, such as Valentine Lake in central Newfoundland and Valentine Lake near Hearst, Ont. An elevation with two pronounced summits overlooking Powell River, B.C., is known as Valentine Hill.

Some valentine names honour people. Valentine Creek, which flows north into Lake Diefenbaker in Saskatchewan, is named for George Valentine, an early settler. Valentine Lake, southwest of Newcastle, N.B., derived its name from A. Valentine Mitchell, a trapper who lived near it and adjacent Mitchell Lake at one time.

Among Newfoundland's many delightful names is Cupids, a town of 870 people located on the west side of Conception Bay, 30 kilometres due west of St. John's. John Guy of Bristol, who was appointed governor of Newfoundland in 1610, chose Cuper's Cove for the centre of a colony of thirty-nine settlers. Possibly because of the practice of suppressing the *r* by people in southern England, the forms Cupid's Cove and Cupids easily evolved, the latter form noted in 1630 by Nova Scotia–founder William Alexander. Considering that Cupid was the Roman god of love, it is endearing to know that the wife of Nicholas Guie (not known to be related to the governor) gave birth at Cupids in the spring of 1613 to the first white child born in Newfoundland.

In Ontario, Cupid Island is in Georgian Bay's Thirty Thousand Islands, and Cupids Rock is in the St. Marys River southeast of Sault Ste. Marie. The Greek equivalent of Cupid is Eros, and this is reflected in the name Eros Lake, southeast of Geraldton, Ont. Beside it is Erato Lake, given for the Greek Muse of lyric poetry.

In matters of the heart, Newfoundland stands out again as the province with the most appealing names. On the east side of Trinity Bay are Heart's Content, an incorporated town, noted by John Guy in 1612 as 'Hartes content'; Heart's Desire, also an incorporated town, possibly associated with a seventeenth-century vessel by the same name; and Heart's Delight, united in 1972 with nearby Islington to form a town with a population in 1991 of 880. On the west side of Trinity Bay is the community of Little Heart's Ease, with a population of 430.

The words *heart* and *coeur* occur in more than 100 names across Canada, often because of the shape of the feature. Noteworthy is Heart Shoal in Georgian Bay, whose outline on charts at the 10-fathom level is distinctly heart-shaped. Hearts Hill, a hamlet southwest of North Battleford, Sask., is adjacent to a range of hills with the configuration of a heart. Also in Saskatchewan, in Prince Albert National Park, is Hanging Heart Lake, whose northern part is shaped like a heart, although there is a legend that a heart was once found hanging from a tree. In Alberta, Heart Lake Indian Reserve is located beside a heart-shaped lake with a long point extending from its north side. Near Mount Waddington in British Columbia is Heartstone Peak, a mountain named for the large heart-shaped outcrop apparent on its south side.

At Motion Head in Newfoundland, a few kilometres 'up the shore' (actually south) from St. John's, is Bow and Arrow Shoal. If it could be aimed northwest, it would point at Merrymeeting Point, 4 kilometres away; or to the southwest for the same distance, at Hearts Point.

Except for Prince Edward Island and the Yukon, each of the provinces and territories has at least one feature with the words *love*, *lovers*, or *amour*. Both Newfoundland and Nova Scotia have little bays called Lovers Cove. Ontario has two narrow, secluded channels called Lovers Lane, one in the Thousand Islands of the St. Lawrence, the other in Georgian Bay's Thirty Thousand Islands. It also has a Lovers Isle on the west side of the Bruce Peninsula and a Lovers Creek near Barrie.

Two lakes with *love* in Manitoba are named for people: Love Lake near Neepawa for John Love, a homesteader; and Love Lake near Sherridon for Ernest Love, a mine official who was once chased by a bear when he was fishing there.

North of Nipawin, Sask., is a village called Love, named in 1930, possibly for an official of the Canadian Pacific Railway, which passes through the community. There is another story of a lumberman becoming captivated by a young woman who cooked for logging crews at this rail siding, but it has the marks of a tall tale evolving from a name already given.

Québec has several features with *amour*, including Havre des Belles Amours, Ruisseau d'Amour, Baie des Amoureux, and Lac de l'Amour. In Labrador, adjacent to the Strait of Belle Isle, is a place called L'Anse-Amour but, alas, this is likely a misnomer, as the adjoining bay is called Anse aux Morts, perhaps recalling multiple drownings there.

A number of great lovers in history and legend are recalled in place names. On Vancouver Island, the first couple of the Creation are remembered in Adam River and Eve River. (On the current large-scale topographical map of the area, the compiler left the single river formed by the two unnamed, shrewdly leaving it to the map reader to discover which is tributary to the other!) Between the two rivers are prominent peaks called Mount Romeo and Mount Juliet.

In the Coast Mountains north of Vancouver, among a group of peaks named for classical figures, are Mount Eurydice and Mount Orpheus, separated by Styx Glacier. These names are drawn from the legend of the eternal separation of Orpheus from his great love, Eurydice, by the River Styx. Among the highest peaks of the northern Rockies in northeastern British Columbia are Mount Ulysses and Mount Penelope, named in 1961 and commemorating the Greek legend of Odysseus (Ulysses in Latin) and his faithful wife.

Now, for that favourite Valentine (Ont.) girl, send her a Bouquet Point (P.E.I.) of Flowers Cove (Nfld.) and a Gift Lake (Alta.) of a Box Canyon (B.C.) of Chocolate Cove (N.B.). She will send you back a pretty Card Lake (N.S.) edged with Lacey Point (N.W.T.). After that you

will go together to Dancing Hill (Man.) at Happyland
Creek (Sask.), where you will exchange a Secret Creek
(Yukon) and Lac Kiss (Qué.).

Giving the Devil His Due

Name givers and explorers have largely bypassed the Cre-
ator in Canada's place names. Gods Lake in Manitoba,
Bay of Gods Mercy at the north end of Hudson Bay, and
Islands of God's Mercie in Hudson Strait are rare excep-
tions. In contrast, the Devil and his associated names –
Satan, Diablo, Mammon, Lucifer, Beelzebub, Sorcerer,
and Windigo/Wendigo – have been widely honoured in
Canadian place names. His traditional homes – Hell,
Hades, and Enfer – are also prominently recorded from
Newfoundland to the Yukon.

Newfoundland has thirty official 'devil' names, with several places called Devils Cove. Some of the more imaginative applications are Devils Dancing Place, a marsh on
the Avalon Peninsula; Devils Dancing Table, a hill on the
south coast; and Devils Dressing Place, another hill, this
one beside White Bay on the north coast of the island.
The province also has two places called Devils Kitchen,
as well as a Devils Knob and a Devils Lookout Island.
The French form *diable* occurs in Diable Bay and L'Anse
au Diable Brook. 'Hell' turns up in Newfoundland names
twelve times, including Backside of Hell Cove adjacent
to Granby Island, Labrador; Hell Fire Pond on the Avalon
Peninsula; and Hell Grapple Head on Black Island in the
Bay of Exploits. Hells Al, a hill on the Avalon Peninsula,
was found by Memorial University students in 1981; the
name's significance was not determined. The Torngat
Mountains in northern Labrador derive their name from
the Inuktitut for 'home of the spirits.'

Prince Edward Island has only a single devilish name: Devils Punchbowl Provincial Park, at the site where more than 100 years ago John Hawkins lost a puncheon of rum in a deep hole and then recovered it.

There are forty names with devil in Nova Scotia. Among them are The Devils Burrow, a marsh near Windsor; Devils Cupboard, a cove on the eastern shore; Devils Funnel Stillwater, a pond near Liverpool; and Devils Limb, an island on the south shore. Hell names are found in Hell Rackets, a reef in Mahone Bay; Hells Gates, a channel in Medway Harbour; and Helluva Hole, a pond near Windsor. Main-à-Dieu, in Cape Breton County, appears to mean 'hand of God,' but is really derived from a Micmac word for the Devil.

New Brunswick has eighteen devil names, examples being: Devil Pike Brook in Kings County; Devils Back Brook in Northumberland County; Devils Elbow Rapids in Restigouche County; Devils Half Acre, a hill in Albert County; another Devils Half Acre, a shoal in Passamaquoddy Bay; and Devils Hand, an 8-metre-high rock in Charlotte County, with huge finger grooves. Hellcat Brook, Hells Gate Rapids, and Hells Kitchen, a deep ravine in Fundy National Park, are examples of the province's eight hell names.

Québec has honoured the prince of demons in sixty-six place names, most of them in the French *diable*. Lac Bat-le-Diable, near Havre-Saint-Pierre, commemorates the achievements of one William Cormier, a local hunter and fisherman who was given the nickname which means 'beat the Devil.' Other *diable* names include Crique du Diable in Labelle County, Pointe au Diable in Soulanges County, Pont du Diable in Frontenac County, and several Rapides du Diable, Rivière du Diable, and Ruisseau du Diable. Québec's twenty-three hell names are mostly with the French *enfer*, although there is a Lac Helluva near Schefferville. The province also has a Lac Hades, a Lac Lucifer, and a Mont du Sorcier. Windigo, the name for mythical cannibals of the Ojibwas and other Indians, occurs in twenty names in Québec.

Ontario has given the Devil his due in seventy-eight places. My first encounter in the 1940s with a devil place name was the precipitous Devils Glen near Collingwood. I was told it was so named because a wrong step would surely lead to death. Then there is Devil Door Rapids, Devils Cellar Rapids, Devil Shoepack Falls, Devil's Warehouse Island, and Devils Punchbowl Lake. Hell occurs in seven names in Ontario, including Hellangone Lake in Parry Sound District and Helldiver Bay in Kenora District. Windigo, or Wendigo, is reflected in thirty-two names; Windigo Lake, Wendigo Lake, and Windigo Island each occur several times. Ontario also has three names with Hades, one being Hades Islands in Lake of the Woods. And there are four Styx names; River Styx is a treacherous area in the Cataraqui River section of the Rideau Canal system.

The Devil has nineteen names in Manitoba. Interesting ones are Daredevil Hill near Neepawa; Devils Punch Bowl, a crater-like ravine near Brandon; and Devils Portage near The Pas. Manitoba has two features called Windigo Lake as well as a Wendigo Beach, Wendigo River, and Wendigo Point.

Saskatchewan has recognized the Devil in eight names, among them Great Devil Rapids and Little Devil Rapids on the Churchill River. Helldiver Lake is near Cumberland House. Hellfire Creek, close to the U.S. border south of Gravelbourg, is said to have been named by a homesteader who found the area 'as hot as hell's fires.'

Alberta also has eight Devil names, including Devil's Bite, a hill southwest of Calgary with one side gouged out, and Devils Thumb, a mountain near Lake Louise. Hell-Roaring Falls is a tributary of the Smoky River, south of Grande Prairie.

The rugged landscape and tumultuous rivers of British Columbia have evoked the Devil in twenty-nine place names. Among them are Devils Claw Mountain in Cassiar District, Devils Club Mountain in Cariboo District, Devils Den Lake in Alberni District, Devils Spire in Kootenay District, and Devils Thumb in Cassiar District. (Devil's Tongue, Devil's Tooth, and Devil's Rectum are unofficial names in the province.) In 1960, some mountains in an area of the Coast Mountains known as the 'White Inferno' were named for the mythical chief lords of Satan: Beelzebub, Azazel, Belial, Dagon, Moloch, and Rimmon. Mount Satan and Ogre Mountain also occur in the same group. North of the group is Purgatory Glacier and Styx Mountain. Also in the province are Lucifer Peak, Sorcerer Mountain, and Witch Spirit Lake. Hell appears in fifteen names in British Columbia, including the turbulent Hells Gate in the Fraser Canyon, Hell Gate in the Grand Canyon of the Liard, Hell Raving Creek in the Coast Mountains, Hellroarer Creek east of Okanagan Lake, and Hellsgate Slough beside the Skeena River. A set of dangerous rapids on the North Thompson River is called Porte d'Enfer Rapids.

In the Northwest Territories, three names pay respect to the Devil. Devil Island recalls the 1900 expedition of the Norwegian explorer Otto Sverdrup, which faced starvation on this island between Devon and Ellesmere islands. Hell Gate, in the same area, was also named by Sverdrup, who described the passage as a surging mixture of raging water. Hell Roaring Creek is a tributary of the South Nahanni River, and Hell's Gate Rapids is a variant for Figure of Eight Rapids on the same river. Tuurngatalik Island, on the south side of Baffin Island, gets its name from the Inuktitut expression 'it has devil spirits.'

The Yukon has three Devil names: Devilhole Creek, Devil's Club Creek, and Devils Elbow. Hellsgate Rapid is a perilous section of the Yukon River.

A computer search of the Canadian Geographical Names

Data Base produced the lists of devil and hell names. The printouts also dumped out such personal names as Mandeville, Mitchell, and Burchell. When the first printout was made, smoke arose from the computer terminal, burning out a transistor!

A Giggle, er, Gaggle of Ha!Ha!s

The townsfolk of Saint-Louis-du-Ha! Ha! have long endured the amusement and disbelief of visitors, who are curious to learn how the place ever acquired such a comical name, and perhaps wonder which Louis among the saints was distinguished by his laughter. Perched by the side of a 380-metre hill, the village of 1,530 is just off the Trans-Canada Highway, 70 kilometres east of Rivière-du-Loup, Qué.

For many years, it has been speculated that the 'Ha! Ha!' part of the name recalled either a Huron word for 'portage' or an early explorer's exclamation. However, neither claim has any basis in fact.

The French word *haha* really means an unexpected barrier, or a dead end. Its use can be traced to the time of Joan of Arc in the fifteenth century. It was accepted by the French Academy in 1762 as a legitimate word to describe ditches outside openings in a wall around a park. The openings afforded a vista of the surrounding countryside while the hahas marked the park boundaries. On farms and in gardens in the south of England, a ha-ha is a sunken fence that segregates livestock from a manor house without interrupting the view across the estate's fields.

In Canada, the word *haha* first appeared on early maps of New France. A 1686 French map and eighteenth-century English maps show an island, a river, and a mountain called 'Haha' in the Bay of Fundy region.

So where is the unforeseen obstacle for which Saint-Louis-du-Ha! Ha! is named? Eight kilometres east of the village is 40-kilometre-long Lac Témiscouata. As early travellers headed north by canoe, they discovered that the lake curved to the northeast – away from their destination of the St. Lawrence River and Québec City. The little bay on the west side (mentioned in early records as Baie du Ha! Ha!, but never officially named) represented an unexpected and inconvenient dead end for travel by canoe. Travellers were forced to portage 80 kilometres west to Notre-Dame-du-Portage on the St. Lawrence. They walked through the village of Saint-Louis-du-Ha! Ha!, named after its founder Louis Marquis. The municipal parish of Saint-Louis-du-Ha! Ha! was established in 1874.

But why the exclamation marks? It seems they were the result of another interpretation of the origin of the village's name disseminated by surveyors and writers, including Joseph Bouchette, the surveyor general and map maker of Lower Canada in the early 1800s; Bouchette's son, Joseph Bouchette, Jr., the deputy surveyor general; and Arthur Buies, a noted nineteenth-century historian and writer. They wrote that astonished explorers exclaimed 'ha! ha!' when they found their route was blocked, and subsequently named the body of water a 'Ha! Ha!'

A number of place names with the expression Ha! Ha! also dot Québec's Saguenay region. Eighty kilometres from the mouth of Rivière Saguenay, the waterway appears to divide into two major branches. The northern branch leads to Lac Saint-Jean, where the river rises. The southern branch is just as wide, but Baie des Ha! Ha! comes to a dead end within 10 kilometres. The plural form of the name is due to two coves at the head of the bay that act as hahas by giving the illusion of leading to another waterway. Flowing into one of the coves from the south is the 55-kilometre-long Rivière Ha! Ha! It drains two lakes called Lac Ha! Ha! and Petit lac Ha! Ha!

Baie des Ha! Ha! is also a prominent 15-kilometre inlet on the north shore of the Gulf of St. Lawrence. The bay gives the appearance of being the outlet of a major river, but in fact it leads only to several rocky barriers and small streams. The name Baye du Haha was in use as early as 1715. Ha Ha Rock is a 2-metre submerged hazard in Ontario's Georgian Bay.

Newfoundland has two widely separated inlets with 'Ha Ha' as part of their names. Ha Ha Bay is a 4-kilometre inlet near the north end of the Northern Peninsula, 15 kilometres west of L'Anse aux Meadows. A sand bar (or haha) at the south end of the bay, separating it from the appropriately named Isthmus Cove, prevents passage to Pistolet Bay to the south. On the east side of the bay stands Ha Ha Mountain, a 70-metre hill. Ha Ha Point is at the east entrance of the bay. The nearby community of Raleigh was originally called Ha Ha, but was renamed earlier this century by the Newfoundland Nomenclature Board. Several names of French origin in the area – Pistolet Bay, Falaise Point, Piton Point – suggest the bay was named by French fishermen or explorers.

The Ha Ha is an inlet at the town of Burgeo, on the south coast of Newfoundland. The head of this inlet is separated by a narrow isthmus (or haha) from another inlet called Long Reach. The Ha Ha was also likely named by the French during early exploration.

The proper spelling of place names such as Baie des Ha! Ha! has long been a source of debate among historians and map makers. In 1938, the Société Historique du Saguenay determined that 'haha' was the proper form, and encouraged historians to refer to the local inlet as Baie des Hahas. In 1947, Father Victor Tremblay wrote an extensive treatise on the origin of the word *haha* and concluded that the substantial historical and geographical evidence favoured the forms Baie du Haha and Baie des Hahas.

The Quebec Geographic Board (predecessor of the Commission de toponymie) informed the federal names office in 1947 that the correct form for the Saguenay inlet was Baie des Ha! Ha!, although acknowledging that 'haha' was an old French word meaning an unexpected barrier on a route. However, the Ottawa names office advised federal map and hydrographic chart makers that the correct name to use was Ha Ha Bay, the form authorized by Ottawa in 1901. It was only in 1960 that Baie des Ha! Ha! was approved for federal mapping.

Names with Ha! Ha! in Québec and Ha Ha in Newfoundland almost all identify water features that have land barriers. The present erroneous spellings have considerable historical precedence, so it would be most unlikely that the Commission de toponymie in Québec or the Geographical Names Board in Newfoundland would consider 'correcting' such names as Baie des Ha! Ha! to Baie des Hahas, or Ha Ha Bay to Haha Bay.

Saint-Louis-du-Ha! Ha! and The Ha Ha, among a dozen 'haha' place-names, reflect more than 300 years of Canadian heritage – and quite unintentionally provide us with a little surprise and merriment.

Adopting Names of Native Origin and Acknowledging Names Used by Indigenous Peoples

Native Place Names: We All Have Our Favourites

No place names distinguish a country better than those of native origin. And each of us likely has a favourite.

For some, it may be Antigonish, the small Nova Scotia town made famous for the cooperative movement which began there in the early 1930s. Reported to mean 'where the bears tear the branches off trees,' the name more likely means 'flowing through broken marsh.'

Québec is another favourite, meaning 'where the waters narrow,' in reference to the St. Lawrence upriver from Île d'Orléans. Its counterpart in Nova Scotia is Chebucto, the Micmac name for The Narrows in Halifax Harbour. The usual meaning given for Chebucto, 'a great long harbour,' is really just a variation of the idea of a narrow water body. Ontario, a pleasing name to many, is usually considered to be Iroquoian for 'handsome lake,' but may be better interpreted as deriving from the Huron for 'large lake.'

The southern British Columbia names Keremeos and Similkameen are deemed especially pleasing by some. Both are derived from Salish, the first meaning 'wind passage in the mountains,' the latter, 'swimming river.' My own favourite is Kitwanga (pronounced 'KIT-wahn-gaw'), the name of a small community east of Prince Rupert, meaning in Tsimshian, 'people of the place of many rabbits.'

No one can really deny the musical charm and sweet lilt of Athabasca, 'where there are reeds'; Madawaska, 'land of porcupines,' in New Brunswick; in Ontario, Madawaska literally translates as 'reeds at the forks of the river,' but the original name, Matouachita, points to Matououescarine, 'people of the shallows,' who were encountered by Champlain in 1613. Wascana, 'pile of bones,' the Cree name for Regina; Minnedosa, 'swift water' in Sioux, the equivalent of the Cree Saskatchewan; Winnipeg, 'murky water' in Cree, the equivalent of the Sioux Minnesota; Wawanesa, 'whippoorwill,' noted as an insurance company centre near Brandon; Coaticook, 'river of pines,' a town south of Sherbrooke; and Muskoka, the name of a chief given to Ontario's premier cottage country.

Some people, however, dismiss names of native origin because of either their simplicity in meaning or the awkwardness of their pronunciation.

Some names that mean only 'big bay' (Malpeque), 'big water' (Meelpaeg Lake, Nfld.), 'big river' (Mississippi, Koksoak, Yukon), and 'fine river' (Oromocto) are occasionally ridiculed because of their ordinariness. Names that are difficult to pronounce are avoided by many – Musquodoboit, 'flowing out in foam'; Magaguadavic, 'big eels place'; Kashagawigamog, 'long and narrow'; Kaministiquia, 'place of islands in the river'; Illecillewaet, 'swift river'; Auyuittuq, 'place which does not melt' (the national park on Baffin Island); and Chinguacousy, 'young or little pines,' the township surrounding Brampton, Ont., where I was born.

Sometimes similar origins are revealed in names that do not appear to have common roots, examples being Timiskaming, Témiscouata, and Chicoutimi, with their reference to deep water; Baddeck and Petitcodiac, with their characteristic feature of bending sharply; and Saugeen, Mississauga, and Saguenay with their reference to a river mouth.

Most spellings are only imperfect renderings of what natives may have said to explorers, who then provided their interpretations to publishers and map makers. Names with the idea of 'ochre' were variously rendered as Romaine, Onaman, and Wunnammin, all from related languages. Chippewa and Ojibwa are different names for the same language. *The Handbook of Indians of Canada* (1912) lists 169 variants of Ottawa – Ahtawwah through Outaouais to Watawawiniwok.

The varied native languages in Canada have given our toponymy certain distinctiveness and rustic beauty. Increased knowledge of these languages and an appreciation of the nomenclature derived from them are among the elements in the understanding of Canadian geography and history.

Native Names for Native Places

On 1 January 1987, the municipality of Frobisher Bay became officially known as Iqaluit. The name, meaning 'place of fish' in Inuktitut, was long used by the Inuit for their community at this major centre of the eastern Arctic on Baffin Island.

Settlement in the area of Frobisher Bay has its roots in the establishment of a Hudson's Bay Company post on the south side of Frobisher Bay in December 1914, some 125 kilometres southeast of the present municipality. The post, actually a simple 3-metre by 4-metre hut, was moved up the bay to Fletcher Island in the spring of 1915. Five years later it was transferred across the 35-kilometre-wide Frobisher Bay to Waddell Bay. From 1921 to 1949, the post was located on Cormack Bay, some 70 kilometres southeast of present Iqaluit. In the fall of 1949, the Frobisher Bay post was moved to Apex Hill, 6 kilometres southeast of the United States air base, built near the head of the bay in 1942. In 1951, the area of the air base was officially named Frobisher, and that of the trading post was called Frobisher Bay. The latter became Apex in 1965.

In 1971, the municipal hamlet of Frobisher Bay in the area of the air base was incorporated. It became a village in 1974, a town in 1980.

In December 1984, the residents of Frobisher Bay voted 310 to 213 to have the name replaced by Iqaluit. This was subsequently confirmed by the Northwest Territories Executive Council, to take effect on the first day of 1987.

In 1965, the small Inuit community between the townsite and Apex Hill was officially named Ikaluit. As the community is within the town of Iqaluit, this variant spelling was dropped in 1989.

As to the name for the water feature, originally called Frobisher's Strait in 1576 by Martin Frobisher, there are no plans to change Frobisher Bay.

Recognition of native community names in preference to non-native names began in the western Arctic, where Tuktoyaktuk replaced Port Brabant in 1950. Vilhjalmur Stefansson reported that 'Tuktuyaktok,' meaning 'place where there are caribou,' was in use when he was there in the winter of 1907. However, the Hudson's Bay Company introduced the name Port Brabant in 1936, and this was adopted by the Geographic Board a year later. In 1948, postal officials requested the acceptance of Tuktoyaktuk for the new post office, but HBC and the noted ethnologist Diamond Jenness recommended Tuktuk. The board disliked this popular variation of the native name, and adopted Port Brabant for the post office. Two years later the board accepted the local name Tuktoyaktuk for the community and post office.

Much of the recent work in native name restoration has been undertaken by the Commission de toponymie du Québec to reflect more closely the usage of the Inuit. Examples were the change of Port Harrison to Inoucdjouac (although Port Harrison remained the postal name), Notre-Dame-d'Ivugivic to Ivujuvik, and Notre-Dame-de-Koartac to Koartac. Even Port Burwell was changed to Killiniq by the Québec commission, although the community, since abandoned, was in the Northwest Territories.

In 1979 and 1980, the commission decided that the actual names and the romanized spellings used by the native people in their own communities should take precedence. The following year Canada Post agreed to change its postal designations to conform to local preferences. The main changes that resulted in Québec were:

Inukjuak, from Port Harrison (1908) and Inoucdjouac (1965)

Kangiqsualujjuaq, from George River (1876) and Port-Nouveau-Québec (1965)

Kangiqsujuaq, from Wakeham Bay (1930s) and Maricourt (Wakeham) (1965)

Kangirsuk, from Payne Bay (1940s) and Bellin (Payne) (1965)

Kuujjuaq, from Fort Chimo (1830–43, 1866) and Fort-Chimo (1965)

Quaqtaq, from Koartak (1940s) and Notre-Dame-de-Koartac (1961) and Koartac (1965)

Salluit, from Sugluk (1947) and Saglouc (1965).

As early as 1756 there was a trading post at Great Whale River on the east coast of Hudson Bay. The community was renamed Poste-de-la-Baleine in 1965, and the post office was changed to this in 1979. The Québec commission officially recognized the Inuit name Kuujjuaraapik in 1979 for the Inuit part of the village, and Whapmagoostui for the Cree part. Canada Post changed the post office to Kuujjuaraapik in 1992.

How well some of the native names are being received throughout the native communities of the North remains to be seen. In arranging for air travel from Kuujjuaq to other communities, it has been said that some native travellers will use the previous name (George River) to ensure that they get to Kangiqsualujjuaq, if that's where they're going, and not to Kangiqsujuaq.

Elsewhere in Canada, the trend of changing community names to those used by native people, where they form the majority of residents, is slowly picking up.

In British Columbia, the Indian band council of Port Simpson requested in 1985 that its community be changed to Lax Kw'alaams. Meaning 'place of wild roses' in Tsimshian, this name had long been used by the native people. The change was officially made in July 1986, based on agreement by the names committee members for British Columbia and the federal Department of Indian and Northern Affairs. Canada Post also renamed its post office. Port Simpson itself was named in 1831 for Capt. Aemilius Simpson, who was then employed in the Nass River area in the marine service of the Hudson's Bay Company.

In 1989, the name of the hamlet Eskimo Point, N.W.T., on the west coast of Hudson Bay, was changed to Arviat. In 1992, Spence Bay, N.W.T., at the south end of Boothia Peninsula, became Taloyoak, and the Dene name Lutselk'e was substituted for Snowdrift, on the southeastern shore of Great Slave Lake.

By the end of the century there may be few English and French names of native communities left in Canada. As reviews are made of each community name, don't be surprised to see Cambridge Bay become Ikaluktutiak, Coral Harbour change to Salliq, Hall Beach to Sanirajak, Resolute to Qausuittuq, and Chesterfield Inlet to Igluligaarjuk. Some other Dene community names may also be changed, such as Nahanni Butte to Tthenaagoo and Fort Norman to Tulít'a.

Since our adjustment to Tuktoyaktuk is complete, and since references to Inukjuak and Kuujjuaq can usually now be made without adding their former names, we shouldn't worry too much as more and more changes are made from English and French names to native ones.

Miramichi: Jacques Cartier in the 'Land of the Micmacs'

One of the intriguing names of Eastern Canada is Miramichi. The name is best known as that of a river which drains a basin of 12,740 square kilometres in New Brunswick. Its principal branches are colloquially called the 'Sou'West,' the 'Nor'West,' and the 'Little Sou'West.' Miramichi is also a component of the longest geographical name in Canada: Lower North Branch Little Southwest Miramichi River.

In the form 'the Miramichi,' the name applies to a broad region of rugged terrain and dense woods from Boiestown to the towns of Newcastle and Chatham and beyond. The name occurs in the village Nelson–Miramichi, opposite Newcastle; and in the community of Miramichi, east of Chatham, where a post office by that name existed from 1940 to 1970; a century earlier another post office by that name served the Chatham area.

Miramichi has even been applied three times beyond New Brunswick: to Pembroke, Ont., which briefly was called Miramichi in the early 1800s; to a brook and a small community south of Inverness on Cape Breton Island; and to a pond in Massachusetts.

One of the original 1867 House of Commons ridings was Northumberland–Miramichi. In 1988, it became simply Miramichi. Three of the fifty-eight provincial constituencies have it as part of their names: Miramichi Bay, Miramichi–Newcastle, and Southwest Miramichi.

Miramichi has its roots in the 1534 voyage of Jacques Cartier. Although his narrative makes no mention of it, maps derived from his historic voyages are the first to record it in the form of *Merchemay* (1541) and *Mecheomay* (1550). Similar forms appeared on later maps and documents, occurring as *Misamichy* on Samuel de Champlain's 1632 map, *Mizamichi* on Nicolas Sanson's 1656 map, and *Mizamichis* on Chrestien LeClercq's 1691 map.

Meanwhile, in 1632, Jean Guérard produced a map on which he inscribed *Grand Miramichi* (for today's Restigouche River) at the head of Chaleur Bay, and *Petit Miramichi* in the area of the present Miramichi. *Lustagooch* ('good river') and *Lustagoocheech* ('little good river') are the Micmac names for the Restigouche and the Miramichi, respectively.

The form with the 'r' on Guérard's map may have been a misprint, but it was repeated by Charles Lalement in 1645 and 1659, by Nicolas Denys in 1672, and by his son Richard, the first European settler in the Miramichi. Thereafter, map makers gave precedence to Miramichi.

In a thorough analysis of the roots of the name, William Francis Ganong concluded in 1926 that Cartier had learned it from the Montagnais Indians in the area of Natashquan, opposite Anticosti Island on Québec's North Shore. On telling them where he had sailed, they probably said that Cartier had been in the 'land of the Micmacs,' or, in their words, 'Maissimeu Assi.' This expression was then transformed into Mecheomay and related forms.

This derivation certainly seems to have more merit than several other origins given in various references, such as 'happy retreat,' 'ugly beaver,' 'place of many berries,' and 'river of many branches.'

Britain's redoubtable Lord Beaverbrook was raised in Newcastle, where his father, William Aitken, was a Presbyterian minister. When raised to the peerage in 1917, he intended first to call himself 'Lord Miramichi,' but the eminent Miramichi historian Louise Manny cautioned him that he might become known as 'Lord Merry Mickey,' and thus bring discredit upon himself and the region. He turned then to Beaver Brook, a small village north of New-castle where he had once borrowed a fringed surrey from the Catholic priest for an Orange parade. Thus Max Aitken became Lord Beaverbrook.

The correct pronunciation of Miramichi often distinguishes the natives from the outsiders. By emphasizing the first and last syllables, it closely resembles 'MEER-a-me-SHE.'

Saskatoon: A Home-made Name from a Home-grown Fruit

Saskatoon, Saskatchewan – a handsome prairie city founded on teetotalism has a name that is pure Canadian.

Indeed, what could be more Canadian than Saskatoon? Its naming occurred during a religious service when a branch of delicious berries was presented to the leader of a new settlement on the banks of the South Saskatchewan River.

During the summer of 1881, the government of Canada advertised land on the Prairies for one dollar an acre. In Toronto, some abstemious individuals saw this as an opportunity to establish an alcohol-free community. They banded together to form the Temperance Colonization Society and applied for a block of half a million acres (200,000 hectares) straddling the South Saskatchewan. The following spring, the society's leader, Methodist missionary John Neilson Lake, and a number of society members boarded the Canadian Pacific train for Moosomin in what was then the District of Assiniboia. From there, they journeyed by wagon 430 kilometres to the northwest, arriving at their destination towards the end of July.

On 18 August 1882, Lake chose a site for the centre of the new colony near the present corner of Saskatoon's Broadway Avenue and Main Street, a short distance from the east bank of the South Saskatchewan. In his diary, Lake noted that he planned to name the new settlement Minnetonka. But he did not record why he chose a name meaning 'big water' in Siouan. Perhaps a Sioux accompanied Lake's party and said he knew the South Saskatchewan as *minne tonka*.

On Sunday, 20 August, Lake led a religious service at his camp. According to Adam Turner in his book, *Early Days in Saskatoon* (1932), Gerald Willoughby, a member of Lake's party, brought a branch of reddish purple berries to the service. It seems likely that the branch was given to Willoughby by one of the Cree chain bearers in a survey party that was laying out a plan for the town, and that the Indian told him about the importance of the berry in the native diet and in making pemmican. Willoughby informed Lake that the purple berries were called *misaskwatomina* in Cree.

To Lake, this sounded like *sas-ka-toon* and he announced this would be the name of the new settlement. The literal translation of the native name is said to be 'fruit of the much wood.' Saskatoon berry is also called the early berry, serviceberry, and Juneberry (*Amelanchier alnifolia*).

By the spring of 1883, the *Regina Leader* was carrying advertisements for the 'Temperance Colony, City of Saskatoon.' However, the settlement languished until 1890, when a railway from Regina to Prince Albert was rerouted to cross the South Saskatchewan at Saskatoon. Because it was easier to obtain water for the steam engines on the low flood plain along the west side of the river, the Saskatoon station was constructed there.

The first Saskatoon post office was built in 1884 on the east side of the river at the corner of Broadway Avenue and Eleventh Street. A new post office, called West Saskatoon, was established on the west bank in 1900 to serve the growing community there. Before long, the burgeoning west side had appropriated the name Saskatoon for its post office.

Thomas Copland, a leading merchant and land agent, was asked to resolve the confusion by devising a new name for the east-side post office. His proposal, as reported to the chief geographer of Canada, James White, on 3 November 1905, was to spell Saskatoon backwards, slightly modified, producing Nootaska. The Post Office Department amended it to Nutana, which Copland noted was a great improvement even though it obscured the origin of the name. Later, Adam Turner stated, and many others have repeated, that *Nutana* was a native word for 'first born,' but such a claim has no merit.

Nutana continued as a post office until 1919, when it became Saskatoon No. 1. Nutana remains today as the name of a neighbourhood between the river and the campus of the University of Saskatchewan. It also occurs in the names of twelve businesses and institutions, and in the name Saskatoon Nutana, a provincial electoral district.

In 1903, the villages of Saskatoon and Riversdale on the west side and Nutana were amalgamated to form the town of Saskatoon. Three years later, the now-expanding, self-proclaimed 'Miracle City of the West,' which even billed itself as the 'Fastest Growing City in the World,' was incorporated as a city in the newly created province of Saskatchewan. By 1908, three transcontinental railways – the Canadian Northern, the Canadian Pacific, and the Grand Trunk Pacific – converged on what became known as the 'Railway Hub of the West.' Prone to labels, Saskatoon also is called the 'City of Bridges,' having seven of them over the South Saskatchewan.

In 1921, Saskatoon had a population in excess of 25,000 people, and by 1961, the figure stood at 95,526. The 1986 census recorded Saskatoon as the largest city in Saskatchewan, when its residents numbered 177,641 to Regina's 175,064. By 1991, it had grown to 186,058 (Regina: 179,178).

Saskatoon is an authentic Canadian name acquired from the immediate surroundings of the city. Its uniqueness is emphasized by the tale of two British visitors travelling west by rail. Wondering where they were when the train stopped after crossing a wide river, one of the travellers got off the train to inquire and was told: 'Saskatoon, Saskatchewan.' Reboarding the train, the traveller announced with disappointment: 'They don't speak English here.'

The name Saskatoon also occurs elsewhere in Western Canada. There is a Saskatoon Lake in both northeastern Saskatchewan and northwestern Alberta. In the same area of Alberta are Saskatoon Hill, Saskatoon Lake, and Saskatoon Island Provincial Park. Across the border in British Columbia is Saskatoon Creek. In southern Alberta, near the Crowsnest Pass, is Saskatoon Mountain.

Both the place and the name that John Lake created on the western landscape were symbolically brought to Toronto in the 1950s by the naming of Saskatoon Drive, now in the city of Etobicoke. One can imagine this would have pleased Lake, who died in 1925 in Toronto at the age of 91.

Medicine Hat: Mystery, Romance, and Hints of Magic Below

The story of how Medicine Hat got its name is so intertwined with folk tales that the truth can no longer be authenticated. The most publicized story is that a Cree medicine man had his hat blown into the South Saskatchewan River during a battle with Blackfoot Indians. When that happened, the Cree warriors fled, leaving the Blackfoot to declare the site 'Saamis,' or 'place of the medicine man's hat.'

The Geographic Board report of 1919 published that

account, and it was repeated in 1928 in Robert Douglas's *Place Names of Alberta*. However, both these publications, so as not to show any preference among the tales, presented four other stories:

• A hill east of Medicine Hat was said by Walter Johnson, the first settler there in 1882, to be shaped like a medicine man's head-dress.

• An Indian medicine man took a fancy to a hat taken from a white settler who, together with his companions, had been massacred.

• A brave was rewarded with a fancy head-dress by a medicine man after he rescued a girl.

• An Indian chief had a vision of a figure rising out of the river and wearing the plumed hat of a medicine man.

There are at least two other stories on the origin of the name. One is that a Blackfoot warrior was directed in a dream by a figure wearing a head-dress to drown his betrothed so that he might become a great chief. He drowned her, became a powerful chief, and declared the site 'Saamis.'

The most recent story came to light in 1948. It stated that William Van Horne, the renowned builder of the Canadian Pacific Railway, was told in 1883 by two Métis hunters that a Cree brave named Thunder Bear ran off in 1862 with the young wife of an old Cree chief. The wife is said to have dreamed that if Thunder Bear would give the old chief a war bonnet with the tail feathers of seven eagles, he would leave Thunder Bear in peace at the site where the river (South Saskatchewan) comes closest to the Cypress Hills. When Van Horne was told the story he is said to have remarked: 'That hat was good medicine to appease the irate chief,' and thereupon named the place Medicine Hat.

Shortly after Medicine Hat achieved city status in 1906, Rudyard Kipling paused there on a transcontinental trip. On learning that the area was sitting on top of a huge natural-gas field, he declared that it had 'all Hell for a basement with Medicine Hat for a trap door.'

In 1910, some newcomers to the community suggested that the city should have a more prosaic name, such as Gasburg or Smithville. Members of the city's Cypress Club were outraged, and delegated Frank Fatt, the postmaster, to appeal to Kipling for support in retaining the original name. Kipling responded forthwith from England:

'To my mind,' he wrote, 'the name of Medicine Hat ... echoes the old Cree and Blackfoot tradition of red mystery and romance that once filled the prairies. Also it hints at the magic that underlies the city in the shape of your natural gas.

'Believe me, the very name is an asset, and as years go on will become more and more of an asset. It has no duplicate in the world; it makes men ask questions, and ... draws the feet of the young men towards it. It has the qualities of uniqueness, individuality, assertion and power. Above all, it is the lawful, original, sweat-and-dust-won name of the city, and to change it would be to risk the luck of the city, to disgust and dishearten old-timers, not in the city alone, but the world over, and to advertise abroad the city's lack of faith in itself.

'Men do not think much of a family which has risen in the world, changing its name for social reasons. They think still less of a man who because he is successful repudiates the wife who stood by him in his early struggles. I do not know what I should say, but I have the clearest notion of what I should think of a town that went back on itself ...

'Forgive me if I write strongly, but this is a matter on which I feel keenly ... I have a large stake of interest and very true affection in and for the city and its folk.

' ... The Calgary Herald writes [that a new name would have] a sound like the name of a man's best girl and looks like business at the head of a financial report.

'But a man's city is a trifle more than a man's best girl. She is the living background of his life and love and toil and hope and sorrow and joy. Her success is his success; her shame is his shame; her honour is his honour; and her good name is his good name.

'What, then, should a city be rechristened that has sold its name? Judasville.'

In Canso, Survival Is a Tradition

Canso, N.S., knows how to survive adversity. The burdens it has shouldered in its long history – isolation, harsh climate, shallow soils, unreliable fish stocks, depressed fish prices, oil spills, drownings, and fish-plant closings – have strengthened its fibre and durability. As recently as 1990, the community had to fight for its survival through a year-long campaign to reopen its fish plant: the tenacious effort restored 500 jobs and impressed Canadians from coast to coast.

Canso is located at the seaward end of Chedabucto Bay's south shore, 200 kilometres northeast of Halifax. Several islands shelter its harbour from the open waters of the bay and the Atlantic Ocean. The town has a population of 1,230, with another 500 in the adjacent communities of Hazel Hill, Tittle Road, and Durells Island.

European fishermen were attracted to Canso's sheltered harbour from the first decade of the 1500s. For the next 200 years, French, Portuguese, and Basque fishermen built wharves, fish flakes, and shelters on the shores of the islands and mainland, and fished for cod. The English took over Canso when most of Acadia was transferred to Britain in 1713 by the Treaty of Utrecht. Fishermen, merchants, and traders from New England – with the protection of a British garrison – developed a prosperous fishery on Grassy Island in Canso Harbour, and English records declared it to be 'the best and most convenient fishery of any part of the King's dominions.'

Those advantages also marked Canso as a military target. In 1744, French forces from Louisbourg, Cape Breton Island, captured and burned the settlement, calling down the wrath of both the English and the New Englanders. A British fleet with New England militia attacked and captured the Louisbourg fortress the following year – after training on Grassy Island. The island, which has remained largely undisturbed for nearly 250 years, is now a national historic site.

Canso was razed again during the American Revolution when privateers, led by the notorious John Paul Jones, attacked the community in 1776. The devastation discouraged settlement, and even twenty-five years later there were only about six families living in the area. Permanent settlement finally began around 1812, a 'way office' for mail transfer was established in 1834, and by mid-century the population had increased to 250 families. Two cable companies operated their headquarters in Canso and neighbouring Hazel Hill – for communications with Europe – from 1881 to 1961, providing a source of employment aside from fishing and fish packing. Canso was incorporated as a town in 1901.

Canso's name is derived from the Micmac language. Rev. Silas Rand a nineteenth-century authority on the language, gave the native word as *camsook* or *kamsook*, meaning 'opposite the lofty cliff.' In a 1914 study of Canso, Dr. William F. Ganong, a renowned authority on Maritime native names and their meanings, said the root *kam* meant 'across' or 'beyond,' and *sook* meant 'cliff.' Ganong concluded that the line of cliffs on the south shore of Chedabucto Bay provided the source for the name, and this conclusion has been repeated in a number of studies of place names. However, residents suggest the name may owe its origin to a mirage, seen from the Canso shore, of an impressive height of land on Isle Madame, 13 kilometres to the north. Although this hill is only 65 metres high at Cape Auguet, its image – seen over water – seems magnified under certain atmospheric conditions that distort light rays.

The Micmac origin was noted as early as 1609 by the French writer Marc Lescarbot in his *Histoire de la Nouvelle France,* but that did not prevent later searches for a European origin. At least one writer linked the name to the Spanish *ganso* for 'goose.' Others have suggested it was derived from the name of a French explorer called Canse, plus *eau* for 'water' – a mystifying hypothesis, since there is no evidence such an explorer ever lived. Lescarbot was the first to use the French transliteration – 'Campseau' – to describe the harbour, the present Chedabucto Bay, and the narrow strait separating Cape Breton Island from the mainland. Samuel de Champlain referred to 'Port de Canseau' in his *Voyages* (1613) in reference to the harbour. In the 1632 edition of his *Voyages,* 'Canseau' is used for the harbour and strait, 'Campseau' for the bay. Colonizer Nicolas Denys used 'Campseaux' for all three features in his 1672 account.

The use of 'Canceau' for present Cape Canso (the outer point of Andrew Island, 5 kilometres southwest of the town) first appeared on hydrographer Jean-Baptiste-Louis Franquelin's 1686 map of Acadia. Later editions of the map and one by Guillaume Delisle (1703) spelled the cape's name 'Camseau.' Map maker Jacques-Nicolas Bellin used 'Canseau' on his 1744 map of Acadia for the harbour, cape, and strait, and this spelling prevailed thereafter on French maps.

The earliest appearance of the name in an English document is on a Herman Moll map of 1715, when he used 'Canseaux' for the strait. The change to today's spelling came in 1749, when Nova Scotia surveyor general Charles

Morris substituted 'Canso' for the French version, and this prevailed as the official form.

Strait of Canso, for the body of water between Cape Breton Island and the mainland, was first used in 1776 by chart maker Joseph F.W. DesBarres, and it ultimately replaced 'Gut of Canso' on maps and marine charts by about 1865.

Canso has much to offer inquisitive travellers, even those who arrive in search of the Canso Causeway, which is some 100 kilometres northwest of the town, by road. The causeway joining the mainland to Cape Breton Island was built in 1955, and perhaps should have been called the Strait of Canso Causeway, or Road to the Isles Causeway, to avoid confusion with the distant town.

Canso's boosters are proud to show visitors the Whitman House Museum, the Seafreez fish-packing plant, the graceful Star of the Sea Roman Catholic Church, the Grassy Island visitor interpretation centre, and the impressive seamen's memorial. Knowledgeable residents talk proudly about the first mass celebrated in Nova Scotia (1611) and the first Anglican church built in Canada (1720) – both in Canso. They recall the survival instincts of the little town where, in the Dirty Thirties, Fr. Jimmy Tompkins publicized the poverty of Maritime fishermen: he later introduced the concept of credit unions to the province. They also have no doubt that Canso will continue to be a proud, 'can so' community.

We Have 'Honoured' the Moose 662 Times!

Naming geographical features for wild animals was one of the commonest ways of differentiating elements of the landscape in the early exploration and settlement of North America. One animal that attracted much attention was the moose, a large, somewhat grotesque member of the deer family, similar to the European elk. The Algonquian-speaking tribes called it *moos*, meaning 'browser,' describing the moose's habit of stripping the tender bark and low branches of trees.

When the English explorers encountered the animals in the early 1600s in New England, they initially described them as 'moose-deer.' Eventually the shortened form 'moose' was used throughout the continent for the rather graceless animal with ungainly legs and drooping muzzle. The same animal acquired the identity of *orignal* in French, a Basque word for what the French call *cerf* ('red deer') in both France and Canada.

As well as achieving prominence on coats of arms, coinage, and bottled beverages, the moose has been 'honoured' in the names of 662 official names in Canada, concentrated in a wide band across Northern Ontario (166) and central Québec (109), and in mainland Nova Scotia (117).

The oldest 'moose' name in Canada may be Moose River in Northern Ontario, known in Cree as Mons Sipi. The area was once occupied by an Algonquian-speaking tribe called Monsoni ('moose people'). Thomas Gorst mentioned 'Moose Sebee' in his 1670–1 journal. On Moose Factory Island, 20 kilometres from the river's mouth, the Hudson's Bay Company established in 1673 its second trading post, Moose Fort (the first was Fort Rupert). In 1730, the post was moved farther upriver on the island, and today is the home of approximately 1,000 Cree.

Opposite Moose Factory Island on the west bank of Moose River, where Revillon Frères once had a trading post called Moose River Post, is Moosonee, a community of 1,250 people.

Moosonee, from the Cree name for Moose Factory, became the terminus of the Temiskaming and Northern Ontario Railway (now the Ontario Northland) in 1932. It is the destination of the popular summer tourist excursion, the Polar Bear Express. The Diocese of Moosonee was established in 1872 by the Anglican Church at Moose Factory. The diocesan centre is now based in Schumacher, a community in the city of Timmins.

Moose Jaw, Sask., has often been called the most extraordinarily crazy name for a town in the world. Moose Jaw River, a tributary of the Qu'Appelle River, was first recorded as Moose Jaw Creek by John Palliser in 1857.

Suggestions that the name commemorates the repair of a cartwheel with a moose's jaw by a titled Englishman (who may have been Lord Dunsmore or the Earl of Musgrave or Lord Milton) are considered to be mythical. The preferred origin is the shape traced by the river as it flows first northwest, then, within the city of Moose Jaw, east and north. One of the earliest settlers to arrive in the area of the city in 1882, James (later Senator) Ross claimed that the formation of the hills as seen from the river's mouth had the shape of the jaw of a moose.

Moose Jaw was incorporated as a town in 1884, and as a city in 1903. The Geographic Board approved the forms Moosejaw Creek and Moosejaw for the town in 1901. In 1931, the board corrected its record of the city's statutory name to Moose Jaw. In 1967, the name Moose Jaw River replaced the earlier decisions of Moosejaw Creek (1901) and Moose Jaw Creek (1952).

The town of Moosomin, 220 kilometres southeast of Regina on the Trans-Canada Highway, received its name as a CPR station in 1882. It was given in honour of a prominent Cree leader, whose name is also commemorated in the name of Moosomin Indian Reserve north of North Battleford, Sask. The name is also the Cree word for mooseberry, a low-bush berry of the Prairie provinces.

In the early 1800s, the site of the town was the crossing of a trail leading to Moose Mountain, a prominent elevation in southeastern Saskatchewan. In 1947, a federal electoral district was named Moose Mountain. In 1974, it was joined to Qu'Appelle to become Qu'Appelle–Moose Mountain, and, in 1988, it was renamed Souris–Moose Mountain.

L'Orignal, an attractive village in Eastern Ontario, with a population of 2,175, is the county seat of the United Counties of Prescott and Russell. It is located on the Ottawa River almost midway between Ottawa and Montréal.

The name may be traced to the Seigniory of Pointe-à-l'Orignal, granted to François Prévost in 1674. The point, east of the village, possibly named by voyageurs, is now called Grants Point. It is variously said to be the site where a moose or deer skeleton was discovered, or where the moose crossed the Ottawa River at this narrow place above the storied Long Sault, made famous as the last stand of Dollard des Ormeaux.

In many of the early land records, the name was also spelled L'Orignac. Frequently the name of the village has also been misspelled L'Original, even on postmarks.

Moose Creek is a small community 46 kilometres southwest of L'Orignal. The small creek, a tributary of the South Nation River, is said to have a place that rarely freezes where moose used to gather in the winter. The current post office sign fuses the two words into Moosecreek.

Moose River Gold Mines, about 65 kilometres northeast of Dartmouth, N.S., were mined from the 1870s to the 1920s. The place became famous in 1936 when three Toronto men, exploring the possibility of reopening the mines, became trapped by a cave-in. After eleven days, while the ordeal was followed by millions through newspaper accounts and the first continent-wide use of radio broadcasts, two of the men were brought out alive. Nearby is Mooseland, where a post office was opened in 1877. Its current population is about 80.

Nova Scotia had two post offices called Moose River, one in Pictou County from 1874 to 1943, the other in Cumberland County from 1882 to 1950. The population of each is now smaller than 25. Near Digby is a small stream called Moose River, identified as 'R de l'Orignac' on Lescarbot's 1609 map.

Some moose were transferred from the Maritimes to the island of Newfoundland in the 1870s and at the turn of this century. Their occurrence likely accounts for the seventeen geographical features with moose, mostly between Corner Brook and Grand Falls-Windsor.

The moose – an imposing beast of the Canadian woods and wilderness – is prominently reflected in the names of geographical features, from Moose Ear Pond in Newfoundland to Moose Bath Pond in B.C. and Moosehide Hills in the Yukon. The names – 662 of them – reveal the distinctive character of Canada's names.

Examining the Names of Particular Places

Cupids, Nfld.: Britain's First Canadian Colony

During a May 1991 visit to Newfoundland, I had the pleasure of touring the old town of Cupids. It has the distinction of being the first year-round British colony in what is now Canadian territory, having been founded by John Guy as the Seaforest Plantation in August 1610.

Guy's achievement is little known outside Newfoundland, and even within the province other events – the 1,000-year-old Viking settlement at L'Anse aux Meadows; Marconi's 1901 transatlantic radio broadcast at Signal Hill in St. John's – have received greater attention.

Guy was a city councillor in Bristol and a master of the Bristol Society of Merchant Adventurers. In 1608, the same year Samuel de Champlain founded Québec City in the name of France, Guy made a reconaissance of Conception Bay. On his return to England, he persuaded forty-eight investors to join him in a company to establish a plantation on the west side of the bay. In May 1610, the Privy Council endorsed his proposal, with the condition that his colony not interfere with the established fishery.

In early August, a ship carrying Guy and thirty-nine artisans – carpenters, stonemasons, shipwrights – sailed into the 'harbour here called Cuperres coue,' on a short arm of Bay de Grave, 35 kilometres west of St. John's. According to local history, the site was proposed by a man named Daw, whose ancestors reportedly had a fishing operation as early as 1522 at Ship Cove, on the north side of Bay de Grave.

Cupers Cove, as Guy later wrote it, likely owes its name to the practice of fish packers sending coopers to the well-treed slopes to cut wood for staves to make barrels for pickling fish. Cuperts coue, Cubitts Cove, and Coopers Cove are early variations of Cupids Cove, which came into use on maps and charts in the last quarter of the seventeenth century.

Selecting a site beside a small brook near the head of the cove, Guy set his artisans to work building a house, workshop, storehouse, forge, and barn, all enclosed by a stockade measuring 27 metres by 37 metres and protected by three cannons. They also built a wharf and a store on the lagoon at the head of the cove, as well as six fishing boats and a 12-ton shallop.

In October, Guy sent the company a glowing report on the abundance of fish and the industrious settlers. A treatise on overseas ventures, published in London three months later, noted that Guy's 'plantacon is very honest peacefull and hopefull and very lykelye to be profytable.'

Guy returned to England in the fall of 1611 with prospects of opening new plantations at Renews, south of St. John's, and on Trinity Bay. He returned to his colony in the spring of 1612, accompanied by sixteen women, presumably wives of the artisans, and was joined later by six apprentices. By year's end there were sixty-two colonists in the plantation.

Following two years of good fortune and mild winters, the colony was plagued by problems in 1612. Guy's expansion plans had to be curtailed because of danger posed by pirates based at nearby Harbour Grace. Conflicts also arose between the colonists and fishermen from Devon and Cornwall, whose supporters in England denounced Guy's colony in the House of Commons. The severe winter of

1612–13 caused considerable illness, eight deaths, and the loss of most of the livestock, and investors soon became disillusioned with the colony's meagre returns.

One bright note was struck on 27 March 1613, when a weather log incidentally made note of the first-recorded white child born in Newfoundland. The father was Nicholas Guie, whose relationship to John Guy is unknown.

Two days after the child's birth, John Guy departed for London, never to return. He was elected mayor of Bristol in 1618 and represented the city for two terms in the House of Commons before his death in 1629. The colony was governed from 1615 to 1621 by Capt. John Mason, who during that period made the first English chart based on his hydrographic survey of eastern Newfoundland.

It was long assumed by historians that the colony at Cupids Cove was abandoned sometime after 1621, but archaeological evidence has revealed continuous occupancy, with a sharp population decline after 1750. The population of Cupids rose to 840 in 1836, and peaked at 1,424 in 1884. The current population is 868.

In 1910, on the tercentenary of Cupids's founding, a monument near the site of the original stockade was erected by the Newfoundland Historical Society. The City of Bristol donated a plaque for the monument, and the Old Colony Association (Newfoundland expatriates in Toronto) raised a 7- by 11-metre Union Jack – then believed to be the second-largest in the Empire – on a 41-metre pole half a kilometre east of the monument. Seventy-five years later, a new and larger Union Jack was donated by H.B. Dawe, owner of the local fish-packing plant; it is flown on holidays and other special occasions. Seeing the Union Jack fly in the stiff offshore breeze in 1991, I imagined the same scene in the days of the Seaforest Plantation, and marvelled at the fortitude of the colonists.

Since the early 1970s, the Cupids Historical Society and the municipality have urged the federal government to build a modest museum or interpretation centre in Cupids, without success. With the 400th anniversary of Cupids's founding in 2010, there is ample time to raise funds and draw plans for such a museum, which would be a fitting tribute to the accomplishments of those early New World settlers.

Acadia: A Land without Boundaries

To some, Acadia is a remote corner of New Brunswick, to others, a historic area of Nova Scotia's Annapolis Valley. Many believe it includes the three Maritime provinces and even extends into Québec. Although it is not shown on modern maps, Acadia occupies a special place in the hearts and minds of more than a quarter of a million people who proudly proclaim their Acadian heritage with a flag, an anthem, and a national day.

There is confusion about Acadia's origin and meaning, and few people agree on the exact area it encompasses. Yet it is a name of extensive geographical, historical, and cultural significance.

The name of Acadia can be traced to the discoveries of Giovanni de Verrazzano, who explored the coast of North America in 1524. He was struck by the beauty of Chesapeake Bay, calling it Archadia, a variation of Arcadia, the pastoral paradise of the Greek and Roman classics.

If Verrazzano produced a map of his voyage, none has survived. However, the places he named during his travels are shown on a 1527 map by Vesconte de Maggiolo, although Arcadia does not appear on it. The variation, Larcadia, first appeared on a 1548 map by Giacomo Gastaldi. He located it near what we now call Cape Cod. In the 1560s, another Italian map shifted Larcadia to the northeast, where it supplanted Tierra de los Bretons. In 1575,

French historian André Thevet changed the name to Arcadie.

In 1599, King Henry IV of France appointed Pierre Chauvin de Tonnetuit lieutenant-general of Canada, the coasts of 'Lacadie' and other areas of New France for ten years. This commission was transferred to Pierre du Gua de Monts four years later. De Monts used Lacadie in his petition to the king to undertake the exploration and colonization of New France.

A 1601 map by French cartographer Guillaume Levasseur used the name Coste de Cadie for what is now Maine. Two years later, Samuel de Champlain wrote a report entitled *Des Sauvages* in which he used Arcadie for the area we now call the Maritimes. In the early years of the seventeenth century, the form l'Acadie became common in documents and on maps referring to Port-Royal and other settlements around the Bay of Fundy.

From the late 1620s to 1763, Acadia was an undefined territory east of New England and southeast of New France. The inhabitants of French extraction, cut off from other French colonies and with little immigration from their homeland, developed a distinctive Acadian culture. After their forced expulsion to the United States and Europe in 1755, and the subsequent return of many to the region, their Acadian heritage was reaffirmed.

After 1763, the name Acadia was superseded by Nova Scotia, which applied to New Brunswick and peninsular Nova Scotia as we know them today. Later, Cape Breton Island, Prince Edward Island, the southern Gaspé coast, and even Îles de la Madeleine were considered parts of Acadia.

Recent writers, such as Naomi Griffiths and Jean-Claude Dupont, often acknowledge the European evidence of Acadia's origins, but then proceed to suggest the name is derived from a native name for their lands, or from the Micmac expression for 'plenty,' 'fertile,' or 'camping place.'

The first reference to a possible Micmac origin may have been made by Thomas Chandler Haliburton, a Nova Scotia writer, judge, and politician, in his *A General Description of Nova Scotia*, published in 1823. In 1849, Nova Scotia scientist Abraham Gesner stated in *The Industrial Resources of Nova Scotia* that 'the terms Cadie and l'Acadie have evidently been derived from the Micmac ākăde – a place.'

The first protest against the aboriginal origin for Acadia was lodged in 1896 by the renowned New Brunswick naturalist William F. Ganong, in the *Transactions* of the Royal Society of Canada. But twenty years later, he was disappointed to learn that few scholars agreed with him.

After 1917, most historians and writers acknowledged the European source as being correct, although historical geographer Andrew Clark wrote in 1968: 'Perhaps the most sensible conclusion is that the cartographic ancestry of Arcadie for various parts of the coast of eastern and northeastern North America prepared the way for the acceptance of "Cadie", "La Cadie", "L'Acadie" and so "Acadie" from its Indian source.' I believe the converse is true: place names ending with the Micmac expression *a-kaa'-di-k*, meaning 'occurrence place,' were spelled with the suffix *-acadie* by early explorers and map makers, reflecting the region's name of European origin. A few examples of such renditions are Chebenacadie (for Shubenacadie River, N.S.) and Tracadie (for Tracadie Bay, P.E.I.), shown on a French map drawn in 1744.

Acadians have contributed substantially to the Cajun culture of Louisiana, where there is a parish called Acadia. Acadia National Park is in the state of Maine, east of the mouth of the Penobscot River. As well, Acadia and Acadie have survived in numerous place-names, including Acadieville, N.B., L'Acadie, west of Saint-Jean-sur-Richelieu, Que., and New Acadia, P.E.I. Acadia University in Wolfville, N.S., received its charter as Acadia College in 1841.

From 1924 to 1966, Acadia was a federal electoral riding in central Alberta; it probably received its name from the little community of Acadia Valley, 150 kilometres northeast of Medicine Hat, where Nova Scotians had settled in 1910. In 1990, the federal riding of Gloucester, N.B., was changed to Acadie–Bathurst to reflect its culture. The riding embraces the Acadian Peninsula, where more than 60,000 Acadians live.

Some contemporary writers have suggested that New Brunswick, where the vast majority of Acadians live today, is the centre of modern Acadia, and have looked to Moncton and its university as its focal point. But the soul of Acadia resides in many small towns and villages, such as Caraquet and Cap-Pelé in New Brunswick; Urbainville in Prince Edward Island; and Pubnico, Comeauville, and Chéticamp in Nova Scotia.

Many may regret that Acadia is not a country, with borders and legal institutions. But as the successor of the fabled beautiful land of the classics, perhaps it is best that modern Acadia resides in the hearts and souls of a people with a proud social and cultural heritage based on nearly four centuries of settlement in Eastern Canada. No matter where Acadians dwell, their rich literature, language, and music will tell them they are in Acadia.

Montréal: A People's City Beneath a King's Mountain

When Jacques Cartier ascended 'the great river of Hochelaga and the route to Canada' in 1535, he arrived at the rapids below the site of the present city of Montréal on 2 October and was greeted by some 1,000 Iroquois, about one-quarter of the estimated population of the region. The next day, with proper decorum, he entered Hochelaga, a palisaded village of some fifty buildings. He then climbed the 223-metre, tree-clad mountain rising behind the village and named it either directly in honour of the king, François I, or indirectly as a feature worthy of the king.

Most scholars believe the name Montréal is a variation of Mont Royal, but few attempt to explain how and when the variation evolved. Some note that one of Cartier's companions on the 1535 voyage was the son of the Seigneur of Montréal in Languedoc, France, and suggest Cartier chose the name in honour of his family. Others connect the name with Cardinal de Médicis, Bishop of Montreale in Sicily. Still others look to a number of places with similar names in France and Spain, noting that they all have a location overlooking the countryside and concluding that Cartier gave the name as a generic term for a place with a distinctive mountain.

Jean Poirier of the Commission de toponymie du Québec has thoroughly investigated Mont Royal's and Montréal's linguistic and toponymic roots, and has concluded that Montréal is derived from Cartier's name for the mountain.

The earliest reference to Montréal is found in a 1575 atlas by François de Belleforest, where the text, in a clear reference to the Iroquois village of Hochelaga, notes the 'ville les Chrestiens appelerent Montreal.'

The evolution of Montréal from Mont Royal has two explanations. First, in sixteenth-century France, the words *royal* and *real* had the same meaning. For example, Cartier named a Newfoundland headland C. Royal in 1534; on a 1546 French map by Pierre Desceliers, it appears as C. Real.

Second, atlas maker Belleforest relied on a 1565 Italian translation of Cartier's writings. In it a plan of Hochelaga identifies the mountain as Monte Real. The reason for the use of *real* in place of the Italian *reale* is unknown, but may have been inspired by a Spanish or Portuguese map or document. As Poirier contends, it is easy to conclude that Belleforest was only writing another form of Mont Royal.

In 1612, Samuel de Champlain referred to the mountain as montreal. Twenty years later, he wrote of the Isle de Mont-real. In 1637, the Jesuit Relations referred to 'la grande Isle nommée de Mont-Real.'

In May 1642, Paul de Chomedey de Maisonneuve and a party of thirty-nine men, two priests, and nurse Jeanne Mance (founder of Montréal's first hospital) arrived at Hochelaga to establish the missionary colony of Ville-Marie and convert the Indians to Christianity. A year earlier, New France's Governor Montmagny had warned him of the danger of Indian attack, but Maisonneuve would not be turned back, insisting that he had been instructed by the Société de Notre-Dame de Montréal in France to start a settlement there, and he would proceed even if all the trees on the island were to change into Iroquois!

Maisonneuve wrote of the colony of 'Ville marie en l'isle de Montréal en la nouvelle-france' in 1642, but Ville-Marie was superseded by Montréal in the early 1700s. As early as 1684, military officer and author Baron Lahontan wrote that 'this city is called Ville-Marie or Montréal.' In 1703, he signed a letter simply 'À Montréal.' In 1709, Jesuit Father Camille de Rochemonteix wrote that 'this city is situated on an island and has two names, which are Montreal and Ville-marie, the one by popular usage, the other by the priests of the seminary located there. The first name, Mont-royal, describes a large mountain in the central part of the island; by corruption, the mountain, the island and the city were called Montreal.'

Montréal was incorporated as a city by royal proclamation on 7 May 1792. Two hundred years later, the Montréal Urban Community has a population over 1.75 million. The city of Montréal, one of twenty-nine divisions of the urban community, has a population of 1,017,666. Montréal-Nord, Montréal-Ouest, and Montréal-Est have populations of 85,500, 5,180, and 3,770, respectively. The Town of Mount Royal, on the north side of the mountain, has a population of 18,500 in an area of less than 8 square kilometres.

'My Canada includes Québec' is a popular appeal from the four corners of Canada to the people of Québec to continue contributing their culture and passion for life to this great land. Because Montréal has endured for 350 years as Canada's spiritual centre, my Canada must continue to embrace Montréal.

Meech Lake – of Accord Fame – and Other Lakes Nearby

Nestled in the forested hills of Gatineau Park, less than a half-hour's drive northwest of the Parliament Buildings, is a chain of three lakes. Two have achieved national prominence: Meech Lake because it is beside the Thomas L. Willson House where the 30 April 1987 constitutional accord was signed; Harrington Lake because the house at its southern end became the prime minister's country retreat in 1959.

Meech Lake gets its name from Asa Meech (1775–1849), a Congregational minister in New England from 1800 to 1821 before moving his family to Hull Township in Québec. Three years after settling at the lake, he was granted 200 acres (80 hectares) and began clearing a farm. As well, Meech continued to minister in the area of Aylmer, Hull, and Chelsea, and gained a reputation for intellectual ability and spiritual influence. His original house, extensively remodelled over the years, has been preserved by the National Capital Commission (NCC).

On an 1870 plan made by Eugène Taché, the lake is called 'L. Charité,' and is said to have been named either for a French settler, François Lacharité, or for an Irishman whose name may have been Lacharity. Asa Meech's name was also attached to the plan, but for some reason it was spelled Meach, and this misspelling was confirmed by the Geographic Board of Canada in 1931.

In 1951, Marion Meech, a descendant of Asa, and some others asked the Canadian Board on Geographical Names to respect the correct spelling of Meech. The board, basing its decision on the long-established use of 'Meach' on maps, decided to maintain this version.

In 1982, the NCC sent the Commission de toponymie du Québec a copy of Asa Meech's will and other documents noting the spelling of Meech's name. The provincial commission was persuaded, and corrected the name to Lac Meech. Although it was thought that it would take some time to convince the public to make the switch, the change was almost immediately accepted by map makers and by the media. And, of course, publicity about the Meech Lake Accord has thoroughly imprinted the name (and correct spelling) in the minds of people all across Canada.

Harrington Lake, which is immediately northwest of Meech Lake, was a bird sanctuary and then the private estate of Col. Cameron M. Edwards prior to its acquisition by the Federal District Commission (predecessor of the NCC) in 1951. The name would appear to be a corrupted form of the name of John Hetherington, a son-in-law of Asa Meech. Hetherington, who was raised nearby, is thought to have built a house near the outlet (southeast end) of the lake at some time before 1850, although he is not mentioned in the 1861 census for the area. His brother, Joseph, lived nearby at the head (northwest end) of Meech Lake.

Eardley Township, in which the lake is located, was surveyed in 1850, and 'Harrington's Lake' is shown on the plan. The first grant in the township was given in 1860 at the head of the lake to James and David MacLaren, who sold the property to Louis Mousseau seven years later.

Although official plans and maps up to 1951 showed the name Harrington Lake, and this was used by local people, visitors, and residents of Ottawa and Hull were more familiar with Mousseau Lake or Lac Mousseau. Even Colonel Edwards called it Lac Mousseau. Letters to the *Ottawa Journal* and to the federal names board resulted in a review of the name of the lake. Arguing that the name of the first settler had priority, and long-established usage on maps should take precedence, the board decided to retain the name Harrington Lake.

In 1959, when the Prime Minister's Residence Act was passed, the form Harrington Lake (Lac Mousseau) was used in the English text, and the reverse in the French. This prompted the names authority in Québec to adopt Lac Mousseau (Lac Harrington) in 1962. This double form was subsequently shown on topographical and NCC maps.

Fearing that Harrington would disappear from maps, the Historical Society of the Gatineau in 1969 urged the adoption of Harrington Creek for the drainage of Lac Philippe into Lac Mousseau, and from there into Meech Lake. But the Commission de toponymie du Québec approved Ruisseau Mousseau, stating that the name Lac Mousseau (Harrington) would sufficiently honour the memory of the first settler. The society then asked for the approval of Harrington Ridge for the height of land west of the lake, but no action was taken on this proposal.

In 1987, the Commission de toponymie du Québec published a new gazetteer and omitted all mention of the name Harrington, not even as a cross-reference to Lac Mousseau. Questioned about this, the commission stated that it regards bracketed forms as transitory, and such forms were eliminated in the 1987 gazetteer. Thus, Harrington Lake no longer has official status for the lake, and although Lac Mousseau will likely attain wide use, it is not expected that the old name will be forgotten because of its association with the prime minister's country retreat.

The third lake, Lac Philippe, is one of the most popular in the national capital area for swimming, canoeing, and camping. It is on the 1850 plan of Eardley Township as Philip's Lake, and the form Philips Lake occurs on later maps. However, the Geographic Board of Canada endorsed the form Lac Philippe in 1931, and this is universally used by both English and French speakers. The lake may be named for either John Philippe, who had a farm nearby according to the 1861 census, or another farmer named James Philippe, who lived a few kilometres to the north.

While Lac Philippe and Meech Lake are open to the public, Harrington Lake/Lac Mousseau is the prime minister's private domain.

Flin Flon: A Strange 'Professor' on Even Stranger Ventures

If names can be said to express a character of their own, surely the name Flin Flon evokes a feeling of adventure and vitality. The very sound of the name conjures up images of rugged rocks and wild waters.

On a winter's day in January 1915, so the story goes, Tom Creighton, a prospector and woodsman, went hunting for moose along the Saskatchewan–Manitoba border near the 55th parallel. He fell through the ice of a lake and on reaching shore he and his companions started a fire to help him dry out. The fire's heat melted a hole and through it they glimpsed a glint of gold. They proceeded to stake out claims.

This tale may be more fanciful than real. The truth may be that Creighton and his party were led to the deposit by David Collins, a Métis trapper and amateur prospector.

In the summer of 1915, Creighton and his associates – Dan Milligan, Dan and Jack Mosher, and Leon and Isador

Dion – went back to work on their claim. When Jack Mosher brought some gold out of a hole, Creighton exclaimed: 'That must be the hole where old Flin Flon came up and shook his whiskers, so what do you say we call the discovery Flin Flon?'

And who was Flin Flon? He was the hero of an adventure novel, *The Sunless City*, a dog-eared copy of which had been found the previous year by Creighton on a portage between the Churchill River and Lac la Ronge in Saskatchewan. The book had been read and reread, although the last pages were missing, leaving a mystery for our northern travellers as to the fate of the novel's hero.

The principal character in the tale was blessed with the unlikely moniker, Professor Josiah Flintabbatey Flonatin, or Flin Flon for short. His strange adventure to the bottom of a lake in the Rocky Mountains in a submarine was written by Joyce Emerson Preston Muddock, and published by F.V. White of London in 1905. The paperbound edition, which Creighton likely had, was printed in 1911.

The professor, a member of a so-called Society for the Exploration of Unexplored Regions, discovered a strange city abounding in gold. On learning that the city was ruled by strong women with men as their servants, he escaped back to the surface through an inactive volcano.

In 1932, Jack Carr, head of research for Hudson Bay Mining & Smelting, tried to secure a copy of the novel. After writing some 850 letters, he finally obtained a copy from a London bookdealer for a few shillings. In 1942, George Cole, Manitoba's director of mines, reported that only three copies were known to exist: Carr's copy (in the National Archives of Canada since the 1960s), another with a second official of the mining company, and a third in the British Museum.

Flin Flon, Man., a city of nearly 7,500 people, is located just east of the Saskatchewan–Manitoba boundary. A small part of the city, with a population of 330, is in Saskatchewan, where the boundary makes a 2.5-kilometre adjustment to the west. Nearby, to the southwest, is Creighton, Sask., a town of about 1,700 people, founded in 1948 and named for Tom Creighton, who died in 1949 aged 75.

In 1962, on the fiftieth anniversary of the extension of Manitoba to the 60th parallel of latitude (the boundary between the western provinces and the territories), a prominent statue of the adventurous Flintabbatey Flonatin, designed by cartoonist Al Capp in his noted Dogpatch style, was unveiled at the entrance to the city of Flin Flon.

Lake Laberge (Rhymes with Marge) and Other Yukon Names

The harshness of an unforgiving northland combined with frontier hardship and adventure are reflected in the many ballads and poems of Robert Service. Many young Canadians are nurtured on the verses Service wrote during the early years of the twentieth century, and acquire a yearning to discover more about the people who were lured by the spell of the Yukon, as revealed in these lines:

The Northern Lights have seen queer sights,
But the queerest they ever did see
Was the night on the marge of Lake Lebarge
I cremated Sam McGee.

In the 1860s, the Western Union Telegraph Co. engaged American naturalist William H. Dall to explore a route for a line in the Yukon River valley. The first large expansion of the river below Whitehorse Rapids he named for fellow explorer Michael Lebarge. Neither is believed to have seen the lake, but heard of it from Indians. The United States Geographic Board adopted the name Lake Lebarge, as well as other names in the Yukon given by

Dall and Lt. Frederick Schwatka, and this, incidentally, was what prompted Canada to set up its own names board in 1898.

The Canadian authorities consulted church officials in 'Lebarge's' home town of Chateauguay, Qué., and received a reply from the explorer himself pointing out that his correct name was Michel Laberge. The lake's name has been officially spelled 'Laberge' since 1898, but its pronunciation still rhymes with 'marge.'

Service's poems broadcast the name Yukon to the world. As a name, it is simply the Kutchin Indian word for 'the greatest river.' The river was named Youcon in 1846 by the Hudson's Bay Co. trader John Bell. In the area of Lake Laberge it was known in the 1800s as Lewes River, named by Robert Campbell in 1843 for John Lee Lewes, then the Hudson's Bay Company chief factor at Fort Simpson on the Mackenzie River. In 1883, Lt. Schwatka substituted Yukon for Lewes. It was not until 1949, however, that the Canadian names authority dropped the name Lewes which, until then, was the official name for that portion of the Yukon River upstream from its juncture with the Pelly River.

The name Yukon was assigned to a district of the Northwest Territories in 1895; the district became a separate territory in 1898, with its seat of government at Dawson City. The capital was moved to Whitehorse in 1951.

In several of his poems Service included the name Klondike, a name synonymous with gold fever. His ballad 'The Trail of Ninety-Eight' mentions several other Yukon names. It ends with the lines:

There were the tents of Dawson, there the scar of the slide;
Swiftly we poled o'er the shallows, swiftly leapt o'er the side.
Fires fringed the mouth of Bonanza; sunset gilded the dome;
The test of the trail was over – thank God, thank God,
                                        we were Home!

The early miners had difficulty pronouncing the Kutchin 'Thron-duik,' the native name for the tributary river that joins the Yukon at Dawson City, and took to calling it Klondike. The Indian word is said to describe the practice of the Kutchins of driving stakes into the riverbed to trap migrating salmon.

Rabbit Creek was renamed Bonanza Creek in 1896 after the discovery of gold there by George Carmack, Skookum Jim Mason, and Tagish Charlie.

After the gold rush the prominent hill overlooking Dawson City became known as Midnight Dome. Many people of Dawson City climb the hill on 21 June to watch, on or about midnight, as the sun barely sets before rising again.

In 1968, Robert Service's name was given to two features northeast of Dawson City. Mount Robert Service and Robert Service Creek will leave Service's name indelibly imprinted on the Canadian landscape.

Observing Selected Names in Particular Regions

Captain Vancouver's Legacy

In June 1792, British navigator Capt. George Vancouver sailed into Burrard Inlet and observed the forested setting where Canada's third-largest city stands today. Vancouver was almost fifteen months into one of the longest hydrographic surveys ever undertaken – four years, eight months, and twenty-nine days. His instructions were to survey the northwest coast of North America – from Mexico's Baja California to Alaska's Cook Inlet – to determine if a passage joined the Atlantic to the Pacific. But there was another purpose to his voyage: to ensure British control over part of the northwest coast.

Spain had tried to control the entire area from California to Alaska during the 1780s, while British traders were building a lucrative fur trade with Asia. In 1789, the Spanish seized two British merchant ships in Nootka Sound, claiming they were trespassing, and Britain prepared for a war. Realizing it could not mount a successful campaign, Spain agreed to the Nootka Convention in October 1790, forcing it to abandon its right to sole occupation of the area and return the merchant ships to Britain.

Vancouver, then commander of the sloop *Discovery*, set sail from England on 1 April 1791, accompanied by the armed tender *Chatham*. Thirteen months later he sailed into what he called the 'supposed Strait of Juan de Fuca,' casting doubt on the truth of de Fuca's 1592 discovery there of a great passage into a broad sea with many islands. He spent May exploring Puget Sound, naming it and nearby Mount Baker, in Washington state, for two of his officers. Then he went ashore on King George III's birthday and named 'The Gulph of Georgia' – changed in 1859 to the Strait of Georgia – in his honour.

But when Vancouver met Spanish explorers Dionisio Alcalá Galiano and Cayetano Valdés in late June, he was dismayed to learn that another Spaniard had already named the gulf Gran Canal de Nuestra Señora del Rosario la Marinera. Although Vancouver favoured recognizing names given by previous explorers, in this case he shifted the Spanish name to a narrow strait nearby so Britain could lay claim to the gulf. In 1859, Capt. George Richards named the small strait after Capt. Alexandro Malaspina, commander of the Spanish settlement on Nootka Sound in 1791, and leader of Spanish exploration in the North Pacific.

Vancouver, Galiano, and Valdés agreed to work together in surveying the waters northwest of the Strait of Georgia, with Vancouver and his crew concentrating on the deep fiords. They spent the summer of 1792 charting the heads of Jervis, Bute, Knight, and Rivers inlets and the many intricate channels and narrows between Vancouver Island and the mainland. James Johnstone, the *Chatham*'s master, discovered that the strait Vancouver had named for him led to the Pacific. And northwest of Johnstone Strait, Lieut. William Broughton, commander of the *Chatham*, charted the waters around a group of islands which Vancouver called Broughton Archipelago.

In late August 1792, after exploring as far north as Burke Channel near Bella Coola, Vancouver sailed south to Nootka Sound to negotiate the land transfer from the

Spanish to the British. But despite a cordial greeting by the Spanish commander Juan Francisco de la Bodega y Quadra, the two could not agree on the terms of transfer, and referred the matter back to their respective governments. Regardless, the two became friends, and Bodega (addressed incorrectly as Quadra by Vancouver) recommended that a prominent feature be jointly named after them. Having discovered that Nootka was on a huge island, Vancouver called it Quadra and Vancouver's Island, but the name Quadra soon fell into disuse. In 1903, the Geographic Board assigned the name Quadra to another island between Vancouver Island and the mainland.

After wintering in the Hawaiian Islands, Vancouver returned to the northwest coast in May 1793 to survey the many canals, channels, inlets, and sounds from Burke Channel to Revillagigedo Island near the southern tip of the Alaskan Panhandle.

While most of the names Vancouver gave in 1792 and 1793 honoured his officers and prominent men in the British Admiralty and navy, he also chose the surnames of noted political leaders for several features: Pitt, Hawkesbury, and Dundas islands; Grenville Channel; Portland Canal; and many others.

After another winter in the Hawaiian Islands, Vancouver resumed his survey in the spring of 1794, exploring the coastline from Alaska's Cook Inlet south to Point Conclusion, on Baranof Island in the Alaskan Panhandle. On completing his survey, and convinced there was no passage between the Pacific and the Atlantic or an inland sea, Vancouver mapped the west coast of the Queen Charlotte Islands before returning to Nootka Sound. With no further instructions from Britain regarding negotiations with the Spanish, Vancouver sailed home.

By the 1860s, some seventy years after Vancouver explored Burrard Inlet, two towns – Gastown and Hastings –

had been founded on its south shore. Then, in 1870, residents of Gastown renamed it Granville in honour of the British colonial secretary. The city that evolved might have remained Granville if it had not been chosen as the terminus for Canadian Pacific's transcontinental line in 1881, and if CP's general manager had not been William Van Horne. Van Horne, like Vancouver, was of Dutch ancestry, which led him to declare in 1885: 'This is destined to be a great city, perhaps the greatest in Canada. We must see that it has a name that will designate its place on the map of Canada. Vancouver it shall be, if I have the ultimate decision.' On 6 April 1886, Vancouver was formally incorporated as a city.

Several features along the west coast also honour the eighteenth-century navigator. In 1860, Capt. George Richards named Vancouver Bay in Jervis Inlet, where Vancouver stayed overnight on 17 June 1792. Vancouver River flows into the bay from the east. There is another Vancouver Bay at the entrance of Bute Inlet. And Vancouver Rock in Milbanke Sound, which Vancouver described in his journal as a 'very dangerous sunken rock,' was named in 1866 by British hydrographic surveyor Capt. Daniel Pender. Mount Vancouver, a peak of 4,828 metres near the Alaska–Yukon border, was named in 1874 by William H. Dall, scientific director of the Western Union Telegraph expedition.

Vancouver's meticulous survey helped maintain Britain's claim to part of the coast and ensure the eventual expansion of Canada to the Pacific. Along the way he also enriched Canada's toponymy: the names he gave and the many Spanish names he preserved on his charts were widely disseminated on Arrowsmith maps and British Admiralty charts. The only criticism of his naming practices is the almost total disregard of native names, although he and his officers frequently had friendly encounters with native people.

Mackenzie Expeditions Left a Trail of Names

During the summer of 1789, a young Scottish fur trader and explorer reached the shores of the Arctic Ocean after an epic journey down Canada's longest river. Four years later he led a party of ten men on an arduous journey over the Rockies and the Coast Mountains to the Pacific. These exploits at the end of the eighteenth century should be well known and the fur trader extolled as one of the greatest explorers of all time. But most Canadians know very little about the adventures of Sir Alexander Mackenzie.

Mackenzie was born in 1764 in Stornoway on the Isle of Lewis in Scotland. Ten years later his widowed father, Kenneth, emigrated with his young family to New York where his brother, Murdoch, had a successful business. The father remained loyal to the Crown during the War of Independence, becoming an officer in the King's Royal Regiment. During his absence, Alexander was cared for by two of his father's sisters in Johnstown, N.Y. In 1778, they sent him to school in Montréal.

The next year, Mackenzie, then fifteen, was hired by John Gregory, a Montréal fur trader. Five years later he became a partner in the fur trading firm of Gregory, McLeod & Company, which later was absorbed by the North West Company.

In 1787, the North West Company sent Mackenzie to assist Peter Pond, who was in charge of one of the company's posts on the Athabasca River. Pond, an enigmatic and irascible figure from New England, had arrived in the western interior in 1775 and explored the country around Lake Athabasca (then called Lake of the Hills) and Great Slave Lake. Pond had been told by Chipewyan Indians that the lakes drained north to the 'Ice Sea.' However, when he learned that Capt. James Cook's discoveries on the West Coast suggested a large river draining from the interior, he compiled maps implying a link between Great Slave Lake and 'Cook's River.' Were there such a connection, it might have been a practical fur trading route to the Pacific.

In 1788, Mackenzie succeeded Pond at the Athabasca post and spent the year moving the headquarters to Fort Chipewyan on the south shore of Lake Athabasca, east of the mouth of the Athabasca River. (Fort Chipewyan was subsequently moved again to its present site on the lake's northern shore.) There he planned a mission to determine if Lake Athabasca and Great Slave Lake did drain ultimately into the Pacific.

On 3 June 1789, he set out by canoe, accompanied by four French-Canadian voyageurs, a young German named John Steinbruck, a Chipewyan Indian called English Chief, and a company of wives and retainers. In just forty days, Mackenzie's party reached the Arctic Ocean. From Great Slave Lake to the river's mouth they averaged 120 kilometres a day, one day canoeing an incredible 180 kilometres. Such distances were possible because the river flowed swiftly and had few treacherous sections. Moreover, the company was accustomed to canoeing twenty hours a day, sometimes starting as early as 2:30 a.m. Mackenzie was back at Fort Chipewyan on 12 September after an expedition covering nearly 4,800 kilometres.

Although Mackenzie used the name Grand River – perhaps from the Slavey *Deh Cho* – he derisively referred to it as 'River Disappointment' because it led only to the 'Hyperborean Sea.' When Aaron Arrowsmith made the map for Mackenzie's book *Voyages from Montreal* (1801), the name 'Mac Kenzies River' was shown twice, and Mackenzie, in his own observations on the geography of North America, referred to it as 'Mackenzie's River.' In writing to President Thomas Jefferson in 1807, Joel Barlow noted that the world had 'justly given the name Mackenzie to the great river of the north for the obvious reason, the merit of discovery.' However, when explorer John Franklin canoed the river in 1825 he found the name Great River in general use and urged the universal adoption of Mackenzie River in honour of its eminent discoverer.

During his first voyage of discovery in the Arctic in 1821, Franklin named a small point near the mouth of the Coppermine River for Alexander Mackenzie. Franklin had called it Cape Mackenzie, but in 1965, because the feature was judged by the Canadian Permanent Committee on Geographical Names to be too small to merit the word *cape*, it was altered to Mackenzie Point.

Mackenzie is used in five other names in the Northwest Territories. Mackenzie Bay at the mouth of the river was named officially in 1910, although it appeared on earlier maps. The river flows into the bay through a complex of braided channels of the Mackenzie Delta. This name was used by Hugh Bostock in 1947 and officially approved the following year.

The District of Mackenzie is one of the three statutory divisions of the Northwest Territories, established along with the districts of Keewatin and Franklin in 1895. The districts no longer serve any administrative function but are maintained on maps because they remain in the official description of the Northwest Territories.

While Mackenzie remained curious about the land beyond the mountains to the west of the Mackenzie River, he wrote about them simply as 'the Mountains.' John Franklin in the 1820s and Kaye Lamb, who edited *The Journals and Letters of Sir Alexander Mackenzie* (1970), referred to them as the Rocky Mountains, but the Rockies are not now considered as extending into the Northwest Territories. The system of mountains and ranges from the Liard River in the south to the Ramparts River in the north, and west to the Yukon border, is called the Mackenzie Mountains. They were named officially in 1939 for Alexander Mackenzie – not the explorer but the prime minister of Canada from 1873 to 1878, who, by coincidence, was born in Dunkeld, Scotland, in 1822, the place where the explorer had died suddenly two years earlier while on his way from Edinburgh to his estate at Avoch in Ross-shire.

The Mackenzie Highway was built as an all-weather road in the 1940s from Grimshaw, Alta., to Hay River, N.W.T. Later it was extended to Fort Simpson and Wrigley.

After his journey to the Arctic, Mackenzie, determined to become proficient with surveying instruments, went to London in 1791 to learn more about both navigation and surveying. He returned to Fort Chipewyan in 1792 and that same year travelled to Fort Fork on the Peace River, near the present town of Peace River, to make plans to find a practical route to the Pacific.

On 9 May 1793, now twenty-nine, he set out from Fort Fork accompanied by Alexander McKay, six voyageurs, and two Indian hunters and interpreters. By 1 June he had reached a section of the Parsnip River in present British Columbia. The District Municipality of Mackenzie was created at that site in 1966 as the logging and mining centre for that part of the Rocky Mountain Trench. The pre-planned town now has a population of 5,800.

The most arduous part of Mackenzie's trip was the portage through rough terrain from the head of the Parsnip River to James Creek, Herrick Creek, and then McGregor River, a tributary of the Fraser. (He assumed the Fraser was the Columbia River; Simon Fraser proved otherwise fifteen years later.) Perhaps at the summit – the lakes here are appropriately called Arctic Lake and Pacific Lake – Mackenzie may have been able to see several snow-covered peaks of the Rockies some 100 kilometres to the southeast. In 1916, one of them was named Mount Sir Alexander in his honour. The 3,277-metre mountain is 75 kilometres north of McBride.

By 22 June, Mackenzie had followed the Fraser to a point halfway between the present cities of Quesnel and Williams Lake. Twenty-eight years later the North West Company established Fort Alexandria at this site, naming it for the explorer. The present community of Alexandria has a population of 82.

On the advice of Indians, Mackenzie decided against proceeding farther south on the turbulent Fraser. Instead, he turned back to a river he called the West Road – today it is officially called West Road (Blackwater) River – and worked his way west along an Indian track towards the Pacific. By 17 July, he reached the highest point of his travels. Mackenzie Pass, 1,830 metres, is the summit between the valleys of the Dean River to the north and Bella Coola River to the south. Mackenzie Valley is north of the pass in the valley of Kohasganko Creek, and Mount Mackenzie is to the west. These three names were given by the Department of National Defence while surveying the area in 1953. When Mackenzie had trekked over the pass he saw a 'stupendous mountain' to the south; the official name now is Stupendous Mountain.

Mackenzie reached Bella Coola on 19 July 1793, and continued canoeing to the west until he came to a rock in Dean Channel where he took astronomical observations to determine his latitude and longitude. On the rock he inscribed: 'Alexander Mackenzie, from Canada, by land, the twenty-second of July, one thousand seven hundred and ninety-three.' In 1926, the British Columbia government named the site of the rock Sir Alexander Mackenzie Provincial Park. Mackenzie then returned to Fort Chipewyan, taking only thirty-three days to cover the circuitous 2,000-kilometre route via the Fraser, the Parsnip, and the Peace. Remarkably, on his two journeys to the Arctic and the Pacific, no one accompanying him died or suffered serious injury.

After his two prodigious exploratory trips, Mackenzie

spent much of the next fifteen years in Montréal where he remained active in the fur trade. In 1801, on one of his many trips to London, his *Voyages from Montreal* was published. The book created immense interest in Britain and the United States, and was translated into French, German, and Russian. In 1802, at age 38, he was knighted. After 1808, he remained in Britain, where he married a distant cousin and had three children.

With eleven features named for Sir Alexander Mackenzie in the Northwest Territories and British Columbia, including Canada's longest river, it may well be argued that Mackenzie has been adequately honoured. But other than in schools in Edmonton and Inuvik, the explorer does not appear to have been remembered in the names of the nation's institutions. In July 1989, two hundred years after Mackenzie reached the Arctic, a plaque was unveiled at his Scottish gravesite. Four years later, the words he inscribed near Bella Coola were carved on a granite slab at his grave.

'88 Olympics: Calgary, Kananaskis, and Mount Allan

Holding the 1988 Winter Olympics in Canada vaulted Calgary onto the global scene so that, like Innsbruck or Grenoble, Sarajevo or Sapporo, its name was easily mentioned around the world without reference to region or country.

Calgary was named in 1876 on the suggestion of Col. James F. Macleod, who was assistant commissioner of the North West Mounted Police when a post had been established the previous year where the Elbow River joins the Bow. He chose the name to honour a small place with family associations and happy memories on the Isle of Mull in Scotland. As adduced by the noted historian George F.G. Stanley, the name in Scotland most likely means 'bay farm' in Scots Gaelic. Other suggested origins, such as 'clear running water' or 'cold enclosure,' would appear to have no etymological basis.

Bow River, the principal tributary of the South Saskatchewan River, rises in the Rocky Mountains northwest of Banff. It derives its name from the Indian practice of gathering saplings in the valley to make bows. An Arrowsmith map of 1802 shows Bow Hills, and another Arrowsmith map of 1822 refers to Bow or Askow River. The French word for 'bow' is reflected in the name Lac des Arcs, some 90 kilometres upriver from Calgary at Exshaw. It was named in 1858 by Eugène Bourgeau, the botanist on the Palliser expedition.

Kananaskis River, a major tributary of the Bow, rises about 60 kilometres south of Exshaw in some of the most awe-inspiring mountain landscape in North America. John Palliser named the river in 1858 for an Indian who, according to legend, miraculously recovered from the blow of an axe. In this area, widely known as Kananaskis Country, and 12 kilometres south of Exshaw, is Mount Allan, chosen in 1984 for the '88 Olympic alpine ski events. This 2,800-metre peak was named in 1948 for John Andrew Allan (1884–1955), who had headed the department of geology at the University of Alberta from 1912 to 1949, and had undertaken extensive geological studies in the Rocky Mountains. A 1987 study undertaken for the Stoney Chiniki Band Council revealed the names Châse Tîda Baha ('burnt timber hill') and Watâga îpa ('grizzly hill point') for it. In 1985, the Alberta government chose the name Nakiska for the ski resort at Mount Allan. This name, derived from a Cree expression meaning 'to meet,' refers to athletes from all over the world who came together in February 1988.

Immediately to the west of Mount Allan is Mount Lougheed, which may be the peak named Windy Mountain in 1858 by Bourgeau. In 1886, George M. Dawson recorded the name Wind Mountain for it, and this was made official in 1911 by the Geographic Board of Canada. In 1928, the board renamed the mountain for the late senator Sir James Lougheed (1854-1925), the grandfather of Peter Lougheed. In 1982, the Alberta Historic Sites Board confirmed the name Windtower for the northwesterly peak of the Mount Lougheed massif, and in 1985 restored the name Wind Mountain to its southeasterly peak. Kananaskis Provincial Park, at the head of the Kananaskis River, was renamed Peter Lougheed Provincial Park in 1986 by the provincial government.

Southwest of Mount Lougheed is Mount Sparrowhawk – the original choice for the Olympic downhill ski events – which was named in 1922 for a destroyer that had served in the Battle of Jutland during the First World War. To the south of it are several other named mountains that recall officers, cruisers, and destroyers of the same battle: Chester, Engadine, Galatea, Indefatigable, Invincible, Warrior, Black Prince, Shark, Warspite. And in the same area adjacent to the British Columbia boundary are many other peaks that honour noted foreign leaders of the First World War: Joffre, Foch, Jellicoe, Putnik, Smuts, Leman, Hood, Brock; and Canadian generals: Burstall, Currie, Mercer, Turner. Northeast of Mount Allan is Mount Lorette, named after a First World War battle at Lorette Ridge in France.

Straight south of Mount Allan is Mount Bogart, named for Donaldson Bogart Dowling (1858-1925), who explored this area in 1904 for the Geological Survey of Canada. Dowling named Mount Kidd, the next mountain to the southeast, for John Alfred Kidd, then a trading-post manager at Morley, the centre of the Stoney Indian Reserve west of Calgary.

Across the Kananaskis River valley from Mount Allan is Fisher Range, named by Palliser in 1858 for George Fisher, a British astronomer and a family friend. A prominent elevation of the range, Mount McDougall, was named by George Dawson in 1884 for Rev. George McDougall (1821–76), a Methodist missionary among the Stoneys, and for his sons, David and Rev. John McDougall.

To the north of Mount Allan, and overlooking Exshaw, is Mount McGillivray, which was named in 1957 for Duncan McGillivray (c. 1764–1825), a partner of the North West Company, who travelled through the area in 1801. Just east of Mount McGillivray, a peak with a distinctive V-shaped summit reveals the name given to it in 1957: Heart Mountain. Just west of Mount McGillivray is Pigeon Mountain, named by Bourgeau in 1858, and beyond it is one of the most photographed mountains in the Rockies: The Three Sisters, named by Dawson in 1886 for its three similar peaks. Finally, next in succession are Chinamans Peak, named for a Chinese miner who had climbed it in 1886; and Mount Rundle, named by James Hector in 1859 for Rev. Robert Terrill Rundle, a Methodist missionary to the Indians in the 1840s.

Exshaw was named by Sir Sandford Fleming after a son-in-law, William Exshaw. Five kilometres upriver is Dead Man's Flat, which recalls the killing in 1904 of John Marrett by his brother, François. Canmore is a railway name given in the 1880s by Canadian Pacific, possibly for the Scottish King Malcolm III (d. 1093), known as Canmore, or perhaps for Kenmore in Argyllshire.

The Thousand Islands: There Are Really 1,149

One of the most idyllic regions of North America embraces the Thousand Islands in the St. Lawrence River.

The early French explorers, on ascending the river to Fort Frontenac (now Kingston), were impressed with the great number of islands, and concluded they must number at least a thousand. The French historian Charlevoix noted in 1721 that 'we passed through the midst of a kind of

archipelago which they called Mille Isles. I believe there
are about 500.' A 1727 map by de Léry called them 'Les
Mil Isles.'

Many of the travel brochures claim there are at least
1,800 islands. In the early 1800s, the British and American
boundary surveyors determined that there were 1,692, de-
ciding that any rock with at least one tree could be called
an island.

In 1966, an official count by the Canadian Permanent
Committee's names secretariat revealed 1,015 islands compiled on large-scale topographical maps from Amherst Island west of Kingston to McNair Island at Brockville, a
distance of 80 kilometres.

A methodical check in 1985 of the large-scale navigation
charts puts the number at 1,149 islands and islets. The
number on the Canadian side is 665, with 241 officially
named; on the American, 484, with 126 named.

Numerous rocks barely awash or rocks abutting larger
islands probably account for the previously inflated
numbers.

An Indian legend states that the islands resulted from
an accident when a blanket holding Manatoana, or 'Garden of the Great Spirit,' was dropped by its carriers, breaking the garden into a thousand pieces.

Very few of the Thousand Islands had individual names
prior to the War of 1812. The largest, Wolfe Island, known
to the Iroquois as Ganounkousenot, and to the French as
Grande Isle and Isle Buade, recalls the British general who
led the capture of Québec in 1759. Other prominent British
military leaders from that period honoured in the names
of large islands include Gen. William Howe and Gen.
Jeffery Amherst.

After the War of 1812, Capt. William Fitzwilliam Owen
surveyed the St. Lawrence between Lake Ontario and
Cornwall, and published a series of five Admiralty charts
in 1828. In naming the islands he drew on many elements

relating to British military engagements on the Great Lakes and in Upper Canada, as well as noted British military leaders.

Among gunboats on the Great Lakes during the war, with their names applied in the Lake Fleet Islands, are Axeman, Aspasia, Belabourer, Bloodletter, Camelot, Deathdealer, Dumfounder, and Endymion.

The Navy Islands include the names of officers who distinguished themselves in engagements during the war. Among them are Downie Island (Cmdr. George Downie, killed on Lake Champlain in 1814); Hickey Island (Frederick Hickey, commander of the *Prince Regent* on Lake Ontario); Mulcaster Island (Capt. William Howe Mulcaster, who was severely wounded at Oswego, N.Y.); Spilsbury Island (Capt. Francis Spilsbury, who was involved in several engagements on Lake Ontario); and Owen Island (probably not for Capt. W.F., but for his brother, Sir Edward Owen, who commanded forces on both Lake Champlain and the Great Lakes).

Some of the Admiralty Islands off Gananoque were given names by Owen for prominent figures in the British Admiralty. Among them were islands for the Rt. Hon. Charles Philip Yorke, First Lord of the Admiralty in 1811, and Viscount Melville, the First Lord from 1812 to 1827. Possibly because these islands had local names prior to Owen's survey, his names were not accepted locally; Yorke is Bostwick Island; Melville is Hay Island.

A number of other names assigned by the Owen survey have recently been changed to conform to preferred usage in the area. Among them are Squaw Island (formerly Brock), Leek Island (Thwartway), Tremont Park Island (Tidds), and Sugar Island (St. Lawrence).

The well-known Grenadier Island honours the distinguished British Grenadier Regiment. Known to the Indians and the early travellers as Toniata, the name Grenadier occurs on a map relating to the Treaty of Ghent, 1814.

Captain Owen called it Bathurst Island, probably for the third Earl Bathurst (1762–1834). Grenadier was given precedence in 1909.

Hill Island, crossed by the Thousand Islands (Ivy Lea) Bridge to New York state, honours Gen. Rowland Hill. An 1874 survey by Charles Unwin identified it as Leroux Island, but the name assigned by Owen was confirmed in 1909.

Upriver from Brockville is the Brock Group, where several islands commemorate officers who served with Sir Isaac Brock in the War of 1812. Among them are Myers Island (Lt.-Col. Christopher Myers, commander at Kingston in 1813), Sheaffe Island (Gen. Sir Roger Sheaffe, who succeeded Brock at Kingston), De Watteville Island (Maj.-Gen. Abraham de Watteville), De Rottenburg Island (Maj.-Gen. Francis, Baron de Rottenburg), Cockburn Island (Admiral Sir George Cockburn), Conran Island (Maj.-Gen. Henry Conran), and Stovin Island (Maj.-Gen. Richard Stovin, commander at Montréal, 1812–14).

Many of the islands on the American side reflect a British connection, having also been named by Owen. One of the largest is Wellesley Island, which commemorates Arthur Wellesley, the Duke of Wellington. Others include Carleton Island (Sir Guy Carleton) and Picton Island (Sir Thomas Picton).

One of the most frequently visited American islands is Heart Island (formerly Hart), where George Boldt, owner of the Waldorf Astoria in New York, began but never completed a castle, and where his chef, who became the renowned Oscar of the Waldorf, concocted the famous Thousand Island Dressing.

In 1904, St. Lawrence Islands National Park was established to preserve some of the sensitive ecology of these fragments of the Canadian Shield. The park now includes part of the mainland at Mallorytown Landing, plus all or part of twenty-one islands and eighty-three rocky islets.

Among the Thousand Islands, the complex network of channels includes the intricate Lovers Lane, the narrow Needle's Eye, the sharp-angled Fiddlers Elbow, the curiously named International Rift, and the carefree Wanderers Channel.

Some of the most pleasant-sounding names of Canada are scattered among the Thousand Islands. Included are Kitsymenie, Kalaria, Apohaqui, Minota, Arabella, Beaurivage, and Manomin.

Now, as for the Thirty Thousand Islands in Georgian Bay ... another essay or two perhaps.

Relocating the Lost Villages

The construction of the St. Lawrence Seaway in the 1950s was one of the most ambitious engineering projects ever undertaken in North America. The dams, canals, and powerhouse in the International Rapids section between Montréal and Lake Ontario had a profound impact on the region's physical and human geography. Some 8,000 hectares (20,000 acres) of farmland and all or part of nine villages on the Ontario side of the St. Lawrence River between Cornwall and Iroquois were inundated when Lake St. Lawrence was created. Two new towns, Long Sault and Ingleside, were established, partly of new homes and partly of houses moved from the flooded villages. Morrisburg's business district was moved and all of Iroquois was relocated.

Some of Ontario's oldest and most historic settlements – founded by United Empire Loyalists in the 1780s – were submerged under the waters of the man-made lake. Their names – Mille Roches, Moulinette, Dickinsons Landing, Wales, Woodlands, Farrans Point, and Aultsville – are remembered in the names of streets, roads, and islands, and in the Mille Roches, Moulinette, and Aultsville halls of Cornwall's St. Lawrence College.

Mille Roches (thousand rocks), 8 kilometres west of Cornwall, was adjacent to a rough and rocky section of the river's Long Sault Rapids. From the 1780s to the 1830s, it was a landing place for a brisk business in transferring freight and passengers. Its importance declined when the Cornwall Canal was built in 1836, but it remained a small service centre until the 1950s.

Moulinette, 3 kilometres farther west, was named for the small grist mill built by pioneer settler Adam Dixon, who also built a distillery, a foundry, an Anglican church, and a handsome residence.

Five kilometres southwest of Moulinette was the little village of Dickinsons Landing, where Barnabas Dickinson established a stagecoach line between Kingston and Montréal. When the Grand Trunk Railway was built from Montréal to Toronto in the 1850s, the stop north of the village was called Dickinson's Landing Station. In 1860, the Prince of Wales travelled by train to the station and returned to Montréal by the St. Lawrence River. In honour of his visit, the station was renamed Wales. It eventually grew into a small village.

Woodlands, a little village 4 kilometres west of Dickinsons Landing, was named because it was a firewood supply point for steamers on the St. Lawrence. Three kilometres farther west was the village of Farrans Point, where a Farrand family had lived in the early years of settlement. The last village of the submerged group was Aultsville, named in 1854 for Samuel Ault, who served as an MLA and an MP from 1861 to 1872.

In 1954, the Ontario–St. Lawrence Development Commission was set up to transfer 6,500 displaced residents to the new townsites. The commission decided to build a new town at the west side of Cornwall Township to receive people from Mille Roches and Moulinette, and another town 8 kilometres to the west in Osnabruck Township for the residents of that township whose properties were to be inundated.

The Osnabruck Township council endorsed the name Sunnyvale for its new town in July 1955, but two months later changed it to Avondale. Believing this might be confused with nearby Avonmore, and because there was another Avondale to the east in Charlottenburgh Township, several residents urged the adoption of another name, with Osnabruck, Wales, and Kanata being suggested as alternatives. A vote was held and Wales emerged as the preferred choice, but new opposition soon arose because only one of the former villages was being commemorated in the new town name. The township reeve, Thorold Lake, happened to drive by a house in Aultsville called Ingleside, and suggested this name to the council. This was accepted, and subsequently endorsed by the Canadian Board on Geographical Names, as the Canadian Permanent Committee on Geographical Names was then called.

In early 1956, the Mille Roches and Moulinette Chamber of Commerce proposed Longue Sault as the name for their new town in Cornwall Township, and this was endorsed in July by the township council. The Cornwall *Standard-Freeholder* pointed out that the proper form was Long Sault, in keeping with the rules of the French language, and the Canadian Board on Geographical Names approved this form. However, angry residents claimed long usage of Longue Sault in the community, and mustered ample evidence for their claim. In February 1957, the newly named Longue Sault Chamber of Commerce pressed for reconsideration of the town name, but to no avail.

Names for the twenty-three new islands that would be formed by the flooding were drawn up by the Ontario–St. Lawrence Development Commission in the spring of 1956. Names of villages and prominent persons in the valley's history provided inspiration and the names were endorsed by the Canadian names board. When Lionel Chevrier, then president of the St. Lawrence Seaway Authority, was advised of the new names, he proposed a number of changes, and several of his suggestions were adopted.

The villages of Wales, Mille Roches, and Moulinette are each recalled in the name of an island. Dickinson Island is for Dickinsons Landing. Woodlands Islands – East Woodlands Island, Centre Woodlands Island, and West Woodlands Island – all are named for Woodlands. Farrans Point is remembered in the name Farran Point, a peninsula that extends into the St. Lawrence beside Ingleside. Ault Island, the largest of the Canadian islands created by the flooding, is adjacent to the old site of Aultsville and just offshore from Upper Canada Village, where pioneer buildings and traditions are preserved.

Long Sault Rapids is recalled in the name of the village as well as the Long Sault Parkway, which connects eleven islands in St. Lawrence Provincial Park to the mainland at Ingleside and Long Sault.

In the spring of 1958, James Duncan, chairman of the Hydro-Electric Power Commission of Ontario, proposed naming the new reservoir Lake St. Lawrence. It was approved by the Canadian names board in June, and later accepted by the United States Geographic Board. Some newspapers, including the Cornwall *Standard-Freeholder*, objected to its blandness. (They also reported incorrectly that the official Canadian name was Lake Elizabeth.) Alternative suggestions flooded into newspapers and the Canadian names board; among the more bizarre ones were Lake Elizamerica, Lake Indedom (independence and dominion), Lake Canusa, Lake Uscan, and Lake Canarican, but the original proposal prevailed.

Memories of the submerged communities have been kept alive by the Lost Villages Historical Society, founded in 1977, and its museum, opened in August 1992 at Ault Park, east of Long Sault. Inundation Day has been celebrated twice, first on 1 July 1983, and again on the same day in 1988. Many families were uprooted nearly forty years ago, but the great beauty of the islands and shoreline of St. Lawrence Provincial Park and the charm of Upper Canada Village have provided a large measure of spiritual compensation for the residents of the Seaway Valley.

Great Divide Passes in the Rockies

Some of the most historic place names in Canada are those of the mountain passes on the Great Divide in the Rocky Mountains.

From Akamina Pass near the U.S. border to Monkman Pass in north-central British Columbia, there are seventy officially named passes. North of Monkman Pass, the Great Divide skirts west of the Rocky Mountain Trench and Williston Lake, so that the Rockies in this area cease to be the continental divide between Pacific waters on the west and Atlantic (Hudson Bay) and Arctic waters on the east and north.

Three of the passes are crossed by both railways and highways: Crowsnest, Kicking Horse, and Yellowhead. A highway over the Divide uses Vermilion Pass.

A railway and a highway also go through Pine Pass in the Rockies, but at this point these mountains are not the continental divide.

Another railway was built in 1983-4 through an unnamed pass between Monkman Pass and Pine Pass to serve the Quintette and Bullmoose coal mines at Tumbler Ridge.

Two other passes became well known as routes during the fur trade era: Athabasca and Howse. Monkman Pass has neither a railway nor a highway, although several efforts have been made to link Prince George with Dawson Creek and Grande Prairie by building a road through it.

The area of Crowsnest Pass (elev. 1,357 metres) was explored in 1858 by Thomas Blakiston of the Palliser Expedition and in 1882 by George Dawson of the Geological Survey. In the 1800s, the story was told of 'ka-ka-iu-wut-ishis-tun' by the Cree and 'ma-sto-eeas' by the Blackfoot, both literally meaning 'the raven's nest,' but translated as 'the crow's nest.' The hill where the Indians believed the ravens originally nested is said to be 30 kilometres east of the present Crowsnest Mountain, with the latter having been given that name erroneously by white explorers. The Indians considered the area of the hill to be the 'crow's nest country,' accounting for the transfer of the name to the river and the pass.

Crowsnest Pass attained importance in 1897 when the CPR received a subsidy to build a railway through the pass and to develop the mineral deposits of southern B.C., for which it guaranteed fixed rates for the eastbound shipping of grain and flour. This Crowsnest Pass Agreement, extended in 1925 to all railways leading east to Lake Superior, kept the costs of grain transportation down, but resulted in poor development and maintenance of rail lines. In late 1983, a new 'Crow rate' was worked out to allow the costs of shipping grain to rise, although the railways are still supported by large federal subsidies. At the same time the railways agreed to spend $16 billion by 1992 for new rolling stock and improvement of service.

Vermilion Pass (elev. 1,651 metres) is 42 kilometres west of Banff. It links the Bow River valley in Alberta with the Kootenay River valley in B.C. The name is derived from the red, yellow, and orange ochre beds in mineral springs 9 kilometres southwest of the pass. The springs were frequented through time immemorial by the Kootenay and the Blackfoot for decorative paint.

After Dr. James Hector crossed Vermilion Pass on horseback in 1858, he returned to the east side of the Great Divide by a tumultuous tributary of the Columbia River.

Kicking Horse Pass (elev. 1,627 metres) received its fascinating name when Hector was kicked by his horse and knocked senseless. The river, by association, became the Kicking Horse River.

Although the grade from the top of the pass down what came to be known as 'the big hill' into Field, B.C. (elev. 1,241 metres), was greater than 4 per cent, the Kicking Horse was selected for the first railway route to Vancouver, the CPR completing its line through the pass in 1884. (The grade was reduced to 2 per cent with the building of the famous spiral tunnels in 1909.)

Otto Klotz, who undertook an astronomical survey along the CPR right-of-way in 1886, introduced the name Wapta for the river (from the Stoney word for 'river'), but the Hector name, Kicking Horse, prevailed. The Trans-Canada Highway, opened officially in 1962, traverses the pass.

Howse Pass (elev. 1,525 metres), occasionally touted in recent times as a practical highway route to shorten travel time between Edmonton and Vancouver, was crossed in 1810 by Joseph Howse, a Hudson's Bay Company trader. The pass had been crossed earlier in 1807 by David Thompson, who gave it the name Howse Pass on his 1814 map. Howse had been in charge of Carlton House, near present-day Prince Albert, Sask., from 1799 to 1809. He retired to England in 1815.

Athabasca Pass (elev. 1,748 metres) was crossed by David Thompson in 1811, and became thereafter an important route to the Columbia River system. The pass takes its name from the Athabasca River, which rises southeast of the pass; the name in Cree means 'where the reeds are,' a description of the marshy delta where the river enters Lake Athabasca some 1,000 kilometres away in northeastern Alberta.

At the summit of the pass is a small round lake called Committee Punch Bowl, where Sir George Simpson treated his companions to a bottle of wine in 1825. The name is a tribute to the governing committee of the Hudson's Bay Company.

Yellowhead Pass (elev. 1,133 metres) was not explored until the 1820s, but ultimately became the most important rail and highway pass north of the Kicking Horse Pass. The pass and the B.C. community of Tête Jaune Cache both honour a fur trader.

For many years the names of Jasper Hawes, François Decoigne, and Pierre Hatsinaton were advanced as the 'yellow headed' trader in question; but in 1984 David Smyth, a Parks Canada historian, established beyond doubt that the blond trader involved was really Pierre Bostonais. This mixed-blood Iroquois had worked for both the Hudson's Bay and the North West companies and was killed in the upper Peace River region in 1827.

The pass, called merely a portage during the fur trade era, also became known as Leather Pass in the late 1800s, as hides had earlier been carried through it by traders from the Athabasca River on the east to New Caledonia on the west. Other names noted in the literature include Cowdung Pass, Leatherhead Pass, Jasper Pass, Jasper House Pass, Tête Jaune Passe, and Rocky Mountain Pass.

Sandford Fleming failed in the 1880s to persuade the CPR to follow the route of the Yellowhead Pass, but it was ultimately chosen by both the Grand Trunk Pacific and the Canadian Northern. These were united in the 1920s into the Canadian National Railways, which has continued to use the pass as its main freight route to the Pacific coast. It is also used by Via Rail for passenger traffic between Vancouver, Edmonton, and Winnipeg. As well, the pass is the route of the Yellowhead Highway, which follows the same general route – Winnipeg, Saskatoon, Edmonton, Jasper, and on to the coast.

Monkman Pass (elev. 1,082 metres) was discovered by Alexander Monkman in the winter of 1921–2 while on a trapping and hunting trip. The pass was seriously considered for a railway to the Peace River country of Alberta in 1925.

A new provincial park recently established at the pass, and extensive coal developments north of the pass at Tumbler Ridge, may encourage the opening of a highway through the pass, a route long promoted in the Grande Prairie region.

The names of these seven passes through the Great Divide illustrate the diversity in geographical naming in Canada:

The transfer of a native name from a nearby feature – Athabasca; the translation of a description given by natives – Crowsnest; the occurrence of a decorative paint – Vermilion; an incident – Kicking Horse; a mixed-blood Iroquois fur trader – Yellowhead; a Hudson's Bay trader – Howse; and a hunter and trapper from the region – Monkman.

Of course there are many other pass names (Deadman, Palliser, Assiniboine, Miette, Simpson, to name but a few), and each has its own interesting tale of discovery and exploration.

Commemorating Prominent Individuals and Honouring Certain Family Names

Fraser, a Thoroughly Geographic Name

Fraser is one of the most-honoured surnames when it comes to naming geographical features in Canada. The most prominent feature is the Fraser River, the mighty drainage system of British Columbia.

The name Fraser has its roots in a Norman family whose armorial bearings included the blossom of the strawberry (*fraise*). The first Frasers arrived in Britain with William the Conqueror. They acquired lands in Scotland's East Lothian in the twelfth century, and subsequently spread throughout Scotland. Several Frasers distinguished themselves in military campaigns in Britain's defence of its American colonies in the 1700s, and in the fur trade and related exploratory travels.

One might expect only three or four dozen Fraser names in the Canadian Geographical Names Data Base, maintained by the Canada Centre for Mapping in Ottawa. Surprisingly, there are more than four dozen currently used in British Columbia alone, while Québec has four dozen more, and Ontario and Nova Scotia each have more than three dozen. In total, there are 218 geographical features in Canada with Fraser as part of their names, another 15 names with Frazer, and a further 3 with Frazier. In addition, Fraser (or Frazer/Frazier) occurs as a part of 103 names previously used for features that now have other names.

The Fraser River was named by David Thompson in 1813, five years after Simon Fraser had made his historic journey to its mouth. Alexander Mackenzie had assumed in 1793 it was the Columbia, and Simon Fraser expected he would arrive at the Pacific well below the 49th parallel. Discouraged when he found it was not, he left the river unnamed.

The river is only one of many features in British Columbia named for the illustrious partner of the North West Company. Fraser Lake, 125 kilometres west of Prince George, was named by John Stuart, one of Fraser's clerks. The present village of Fraser Lake on the lake's south shore has a population of 1,300. Fraser's first name is honoured with Simon Bay on the north side of the lake. Fort Fraser, said to be the first settlement in the so-called Oregon Territory, was established in 1806 by Simon Fraser as a fur-trading post at the east end of the lake. The community of Fort Fraser now has a population of 450.

Near the source of the Fraser River in Mount Robson Provincial Park in the Rockies is Mount Fraser (elevation 3,270 metres). Its peaks are named Simon, Bennington, and McDonell in honour of Fraser's first name, his birthplace in Vermont, and his wife's maiden name. Bennington Glacier is on the British Columbia side of the Continental Divide; Simon Glacier and Fraser Glacier drain into Alberta's Simon Creek.

One of the stretches of the Princess Royal Channel between Princess Royal Island and the mainland, 90 kilometres south of Kitimat, is called Fraser Reach. It was named in 1866 for Donald Fraser, then a prominent lawyer and landowner in Victoria.

In Port Alexander, at the north end of Vancouver Island, is Fraser Island, named about 1860 by Capt. (later Admiral Sir) George Richards for Alexander Fraser Boxer, then the master of H.M.S. *Alert.*

Eighty kilometres northeast of Vernon is Bill Fraser

Lake and Bill Fraser Creek, named for a widely admired guide who lived in the area from 1907 to 1963. Mount Fraser and Fraser Creek, 55 kilometres north of Kamloops, also are named for the same Bill Fraser. Fraser Island at the north end of Adams lake, 100 kilometres northeast of Kamloops, was named in 1972 for another Bill Fraser, a logger and forest-service patrolman living at Chase in the 1960s.

On the west side of the Fraser Canyon near North Bend is Fraser Peak, named in 1956 for Trooper William E. Fraser, who was killed in action during the Second World War. Near the British Columbia–Alaska boundary, 30 kilometres north of Stewart, is a 2,440-metre mountain called Mount White-Fraser, named for George R. White-Fraser, a member of the International Boundary Commission, 1904–11. (He served during the First World War in France, and died in 1920.)

Fraser Falls on the Stewart River in the Yukon is named for a member of an 1885 prospecting party. Fraser Creek, 125 kilometres southwest of Whitehorse, was named in 1902 for assistant surgeon S.M. Fraser of the North West Mounted Police, who was a mining recorder and customs officer at Dalton Post from 1901 to 1903.

In 1847, John Rae named Fraser Bay, on the west side of Melville Peninsula in the Northwest Territories, for a friend who was a chief trader of the Hudson's Bay Company (likely Paul Fraser, who lived from 1797 to 1855). Six years later, Elisha Kane, an American explorer, named Cape Fraser on the east coast of Ellesmere Island for Prof. John F. Fraser of the University of Pennsylvania.

Where Hudson Bay and Hudson Strait meet, and off the northwestern tip of Nottingham Island, is Fraser Island. It was named in 1965 for Robert James Fraser (1887–1965), who served as the first Dominion Hydrographer from 1948 to 1952, and was the father of J. Keith Fraser, general manager and publisher of *Canadian Geo-*

graphic, 1982–90. Because Robert Fraser had contributed forty-five years to the hydrographic surveying of Canadian waters, the hydrographic service wanted to reward him with a perpetual memorial in the area of Hudson Bay, where he had undertaken the first hydrographic surveys during the years 1910–14. The Canadian Hydrographic Service first proposed a sea-floor feature, but I recommended selecting the then unnamed island so the name could be displayed on topographical maps.

Saskatchewan has four Fraser features named for Second World War casualties: Fraser Bay, in Reindeer Lake, for Gunner Arthur R. Fraser; Fraser Creek, which flows into the bay, for Pte. Robert W. Fraser; Fraser Lakes, west of Reindeer Lake, for Flight Sgt. John S. Fraser; and Fraser Lake, northwest of Lac la Ronge, for Flying Officer Alexander M. Fraser. Fraser Bay in Otter Lake, an expansion of Churchill River in Saskatchewan, was named in 1964 for a pioneer teacher and missionary, Canon Albert Fraser. Fraser Rapids, on Foster River north of Lac la Ronge, was named in 1966 for James Fraser and his wife who were homesteaders in the Pambrun area southeast of Swift Current.

Three features in Manitoba are named for Frasers killed in action during the Second World War: Fraser Island, in Gilchrist Lake east of Lake Winnipeg, is for Flying Officer John C. Fraser; Fraser Lake, near Lynn Lake, is for Flying Officer Alexander D. Fraser; and Fraser Creek, west of Churchill, is for Flight Sgt. Ian Fraser. Fraserwood, a small community 15 kilometres west of Gimli, was called Kreuzburg until 1918, when the name was changed to honour a local merchant, Samuel J. Wood, and his fiancée, Annie Bell Fraser.

Fraser Township, west of Pembroke, Ont., was named in 1854 for Col. Alexander Fraser of Fraserfield, Glengarry County, who was a member of the Legislative Council of Canada in 1841.

A post office was established in 1882 in the community of Fraserburg, in the present town of Bracebridge, with Alexander Fraser its first postmaster. The name recalls Fraserburgh, Scotland, founded by Sir Alexander Fraser in the late 1500s.

Fraserdale, 110 kilometres north of Cochrane on the Ontario Northland Railway, is named for Alan Fraser, a civil engineer on the railway when it was built north to Moosonee in 1930.

South of Lake Nipissing is Fraser Creek, which crosses land granted to John Burns Fraser in 1886.

Malcolm Fraser acquired the seigniory of Mount Murray, east of La Malbaie in Québec's Charlevoix County, in 1761. He had served with distinction with Wolfe at Louisbourg and Québec, and was wounded in a skirmish at Ste-Foy in 1860. On Rivière Comporté, east of La Malbaie, is a set of falls named for him.

North of La Malbaie are two lakes, 18 kilometres apart, officially called Lac Fraser. The current topographical map (1976) identifies each as Fraser Lake. This happened because of a federal mapping policy, in effect until 1976, that prescribed English generics for English names. I argued, unsuccessfully, that the Frasers of La Malbaie had been intermarried with the French from the early 1800s, and noted that Fraser itself was not an English name. The next edition of the map will portray Lac Fraser for the two features.

Alexander Fraser (1761–1837), a son of Malcolm Fraser, served with the North West Company from 1797 to 1809. He spent the winter of 1797 at Bedford House on Reindeer Lake in present-day Saskatchewan. An island in the lake is named for him. In 1802, he bought the seigniory of Rivière-du-Loup-en-Bas. In his honour the village of Fraserville was established in 1850, becoming a town in 1874. In 1919, the name was changed to Rivière-du-Loup. In the 1871 *Dominion Directory*, the following leaders of the community were noted: Edward Fraser, seignior and president of the Fraserville Institute; William Fraser, seignior and justice of the peace; and Alexander Fraser, advocate. Today, the town has both a Fraserville Street and a Fraser Street.

Several Fraser families from Scotland acquired lands in the Lake St. Francis region of the St. Lawrence River after 1818. In Huntingdon County in Québec, James and Alexander Fraser developed farms adjacent to Pointe Fraser and Ruisseau Fraser. Across the lake on the Ontario side, Donald Fraser purchased an estate in the early 1800s at a site that became known as Fraser Point, and his descendants remained there until 1951. In front of the point are several small islands called crabs; one is known as Fraser Crab.

There are seven streams in New Brunswick called Fraser Brook. One or more of them may be named after Donald Fraser, who established sawmills at River de Chute in 1877 and in Edmundston in 1911. After 1917, Fraser Companies (now Fraser Inc.) set up pulp and paper mills in Edmundston and in Madawaska, Me.

Bishop William Fraser (1778–1851) was the first Roman Catholic bishop of Halifax, although he retained his residence in Arichat on Isle Madame, adjacent to Cape Breton Island. Four of his brothers – Colin, Thomas, John, and David – and a sister, Mrs. Donald Chisholm, established the community of Fraser's Grant, 20 kilometres east of Antigonish. Fifteen kilometres south of Antigonish on the South River, Alexander Fraser installed saw and grist mills in the mid-1800s. The post office there was called Fraser Mills from 1884 to 1937. Sunnybrae in Pictou County, 25 kilometres southeast of New Glasgow, also had a post office called Fraser Mills from 1848 to 1876. Fraser Settlement in the Musquodoboit Valley was the site of a grant given to another Alexander Fraser in 1813.

There are only two Fraser names in Newfoundland, both

in Labrador. Fraser Lake, 100 kilometres north of Churchill Falls, may be named for James D. Fraser, well known
at the turn of the century for his dog teams, which he
used in fur trading on the Labrador coast. Fraser River,
which flows into the Atlantic at Nain, may be named for
James Fraser, who commanded Moravian vessels on the
Labrador coast for some thirty-five years after 1782.

Prince Edward Island only has a single Fraser name,
Mary Fraser Island in Malpeque Bay.

George Dawson, Inspiration for More Than Twenty-five Names

The most brilliant and versatile scientist in Canada a century ago was arguably George Mercer Dawson. Best known
as a geologist, he was also an accomplished botanist, zool-
ogist, ethnologist, historian, geographer, linguist, and yes,
even a toponymist. Add to that explorer, adventurer, diplomat, spellbinding speaker, and pastoral poet, and you
have the quintessential Victorian-era gentleman and
scholar – and a worthy inspiration for the names of more
than twenty-five Canadian mountain peaks, inlets, islands,
settlements, and animals.

The best known are Dawson Creek, B.C., and the Klondike Gold Rush capital of Dawson City, Yukon, which
both commemorate Dawson's pioneering surveys of those
regions. In two instances, Dawson himself gave his name
to the features he encountered. Otherwise, other people
named places after him, an indication of the esteem in
which he was held, and of the nature of the man whose
physical deformities and boundless energies earned him
a number of admiring sobriquets, such as 'Little Giant'
in a 1974 biography by Joyce Barkhouse – 'Little' because
a childhood illness had left him head and shoulders
shorter than an average man, with a hunched back and

weak lungs. Despite these handicaps he never shied from arduous explorations.

Dawson was born in Pictou, N.S., in 1849, the son of Margaret Mercer and John William Dawson, a respected geologist and provincial superintendent of education. In 1855, the family moved to Montréal, where George's father became principal of McGill University and one of the first Canadian scientists of international note.

George Dawson studied at McGill and then graduated first in his class from the Royal School of Mines in London. In 1873, he was appointed naturalist and botanist with the British North America Boundary Commission, and spent two years studying the natural resources along the 49th parallel between Lake of the Woods and the Rocky Mountains. An island in Lake of the Woods he called Middle Island was renamed Dawson Island, possibly by Andrew Lawson, who undertook an extensive geological survey of the area in 1883. Nearby are Dawson Channel and Dawson Bay.

In 1875, Dawson joined the Geological Survey of Canada, established thirty-three years earlier to develop mineral industries in Canada. He became the Survey's assistant director in 1883 and director in 1895, a position he still held at the time of his early death in 1901, at age 52.

Dawson's first assignment with the Survey was a study of the geology of British Columbia. After completing extensive surveys of the southern part of the province, and recommending a route for the Canadian Pacific Railway, he went to the Queen Charlotte Islands in 1878, principally to evaluate the coal deposits there. He also took time to put together a report on the customs of the Haida Indians, and to compile comparative vocabularies of the Haida and adjacent mainland tribes.

During his summer in the Queen Charlottes, Dawson fixed the present written forms of thirty Haida place names, and named another seventy-five features, usually using simple descriptives – Bag Harbour, Slug Rock – but also honouring noted scientists of the day, including Charles Lyell, Thomas Huxley, and Charles Darwin. He named Dawson Head, on a small island on the west side of Graham Island (the largest of the islands), for himself, and Rankine Islands, on the east side of Moresby Island, for his brother and assistant, Rankine Dawson.

In the years following his survey, Dawson was commemorated in the Queen Charlottes by other scientists and surveyors in the names of eight more features: Dawson Inlet and Dawson Harbour (1897), Dawson Islands (1910), Mercer Lake (1914), Dawson Point and Dawson Bay (1921), Mercer Point (1945), and Dawson Cove (1948). In addition, a rare caribou on the islands was identified in 1900 as *Rangifer tarandus dawsoni* by Ernest Thompson Seton, the noted naturalist and nature writer.

In 1879, Dawson undertook an arduous reconnaissance from the mouth of the Skeena River, now the site of Prince Rupert, B.C., inland through the mountains and eventually to Edmonton. In the Peace River country near the Alberta-B.C. border, he assigned the name Dawson's Brook to a minor tributary of the Pouce Coupé River, which flows into the Peace. According to Philip and Helen Akrigg, in their *British Columbia Place Names* (1986), Henry MacLeod, a CPR explorer who met Dawson in the area, may have changed the name to Dawson Creek – the name adopted when a village was established on the site in 1919. The settlement grew, particularly after the railway arrived in 1931, and again after 1942 when it became Mile 0 on the Alaska Highway. Incorporated as a city in 1958, Dawson Creek had a population of almost 11,000 in 1991.

Dawson's most remarkable overland journey was a 2,200-kilometre trip in the summer of 1887 on the Stikine, Liard, Pelly, and Yukon rivers in the Yukon and northern B.C. His carefully prepared map of the Yukon identified the Klondike River as a possible source of gold. When the gold rush brought thousands into the area ten years later, the trader and prospector Joseph Ladue asked William Ogilvie to survey a townsite at the river's mouth. Ogilvie said he would if he could name the town for the finest man he knew. On receiving news of the honour from Ogilvie, the 'Little Giant' pencilled in Dawson City on his map of the Yukon.

Ogilvie had honoured his estimable friend earlier, in 1888, with Mount Dawson, east of Lake Laberge. But Dawson asked two years later to have it called Mount Laurier after Wilfrid Laurier, then leader of the Liberal Party of Canada. Ogilvie may also have named Dawson Range, a chain of mountains southwest of the Yukon River.

In the Selkirk Mountains, east of Revelstoke, B.C., there is another Dawson Range. Its highest point, at 3,390 metres, is Mount Dawson. It was named in 1888 by William Green, a British alpinist and author of a book on the Selkirks.

Dawson Peaks are five summits of a mountain on the west side of Teslin Lake, northeast of Atlin, B.C. The name was noted by John Gwillim in his 1901 report on the Atlin mining district, and may have been given by Arthur St-Cyr, who surveyed the B.C.–Yukon boundary in 1899 and 1900.

Joseph Tyrrell, Dawson's assistant on an 1881 Alberta expedition, explored the area of Lake Winnipegosis in 1889, and named its northwesterly extremity Dawson Bay. Dawson Bay is also a small fishing community on the west side of the bay.

Tyrrell undertook several geological surveys in the Chesterfield Inlet, Thelon and Dubawnt river areas of the Northwest Territories. About 1893, he named Dawson Inlet, on the west coast of Hudson Bay between Arviat and Rankin Inlet.

A 1910 geological map of the Lake Nipigon area portrays several islands and bays with the names of scientists, including Logan, Murchison, and Humboldt. Dawson Island, in the centre of the lake, may have been named by Donaldson Dowling, who surveyed the area in 1894 with William McInnes, and on his own in 1898.

During a zoological survey of the Yukon River in the 1880s, Clinton Merriam, chief of the United States Biological Survey, encountered a new species of mouse and named it *Clethrionomys rutilus dawsoni*. I agree with Barkhouse, who says in her biography that the 'Little Giant' would be more pleased with this honour than any other, given the image of the little animals scurrying freely across the same wild lands he had explored and mapped.

Victoria: The Most Honoured Name in Canada

No individual has been more honoured than Queen Victoria in the names of Canada's public buildings, streets, populated places, and physical features. Her name appears more than 300 times on our maps. This is not surprising given Victoria's long reign during the greatest glory of the British Empire from 1837 to 1901.

Every Canadian can think of at least one public building or street named for her. Among the notable public institutions are Victoria University in Toronto, Royal Victoria Hospital in Montréal, and Victoria General Hospital in Halifax and in Winnipeg. Among Canada's 280 postal divisions, more than half have at least one thoroughfare identified by the name Victoria. Most were named to honour the Queen ... but one that was not is Thunder Bay's Victoria Avenue, named for Victoria McVicar, a Lakehead landowner in the late 1800s, noted for her dealings with some celebrated builders of the West, among them Louis Riel, founder of Manitoba, and William Van Horne, builder of the CPR.

The first honour for Princess Victoria may date from 1829. Pierre-Georges Roy wrote (1906) in a book on Québec's names that Pointe Victoria in the Saguenay had been named that year for her. But a check of mid-nineteenth-century charts and maps has failed to reveal the point so named.

In 1831, John Ross, while searching for the Northwest Passage, entered a small bay on the east side of Boothia Peninsula and named it Victoria Harbour for the thirteen-year-old princess. Subsequently, she formally granted him permission to use her name for this remote and minor water feature in Canada's Arctic. From then on, explorers, map makers, and administrators assigned the name Victoria to a multitude of lakes, points, islands, and other geographical features all over the Canadian map.

On the occasions of her golden (1887) and diamond (1897) anniversaries many more features were named for her. And long after her death, Queen Peak in northern British Columbia was named for her in 1933 because of its associations with nearby Victoria Peak and Consort Peak.

The best-known place named for the British monarch is the beautiful city at the southern tip of Vancouver Island. In 1843, the Hudson's Bay Company resolved to name the new fort overlooking Juan de Fuca Strait for her. Briefly, Fort Albert was substituted, but a terse message from London insisted on the use of Fort Victoria. The townsite of Victoria was established at the fort in 1851–2, and in 1868 the growing city became the capital of the colony of British Columbia, which was to become a province three years later.

Alberta had a Victoria northeast of Edmonton where George McDougall established a mission in 1862 and the Hudson's Bay Company set up a post two years later. In 1887, to avoid confusion with other Victorias, this small community was renamed Pakan, the nickname of a Cree chief. The village of Empress, northeast of Medicine Hat, was named in 1913 in commemoration of the Queen's imperial title received from Parliament in 1876 when Benjamin Disraeli was prime minister.

The Marquess of Lorne and his wife, Princess Louise (the Queen's daughter), wanted to give the name Victoria to the capital of the North-West Territories in 1882, but wisely chose the other half of her Latin title, Regina.

Manitoba has a rural municipality and a lake named Victoria, and another municipality called Victoria Beach.

In terms of geographical names, Ontario is Canada's most 'Victorian' province. It has at least forty-seven distinct features with her name: one county, one township, fourteen populated places, and thirty-one physical features. In fact one does not travel far in Ontario before encountering Victoria Corners, Victoria Square, Victoria Harbour, Victoria Springs, Victoria Lake, or just plain Victoria.

Evidence of Victoria is less apparent in Québec, although the second-largest place in Canada with her name is in that province. Victoriaville, a town of 21,495 people, was named for the Queen in 1861. There are as well seven physical features in Québec with the name Victoria, including Grand lac Victoria at the head of the Ottawa River south of Val d'Or.

The Atlantic provinces have twenty-nine places and features with the name Victoria. Among these are a county in each of New Brunswick and Nova Scotia. Victoria is an attractive seaside village in Prince Edward Island, where there are also places called Victoria Cross and Victoria West. Newfoundland has a Victoria, a town of 1,831; it lies on the west side of Conception Bay about 50 kilometres northwest of St. John's.

Our two northern territories have twenty-two features with the name Victoria. Among them are Victoria Island,

Canada's second-largest island (after Baffin) in the Arctic Archipelago, and Victoria and Albert Mountains on Ellesmere Island.

Fit for the Prince of Wales

A long-established practice in Canada since the early 1700s has been the naming of physical features, museums, theatres, and commercial establishments for the reigning Prince of Wales. The name has also been given to a National Hockey League conference (from 1974-5 to 1992-3), as well as a prestigious annual horse race in Fort Erie, Ont.

The first Prince of Wales to be commemorated in Canada was the son of King George I. Born in 1683, he later ruled Britain for thirty-three years as King George II. The name Prince of Wales's Fort was given, in 1719, to the Hudson's Bay Company's stone-walled post at the mouth of the Churchill River in northern Manitoba. In 1782, a French fleet under the command of Comte de Lapérouse blew up Fort Prince of Wales, as it came to be known. In the 1930s, the fort was restored. Now a national historic site, it is one of the main attractions in the Churchill area.

Perhaps the most distinguished visitor to North America in 1860 was Prince Albert Edward, the eldest son of Queen Victoria and great-great-grandfather of the present Prince of Wales, Prince Charles. He received a tumultuous welcome from the time he arrived in St. John's, Nfld., on 24 July until his departure from Portland, Me., on 20 October. Even before his arrival, the Prince of Wales had been recognized in at least five physical features named for him. Prince of Wales Island, located 1,320 kilometres north of Yellowknife, is perhaps the best known, but it was not the first island in the Arctic to bear his name. When explorer and trader John Rae crossed Melville Peninsula to the Gulf of Boothia in 1846–7, he named an island in the gulf's Committee Bay for the then five-year-old prince. In 1926, the Geographic Board of Canada renamed it Wales Island to avoid confusion with the larger Prince of Wales Island to the west.

In 1850–1, Robert M'Clure wintered in a 275-kilometre-long passage between Victoria Island and Banks Island. He named it Prince of Wales Strait. Although now considered part of the main channel of the Northwest Passage, its first recorded navigation was not until Henry Larsen's RCMP patrol in 1944. In 1852, a high range on Ellesmere Island was named Prince of Wales Mountains after Prince Albert Edward. Finally, Prince of Wales Reach was assigned in 1859 to a long, narrow passage of Jervis Inlet, 90 kilometres northwest of Vancouver.

After visits to Halifax and Saint John in 1860, the prince and his retinue set out for Fredericton. From Saint John, they travelled 14 kilometres by train before boarding a steamer on the Kennebecasis River at Rothesay, newly named for one of the prince's titles, the Duke of Rothesay.

The community of Prince of Wales, 18 kilometres southwest of Saint John, may have been named about this time. Its choice was perhaps reinforced by the settlement of that area in the late 1780s by the Prince of Wales American Regiment, Loyalist soldiers who were granted land there after the American Revolution. The Prince of Wales post office operated there from 1861 to 1950.

After visiting Charlottetown, where a college was named in his honour, the prince went up the St. Lawrence River to Québec City and Montréal. On 29 August, he travelled on the Grand Trunk Railway to Dickinson's Landing, 14 kilometres west of Cornwall, Ont., then returned to Montréal that evening after shooting the Long Sault Rapids. That year, the Grand Trunk named its Dickinson's Landing station Wales.

In 1860, a new road leading north from Orangeville, Ont., was being cut through the woods. On completion of the road, one of the workmen is said to have exclaimed that it was fit for the Prince of Wales – to this day the name remains in use. Streets were also named for the Prince of Wales in St. John's and Montréal.

The second Prince of Wales to make a popular tour of Canada was the eldest son of George V – the son who became Edward VIII, the Duke of Windsor. While the prince was visiting Ottawa in 1919, he endorsed a proposal to name the falls at Hogs Back on the Rideau River for him. At the same time, the provincial highway from Ottawa to the St. Lawrence River at Johnstown, Ont., was officially named The Prince of Wales Highway. Neither name gained public recognition or acceptance. Prince of Wales Falls remains the official designation on maps and in publications about the Rideau River and the Rideau Canal, but it is doubtful anyone outside official naming and mapping offices is aware of it. Although the name of the highway never caught on, that part of Highway 16 between Carling Avenue and Ottawa's southern city limits acquired the name Prince of Wales Drive – a name well known in the national capital region. The Prince of Wales Hotel, the largest all-wood structure in Western Canada, was opened in 1927 in Waterton Lakes National Park.

The current Prince of Wales has been honoured by the Prince of Wales Northern Heritage Centre, a museum of native artifacts in Yellowknife which opened in 1979.

Vanier: Places Honouring an Illustrious Statesman

When the Royal Canadian Geographical Society moved its headquarters from Wilbrod Street in Ottawa to McAr-

thur Avenue in Vanier in 1988, some Society members wondered how far the Society had moved from the nation's
capital. Most were surprised to learn it was only about
half a kilometre to the east.

Located on the eastern bank of the Rideau River, 2 kilometres from its mouth, Vanier was originally settled in
the 1830s, when developer Charles Cummings built a
bridge across the river. The growing community on Montreal Road was called Cummings Bridge for almost half
a century. In the 1870s, it was renamed Janeville, either
in honour of the wife of another settler of the 1830s, Donald McArthur (hence McArthur Avenue), or for the first
child born in the community.

The name Eastview was given on 31 December 1908,
when the communities of Janeville, Clarkstown, and Clandeboye – in what was then Gloucester Township – were
incorporated into a single village with an area of 2.79
square kilometres. Eastview – the name was chosen because there was a view of Ottawa's then eastern limits –
became a town in 1912 and a city in 1963. In 1950, Eastview
applied to the Ontario Municipal Board to annex adjacent
lands in Gloucester Township, but the board gave approval to Ottawa instead, leaving Eastview surrounded by
Ottawa and setting the stage for Vanier's distinction as
Canada's smallest city.

On 1 January 1969, Eastview was renamed Vanier, primarily to honour the first French Canadian to be appointed governor general, but also to give the city a name
with francophone character. Fifty-five per cent of its population of 18,150 is francophone, its street names are
largely French, it is the headquarters of the Association
canadienne-française de l'Ontario and other francophone
groups, and its distinctly French-Canadian atmosphere is
widely known throughout the national capital area.

Vanier's population has steadily declined over the past
thirty years as residents left behind their small, quaint

homes on narrow streets for larger houses and lots in the
suburbs. Down from 24,700 in 1963, Vanier now has the
smallest population of the five cities in the Regional Municipality of Ottawa–Carleton (the others are Gloucester,
Kanata, Ottawa, and Nepean).

More than once – the latest being in the fall of 1992
– provincially appointed commissions have urged amal-
gamation with Ottawa. Even in 1984, a majority of Vanier's
voters recommended joining the capital city, though Vanier city council at the time declined to act. Ottawa provides
Vanier with police service and fire protection but, worried
about increased costs, has resisted annexing its small
neighbour, whose median income is only 70 per cent of
Ottawa's. More recently, Vanier has displayed a renewed
pride in itself, and now seems determined to go its own
way.

Georges Philias Vanier was one of the most admired
governors general to hold that office during Canada's first
century. Born in Montréal in 1888, he studied law at Laval
University before becoming a career soldier. He was one
of the founding officers of the 22nd Battalion of the Canadian Expeditionary Force, and lost a leg during a First
World War battle in France. After the war, the battalion
became the Royal 22nd Regiment (the illustrious Vandoos,
an anglicization of vingt-deux), and Vanier served as its
commanding officer from 1926 to 1928. He distinguished
himself in Canadian diplomatic postings in London, Gen-
eva, and Paris, and recruited French Canadians to serve
in the Second World War. In 1959, he was appointed governor general, the Queen's representative in Canada. In
the third month of Canada's centennial celebrations, the
man who had become renowned for his love of Canada,
and for his deeply spiritual and moral dimensions, died
at Rideau Hall.

Ontario's Vanier is not the only city in Canada named
for the governor general. In 1966, the Québec City suburb

of Québec-Ouest, with an area of 4.68 square kilometres and a population of about 11,000, was renamed Vanier. When the legislation to change Eastview's name was being considered in Ontario in 1968, officials in Vanier, Qué., argued that only one Canadian city should have the name, but the wishes of the Ontario city's residents prevailed.

In Québec, four lakes, a township, a creek, a hill, and an electoral division are named for Vanier. Forty towns and cities in the province have a Vanier street, boulevard, or avenue. Elsewhere in Canada, there are another twenty-six towns and cities with a street, avenue, or drive named for the former governor general.

In the 1950s, what was thought to be a peninsula of Bathurst Island in the Arctic Archipelago was found to be three large islands and two smaller ones. Initially, the names of three American vessels involved in establishing early-warning radar stations across the High Arctic were given by geographer Andrew Taylor to the large islands, but they were rejected in 1960 by the Canadian Board on Geographical Names. The board proposed naming the islands after Vanier and his two predecessors, Vincent Massey and Viscount Alexander of Tunis. In 1962, the federal cabinet approved the proposals and stated the choices would reaffirm Canadian sovereignty in the Arctic. The form Île Vanier was adopted for the largest of the three islands, at 970 square kilometres.

A year later, the small island between Île Vanier and Massey Island was named Île Pauline for the popular and gracious wife of the governor general. Vanier replied that his wife was pleased indeed that the 'baby' island was next to his. Knowing that there was a larger unnamed island between Alexander and Massey islands, he quipped that after 'forty-two years of marriage she still prefers my company.'

As Robert Speaight noted in his book, *Vanier: Soldier, Diplomat and Governor General* (1970), Vanier also mused whimsically about the appointment of an island manager for Île Vanier, the design of an island flag, and the publication of two newspapers, one in English and one in French.

In 1967, the Whitehorse Lions Club proposed naming a mountain overlooking the north end of Kusawa Lake, 55 kilometres west of Whitehorse, for the governor general. A four-member team climbed the mountain on 9 July and erected a cairn at its summit. Some badges from General Vanier's Royal 22nd uniform and some photos of the late governor general were embedded in the cairn by the regiment's Staff Sgt. Albert Bélanger. The Canadian Permanent Committee on Geographical Names endorsed the names three days after the climb. Mount Vanier has an elevation of 1,845 metres and is visible from the Alaska Highway, 20 kilometres to the north.

Also in 1967, a Royal Air Force expedition from Britain climbed a mountain near the north end of Ellesmere Island and named it for Vanier. This second Mount Vanier in Canada's north, approved in 1971, has an elevation of 2,417 metres, just 200 metres lower than nearby Barbeau Peak, the highest mountain in the Canadian Arctic.

The name Vanier is recalled in many other ways in Canada. The Vanier Institute of the Family was established in 1964 by Georges and Pauline Vanier to promote research into the family and study the complexity of modern living and its effects on the integrity of family life. Since 1960, the Institute of Public Administration of Canada has annually awarded the gold Vanier Medal to an individual showing outstanding leadership in Canadian public administration.

A community college in Saint-Laurent, Qué., a western suburb of Montréal, is named Vanier College. Vanier Park in Vancouver is the site of the City of Vancouver Archives, and the Centennial Museum and Planetarium. Nationwide, there are many elementary and secondary schools bearing his name. And each November since 1965, the best of Canada's university football teams compete for the Vanier Cup.

A Mountain for Michener, a Lake for Léger

During the first 100 years of Confederation, more than 100 geographic features – and countless more parks, schools, bridges, and institutions – were named for the nineteen governors general of Canada. Among those most honoured in geographic names are the Earl of Dufferin (eighteen) and the Marquess of Lorne (fourteen). But the story behind the naming of features for the twentieth and twenty-first governors general, Roland Michener and Jules Léger, is one of the more unusual ones.

Daniel Roland Michener, governor general from 1967 to 1974, was born 19 April 1900, in Lacombe, Alta., 130 kilometres south of Edmonton, and raised in Red Deer, 25 kilometres farther south. He had a distinguished career as a parliamentarian, Speaker of the House of Commons, and High Commissioner to India.

Until he died in 1991, Michener was an active senior partner in the Toronto legal firm Lang, Michener, Lawrence and Shaw, and he still followed the vigorous exercise routine that made him one of the more memorable advocates of Participaction, the organization that promotes fitness to Canadians.

In 1977, a proposal was sent by the secretariat of the Canadian Permanent Committee on Geographical Names to the Alberta Historic Sites Board (the body responsible for geographic naming in the province) to name a feature for Michener. The board greeted the suggestion with enthusiasm and proposed it for a prominent mountain 185 kilometres west of Red Deer.

The mountain is located on the south side of Abraham Lake along the upper reaches of the North Saskatchewan River. Its magnificent profile was seldom seen by travellers until the early 1970s, when the David Thompson Highway was built, linking the town of Rocky Mountain House to the Icefields Parkway in Banff National Park. The mountain has an elevation of 2,545 metres and rises 1,220 metres above the lake.

Before proceeding with the name, the board consulted the Stoney tribal council, as the surrounding territory is traditional Stoney land. Although the Stoneys know the feature as îyârhe kta ûtha, meaning 'person who dwells in the mountains,' they endorsed the idea of Mount Michener as its official name.

The naming ceremony took place at Windy Point, on the north side of the lake, on 26 August 1979. After unveiling a plaque, then-premier Peter Lougheed observed, 'We think this mountain ... will be a continual reminder to Albertans and visitors to our province of the outstanding contributions made by Mr. Michener to the life of this country.'

On learning that Michener had been seen jogging beside the highway before the ceremony, Lougheed remarked that he almost expected the athletic 79-year-old to cross the lake and climb to the summit of the mountain. Perhaps that suggestion inspired Michener, because nearly three years later he did climb to the top, accompanied by two mountain guides.

Author Peter Stursberg, in *The Last Viceroy* (1989), claimed that Michener set 'a record as the only person after whom a mountain was named who ever reached its peak.' If he had substituted 'octogenarian' for 'person,' his claim would likely be unassailable.

In 1976, Michener was among the guests of his successor, Jules Léger, during one of Queen Elizabeth's visits to Can-da. During an informal conversation, Léger asked Michener if he knew of a tradition of naming features for governors general during their terms of office, and he understood Michener to say that, indeed, there had been a feature named for him in the North. (In fact, what had been named, earlier in 1976, was the Norah Willis Michener Game Preserve on the Northwest Territories–Yukon boundary – for Michener's accomplished wife.)

Acting on the knowledge that an Arctic island had been named in 1962 for Georges Vanier, and assuming a feature had been named for Michener while he was in office, Government House contacted the Canadian Permanent Committee on Geographical Names to find out when a feature would be named for Léger.

The response was that there was no such established custom. In fact, the committee and most provincial names boards had taken a fairly rigid stance in the 1970s against naming features for living persons. Mount Michener was among the last to be allowed.

When Léger learned in 1979 that a mountain had been named for Michener, he asked when a feature would be named for him, adding that he would prefer a lake in his native Québec. His suggestion was sent to the Commission de toponymie du Québec, but because of the commission's rigid adherence to its principle against naming features for living persons, a decision was deferred.

Léger was born in 1913 in Saint-Anicet, on the south shore of Lake St. Francis, a widening of the St. Lawrence River 60 kilometres southwest of Montréal. After a brilliant diplomatic career, he served as under-secretary of state before being appointed governor general in 1974. Although a stroke impaired his speech and mobility, Léger continued to perform the duties of his office with the quiet dignity for which he had become widely known over the years.

Léger died in Ottawa in November 1980. Two years later, the commission gave the name Lac Jules-Léger to a lake in north-central Québec near the great divide separating the headwaters of the St. Lawrence from the Hudson Bay drainage basin. At her home in Ottawa, Gabrielle Léger, the governor general's widow, was presented with a laminated map of the region surrounding Lac Jules-Léger.

Laurier, Most-Commemorated Canadian

The individual most honoured by names on our maps is Queen Victoria. However, the most-commemorated Canadian is Sir Wilfrid Laurier, who has thirty-seven geographical features named for him, to say nothing of dozens of schools, parks, and streets from Newfoundland to the Yukon.

Laurier – born in 1841 in Saint-Lin, Qué., 35 kilometres northwest of Montréal – was prime minister of Canada from 1896 to 1911. During this time, the Geographic Board was set up to coordinate naming in Canada. Before he died in 1919, at a time when naming for living persons was common, at least eleven communities and features had been named for him. By 1928, the total was up to twenty, and seventeen more were added in subsequent years.

Widely respected in both English and French Canada, Laurier has been commemorated in the names of twelve features in Québec, seven in Ontario, six in British Columbia, seven in the Prairie provinces, three in the Territories, and two in the Atlantic provinces.

In 1896, geologist Robert Bell explored a vast area of west-central Québec surrounding Lac Matagami. South of the lake he observed a mountain, the most conspicuous feature of the landscape, and named it Mount Laurier (officially it is now Mont Laurier) for the recently elected prime minister.

From 1859 to 1902, the area of Laurierville, 65 kilometres southwest of Québec City, was part of the civil parish of Sainte-Julie-de-Somerset. In 1902, the village was incorporated and named for the prime minister. It now has a population of 885.

When the Intercolonial Railway was built from Saint-Hyacinthe to Lévis, one of the stations on the line was Saint-Flavien. Located 48 kilometres southwest of Lévis, the station was renamed Laurier when the Intercolonial became part of the Canadian National Railway system. A village that developed around the station was incorporated as Laurier-Station in 1951. Situated beside the busy Trans-Canada Highway, it now has a population of 2,175.

The area of the present town of Mont-Laurier, 175 kilometres northwest of Montréal, was settled in the late 1800s. The community of Rapide-à-l'Orignal had been established at a stretch of rough waters on the Rivière du Lièvre. In 1909, Curé Génier, the parish priest, urged Québec's premier Lomer Gouin to designate the village as the centre of the new judicial district being planned in the area, and enlisted the support of the prime minister in his cause. As a result, the village was incorporated as Mont-Laurier. Elevated to town status in 1950, Mont-Laurier is now an active commercial and tourist centre, with a population of 7,865.

In 1934, the name Mont Laurier was proposed for a mountain, 16 kilometres north of the community. Pointing out that another mountain near Lac Matagami was already named that, the authorities substituted Mont Sir-Wilfrid.

About 40 kilometres east of La Tuque (north of Trois-Rivières) is a township named Laurier. Within the township are Lac Laurier and Lac Wilfrid, both named in 1948. There is another Lac Laurier in Parc des Laurentides, 35 kilometres south of Chicoutimi. In Parc de la Vérendrye northwest of the town of Mont-Laurier, there is another Lac Laurier, so named in 1973.

In New Brunswick, a post office (now closed), 35 kilometres northeast of Chatham, was named Saint-Wilfred in 1932 in honour of the former prime minister, although his name was spelled incorrectly. In 1958, a small islet in Lockeport Harbour, N.S., was named Laurier Rock.

Laurier Township in the Parry Sound District of Ontario was named in 1878 when Laurier was minister of inland revenue. This appears to be the earliest use of his name for a feature. Within the township, Fox Lake was renamed Laurier Lake in 1951.

At the point where the Spanish River flows into Lake Huron, there are two small islands called Laurier Island and Wilfrid Island. About 20 kilometres northeast of Kenora is a small lake called Laurier Lake, which may have been named at the turn of the century during a railway survey. The lake is drained by Laurier Creek.

Among settlers in an area 45 kilometres southeast of Dauphin, Man., were some Québec farmers who were admirers of Wilfrid Laurier. When Laurier was first elected prime minister in 1896, the name Laurier was substituted for Fosbery.

Laurier Island in Cree Lake in northern Saskatchewan was named in 1938. Laurier Rural Municipality in the area of Radville, Sask., 110 kilometres southeast of Regina, was also named for Sir Wilfrid in 1909.

Alberta also has a Laurier Rural Municipality named for Sir Wilfrid. The municipality, west of the town of St. Paul and 130 kilometres northeast of Edmonton, was named in 1914. There is a Laurier Lake 60 kilometres east of St. Paul.

The earliest use of Sir Wilfrid's name in British Columbia was in 1897, when J.D. Moodie of the North West Mounted Police took an inspection trip from Edmonton to the Yukon. He named Laurier Pass, which traverses the Rocky Mountains 190 kilometres northwest of Fort St. John. In 1913, the peak on the south side of the pass was named Mount Laurier by F.K. Vreeland of New York. Although the Geographic Board was reluctant to have another mountain named for the prime minister, the name was adopted fifteen years later. At the same time, Mount Lady Laurier, 25 kilometres west of the pass, was named for his wife.

A year earlier, in 1927, a mountain rising to 3,580 metres in the Premier Range in British Columbia was named Mount Sir Wilfrid Laurier. The range is directly west of Valemount and 50 kilometres south of Mount Robson, at 3,942 metres the highest peak in the Rockies. Several Canadian prime ministers, and some other first ministers of British Columbia and Great Britain, have been honoured in the names of mountains in the Premier Range rising above 3,050 metres.

Laurier Cove in Tuck Inlet north of Prince Rupert may have been named in 1906 during a survey of the inlet, or in 1910 when the prime minister visited the western terminus of the Grand Trunk Pacific.

In 1888, surveyor William Ogilvie named a mountain overlooking Lake Laberge, 25 kilometres north of Whitehorse, for the indefatigable scientist and explorer George M. Dawson. Two years later, Dr. Dawson insisted that the name be changed from Mount Dawson to Mount Laurier. Later, in 1936, Laurier Creek, which flows west into Lake Laberge, was also named for Sir Wilfrid.

In Québec, two-thirds of the current 89 postal divisions have a thoroughfare named for Sir Wilfrid. Elsewhere in Canada, one-quarter of the 201 postal divisions have a street commemorating the former prime minister. Prominent among them is Laurier Avenue in Ottawa, where Sir Wilfrid owned a large house, now a museum.

Among schools, the most noteworthy is Wilfrid Laurier University in Waterloo, Ont. Founded as Waterloo College, and named Waterloo Lutheran University in 1957, it was renamed for the former prime minister in 1973 when it became a provincially funded institution. There are secondary schools in Ottawa, Scarborough, London, and Calgary named for Sir Wilfrid, and primary schools in Vancouver, Brampton, Ont., and Ste. Rose du Lac, Man., among others named for him (although several spell his first name Wilfred).

One of Ottawa's most distinctive landmarks, the Château Laurier, was opened in June 1912 by Sir Wilfrid, then leader of the opposition. Across the Ottawa River in Hull, the Canadian Museum of Civilization is located in Laurier Park.

Remembering John F. Kennedy

Where were you on that black day in 1963 when the shots rang out in Dallas? For millions around the world, the answer is seared in our memories. It was as if a family member had been cut down at the height of his promise of a more caring society, a greater sense of dignity for the individual.

I heard the heart-rending news on that fateful 22 November in my office on Booth Street in Ottawa, where I was working as a toponymic researcher. I still recall joining with my colleagues to share our anguish and, later, tearfully comforting my wife, who, like myself, was deeply distressed by the assassination of President John F. Kennedy.

Almost immediately, President Lyndon B. Johnson proclaimed the renaming of Idlewild Airport at New York and Cape Canaveral Space Center and Cape Canaveral in Florida for the slain president. In 1973, the name Cape Canaveral was restored for the prominent point extending into the Atlantic Ocean, east of Orlando. The John F. Kennedy Space Center remains the name of the site for spacecraft launchings.

The earliest honour in Canada was Avenue du Président-Kennedy, given on 9 January 1964 by the city of Montréal for a new street south of McGill University, between and parallel to Sherbrooke and Sainte-Catherine. The province of Québec gave the name Route du Président-Kennedy to Highway 173 leading south from Lévis, on the St. Lawrence River opposite Québec City, to the Maine boundary.

In early 1964, the residents of Sevogle, N.B., 21 kilometres northwest of Newcastle, asked the provincial government to change the name of their small community to Mount Kennedy. A year later, the Northumberland County Council and the Miramichi Historical Society expressed their opposition. Nothing more was heard about Sevogle's efforts to sanctify – as I characterize commemorative community names like Mount Kennedy – the late president in the Miramichi.

For several months in 1963 I had been working on names proposed for mountain divisions for a new physiographic map of British Columbia. Specifically, I had been investigating the hierarchy of 'mountains,' 'ranges' within mountains, and each named 'range' within ranges.

In the northern Rockies, 160 kilometres west of Fort Nelson, Mount Roosevelt and Churchill Peak were found to be located in an unnamed range of the Muskwa Ranges. I suggested Statesmen Range for it, with the further suggestion that the unnamed peaks within it be reserved for prominent world statesmen. A few days after Kennedy's assassination I proposed commemorating him on one of the many unnamed peaks in the 'Statesmen Range.'

In early December 1963, the names of Statesmen Range and Mount Kennedy were submitted to the British Columbia representative on the Canadian Permanent Committee on Geographical Names, with the added suggestion that the selected peak might be visible from the Alaska Highway, 40 kilometres north of Mount Roosevelt.

The British Columbia government was not enthusiastic about either proposal, especially the idea of naming a group of peaks Statesmen Range. It did not like the idea of reserving peaks for noted international figures, preferring to have names evolve as the features were climbed by mountaineers or explored by geologists. With some reluctance, it selected a peak for Kennedy midway between Mount Roosevelt and Churchill Peak.

Later, another peak 10 kilometres northwest of Mount Roosevelt, and closer to the Alaska Highway, was selected. Prime Minister Lester B. Pearson wanted to make the announcement on the first anniversary of the assassination.

However, at its annual meeting on 5 October 1964, the Canadian Permanent Committee on Geographical Names, with convincing arguments put forward by its Alberta member (his province had never forgiven Mackenzie King for changing Castle Mountain to Mount Eisenhower in 1948), rejected the naming of a peak for Kennedy. It noted his position in world history could not yet be properly assessed, and pointed out that since few unnamed major peaks remained in Canada, they should be reserved for worthy Canadians.

But Pearson, a great admirer of the late charismatic president, was not to be dissuaded. Since the authority for naming in the two territories was then vested in the federal government, the prime minister suggested a peak in the Yukon in the St. Elias Mountains, near the Alaska boundary. An unnamed peak near Mount Logan was chosen, even though its elevation was found to be only 3,776 metres, making it more than 2,175 metres lower than Mount Logan, the highest point in Canada. On 20 November Pearson made the official announcement in the House of Commons.

Two weeks later, Walter Wood, then president of the American Geographical Society and a veteran mountain climber in Alaska and the Yukon, informed the Canadian government that the peak named for the president was really only a part of the Mount Logan uplift. He suggested selecting one of the highest unnamed peaks in Canada, a distinct mountain 85 kilometres to the southeast, but within 6 kilometres of Mount Alverstone and Mount Hubbard on the United States–Canada boundary.

Bradford Washburn, then director of the Museum of Science in Boston, who had crossed the St. Elias Mountains in 1935 and photographed several lofty mountains en route, also urged Canadian authorities to adopt Wood's proposed peak. On 22 December, the new, higher Mount Kennedy was approved.

In March 1965, Sen. Robert F. Kennedy ascended the peak with seven experienced mountain climbers, and went on record as the first person to reach the 4,238-metre summit. Writing in *National Geographic* (July '65), Senator Kennedy observed that his brother 'would be pleased that this lonely, beautiful mountain in the Yukon bears his name, and that in this way, at least, he has joined the fraternity of those who live outdoors, battle the elements, and climb mountains.' Five years later, Robert Kennedy also was gunned down, another victim of a violent decade for American public figures.

Half the presidents – twenty-one out of forty-two – have been honoured in one or more of Canada's geographical names. John F. Kennedy was the last to receive such an honour. With a policy now in place to limit commemorating of non-Canadians, it is unlikely other presidents will have their names assigned to geographical features in Canada.

Smith: We Are Blessed with 439 of Them!

No other family name is more common in the English-speaking world than Smith. In *The Book of Smiths* (1978),

Elsdon Smith estimates there are 2.8 million people with this surname in the world, with nearly 75,000 of them in Canada. It is the number-one surname in the United States, England, and Scotland, and is probably the leading surname in Canada as well.

Smith and its cognates Smyth and Smythe represent the most prominent family name among Canada's place names. The length and breadth of the country is blessed with 439 mountains, creeks, points, capes, rivers, and populated places with this surname. Not counted are such names as Arrowsmith, Goldsmith, or Sexsmith, but ones like Allansmith River and Ladysmith are included because Smith is a distinct component in the original family name.

Ontario has the largest number of Smith names with ninety, followed by Newfoundland with seventy-one, British Columbia with fifty-eight, and Saskatchewan with fifty-two. Prince Edward Island has no places or features called Smith; in 1765, Samuel Holland named Smith Point in Kings County for one of three officers he had served with, but today the name is unknown locally.

Few of the geographical names with Smith in Canada are particularly prominent, with perhaps only Smiths Falls in Ontario and Fort Smith in the Northwest Territories known fairly widely.

Smiths Falls commemorates Maj. Thomas Smyth, who was granted 400 acres (162 hectares) at the Rideau River millsite in 1804, but subsequently lost his holdings in 1826 to Charles Jones, who sold out to Abel Ward. Ward, who built the first mills, called the new settlement Wardsvile, but the settlers persisted in using Smyth's Falls. Smith's Falls was incorporated as a village in 1854, and as a town in 1882. Although it had long been spelled locally without the apostrophe, a special act of the Ontario legislature had to be passed in 1968 to allow the town to issue debentures in the name of Smiths Falls. A move in the 1930s to call it Rideau City – as a name more suitable for a rising metropolis – failed.

Fort Smith, on the N.W.T.–Alberta border, was established as a Hudson's Bay Company trading centre in 1874, and named for Sir Donald A. Smith, Lord Strathcona (1820–1914), a member of the first council of the North-West Territories and president of the Canadian Pacific Railway. In 1910, Medicine Hat was almost renamed Smithville in his honour. Strathcona in Alberta, Mount Sir Donald in British Columbia, and Strathcona Sound in N.W.T. were also named for him.

Smithville in the Niagara Peninsula was first known as Griffintown, but was renamed by Smith Griffin in the early 1800s for his mother's family. Foxboro near Belleville was called Smithville from about 1800 to about 1860, when the present name was adopted. A few miles to the southwest, near Trenton, is the community of Smithfield, where John Smith was a pioneer settler in 1793, and where Abijah Smith was the postmaster from 1860 to 1870.

On the west side of Peterborough is Smith Township, named in 1821 for Sir David William Smith, surveyor general of Upper Canada, 1792–1804.

The site of Port Hope, Ont., was settled in 1760 by Peter Smith, and became known as Smith's Creek. Subsequently, the place was called Toronto, and then Port Hope in 1817, and the stream was called Ganaraska River, a name of native origin.

The name Smith Sound, suggesting an arm of the sea, occurs no fewer than four times in Canada. In 1616, William Baffin named Smith Sound, one of the narrow channels between Ellesmere Island and Greenland, for Sir Thomas Smith, an English merchant and promoter of exploration into the Northwest Passage. The origins of the same name in British Columbia, Nova Scotia, and Newfoundland are not noted in the records of the Canadian Permanent Committee on Geographical Names.

The naming of geographical features in the 1950s and 1960s for soldiers killed during the Second World War was widely practised by some provinces. Thus were forty features in Canada named Smith or a variant of it. Among Saskatchewan's fifty-two names with Smith are no fewer than five called Smith Peninsula, and four of them honour servicemen who lost their lives. Four features called Smith Lake in Saskatchewan also commemorate Second World War casualties. Smith-Jones Lake in that province was named in 1955 for Flt. Sgt. Henry Smith-Jones, who was killed in Europe in 1943; and Smith-Windsor Islands in Lake Athabasca was given in 1953 for Grenville Smith-Windsor, who was killed in North Africa in 1942.

Among British Columbia's fifty-eight names with Smith is Mount Robert Smith in the Selkirk Mountains, named for a land surveyor killed during the First World War. Mount DeCosmos, west of Nanaimo on Vancouver Island, commemorates William Alexander Smith, but he was better known as Amor DeCosmos when he was premier of British Columbia and a federal MP in the 1870s.

Ladysmith occurs as a place name in Québec, Ontario, and British Columbia. They all commemorate the British victory at Ladysmith, Natal, in 1900. The latter was named in 1851 for the Spanish-born wife of the governor of Natal, Sir Harry Smith, who had rescued her during the sacking of Badajos in Spain in 1812, and later married her.

Unusual names with Smith across the country include Cougar Smith Creek in British Columbia, Canon Smith Lake in Alberta, Smith Coulee in Saskatchewan, Smiths Slough in Manitoba, Smiths Shanty Hill in Ontario, Lac Mackey-Smith in Québec, Billy Smith Rips in New Brunswick, Neddie Smiths Pond in Nova Scotia, and Hick Smith Stillwater in Newfoundland.

From Smiths Falls in Ontario to Fort Smith in the Northwest Territories, it is quite evident that the Smiths have had a lasting and distinctive impact on Canada's history.

Index

aboiteau, 118
aboriginal names, 134–40
Acadia, 8, 14, 159–62
Acadia, Alta., 162
Acadian Peninsula, N.B., 162
Acadia University, N.S., 161
Acadia Valley, Alta., 162
Acadie-Bathurst, N.B., 35, 162
Acadieville, N.B., 161
acronyms, 58–60
Adam River, B.C., 125
Admiralty Islands, Ont., 187
Ainleyville, Ont., 81
Air Line Junction, Ont., 110
Aklavik, Y.T., 47
Akrigg, Philip and Helen, 56, 85, 206
Alberni Inlet, B.C., 92
Alberta Historic Sites Board, 73, 184, 218
Albertan, 42
Alberta River, 70
Albertland, 14
Albertoria, 14
Albona, 14

Aldrich, Cape, N.W.T., 20-1
Alexander Island, N.W.T., 216
Alexandria, B.C., 181
Alexandrina, 14
Allan, Mount, Alta., 183
Alma, N.B., 93
Alma, N.S., 6, 93
Alma, P.E.I., 6, 93
Alma, Qué., 6, 93
Alma Parish, N.B., 6, 93
Amherst Island, Ont., 186
Amherstonian, 42
Amiens, Lac, Qué., 98
Amoureux, Baie des, Qué., 125
Amour, Lac de l', Qué., 125
Amours, Ruisseau d', Qué., 125
Amsterdam, Sask., 82
Anderson Siding, N.B., 98
Anian, Straits of, 90
Annapolis Valley-Hants, N.S., 36
Antigonish, N.S., 29, 46, 134
Anzac, Alta., 85

Anzac, B.C., 85
Anzac Lake, B.C., 85
Anzac River, B.C., 85
Apex, N.W.T., 137
Apex Hill, N.W.T., 136
Apohaqui, N.B., 47
Apohaqui Island, Ont., 189
apostrophe, 60, 229
Aquaforte, Nfld., 47, 55, 88
Aquilonia, 14
Arabella Island, Ont., 189
Arcs, Lac des, Alta., 183
Armentières Channel, B.C.,
    99
Armentières, Lac, Qué., 98
Armentières Rock, B.C., 99
Arras, Lac, Qué., 98
Artois, Canton, Qué., 99
Arviat, N.W.T, 139
Arvida, Qué., 5, 59
Aspasia Island, Ont., 187
Assiniboia, Sask., 31
Assiniboia, District of,
    N.W.T., 31, 142
Assiniboine River, Man.,
    Sask., 31
Athabasca, Alta., 35, 51-2,
    135
Athabasca, District of,
    N.W.T., 51
Athabasca Falls, Alta., 52
Athabasca Glacier, Alta.,
    52
Athabasca, Lake, Alta., Sask.,
    51-2, 177-8, 195
Athabasca, Mount, Alta., 52

Athabasca Pass, Alta., B.C.,
    193, 195
Athabasca River, Alta., 51-2,
    195
Athabaska, Alta., 52
Athens, Ont., 80
Ault Island, Ont., 192
Aultsville, Ont., 189-90, 192
Aussie Creek, Y.T., 86
Australia Creek, Y.T., 86
Australia Gulch, Y.T., 6, 86
Australia Hill, Y.T., 86
Auyuittuq National Park,
    N.W.T., 25, 28, 135
Avondale, Ont., 191
Avonmore, Ont., 191
Axeman Island, Ont., 187
Ayer's-Cliffois, 42
Azazel, Mount, B.C., 129

Baccalieu Island, Nfld., 89
Backside of Hell Cove, Nfld.,
    7, 126
Baddeck, N.S., 135
Bagdad, N.B., 75, 83
Baie des Ha! Ha!, Qué., 131-3
Baie du Ha! Ha!, Qué., 130-1
Bakeapple Bay, Nfld., 121
Balaclava, Ont., 93
Balaklava Island, B.C., 93-4
Baldy Mountain, Man., 23
Ballarat Creek, Y.T., 86
Banff, Alta., 25-6
Banffite, 43
Banff National Park, Alta.,
    25-6

barachois, 117

Barachois-de-Malbaie, Qué., 117

Barachois Outside Pond, Nfld., 117

Barachoix, Nfld., 117

Barasway Cove, Nfld., 117

Barasway de Cerf, Nfld., 117

Barbeau Peak, N.W.T., 23, 217

Barkley, Capt. Charles W., 91

Barrie-ite, 43

Barrio Deadwater, N.S., 116

Barry Head, P.E.I., 55

Barry's Bay, Ont., 5, 57, 62

Bastard Township, Ont., 71

Bat-le-Diable, Lac, Qué., 127

Batawa, Ont., 59

Bathurstian, 43

Bathurst Island, Ont., 188

Bay d'Espoir, Nfld., 45–6

Bay of Fundy, N.B., N.S., 28

Bay of Gods Mercy, N.W.T., 126

Bayollais, 42

Bear River, N.S., 55

Beaurivage Island, Ont., 189

Beauséjour, N.B., 36

Beaverbrook, Lord, 141

Beaver Brook, N.B., 142

Beaver Island, Man., 85

Beaver River, Alta., 39

Beelezebub, Mount, B.C., 129

Belabourer Island, Ont., 187

Belial, Mount, B.C., 129

Bell, Robert, 113–14, 221

Bellechasse, Qué., 36

Belleoram Barasway, Nfld., 117

Belles Amours, Havre des, Qué., 125

Bellevillian, 42

Bellevonian, 42

Bellin (Payne), Qué., 138

Belly River, Alta., 69–71

Bennett Lake. B.C., 85

Bennington Glacier, B.C., 199

Bennington Peak, B.C., 199

Berlin, Ont., 5, 64–5, 81

Berry Head, P.E.I., 55

Bethany, Ont., 78

Bethel, Ont., 78

Bethesda, Ont., 78

Bethléem, Qué., 79

Biencourt, Qué., 121

Bienfait, Sask., 46

Big Tracadie Gully, N.B., 116

Bill Fraser Creek, B.C., 200

Bill Fraser Lake, B.C., 200

Billy Smiths Rips, N.B., 231

Black Georges Savannah, N.S., 118

Black Hummock Gully, Nfld., 116

Black Prince, Mount, Alta., 184

Black Rattle Stillwater, N.S., 116

Blackstrap Coulee, Sask., 114

Blakiston, Thomas, 69, 72, 194

Blind Mugford Tickle, Nfld., 116
Blitzen, Mount, N.B., 119
Bloodletter Island, Ont., 187
blow-me-down, 118
Blue Heaven Lake, Ont., 103
Bocas de Winthuysen, B.C., 92
Bodega y Quadra, Juan Francisco de la, 92, 175
bogan, 117
Bogart, Mount, Alta., 184
Bonanza Creek, Y.T., 33, 172
Bonaventure–Îles-de-la-Madeleine, Qué., 39
Bonavista, Nfld., 6, 29, 87
Bonavista, Cape, Nfld., 29, 89
Bonavista–Trinity–Conception, Nfld., 29, 40
Bonavista–Twillingate, Nfld., 29, 34
Bonbons, Lac des, Qué., 122
Borealia, 14
Bosporus, Alta., 26
Bostock, Hugh S., 23, 179
Bostwick Island, Ont., 187
Bouchette, Joseph, 131
Bouquet Point, P.E.I., 125
Bourassa, Qué., 37
Bourgeau, Eugène, 183
Bow and Arrow Shoal, Nfld., 7, 124
Bow City, Alta., 111
Bowers Lake, Ont., 61
Bow Hills, Alta., 183
Bow River, Alta., 69–71, 182–3
Box Canyon, B.C., 125
brandies, 118
Brandonite, 43
Brandon–Souris, Man., 37
Brandy Brook, N.B., 121
Bras d'Or Lake, N.S., 87, 90
Breadalbane, P.E.I., 47
Breton, Cape, N.S., 28
Britannica, 14
Brock, Sask., 84
Brock Group, Ont., 188
Brock Island, Ont., 187
Brock, Mount, Alta., 184
Brockville, Ont., 43
Brome–Missisquoi, Qué., 35
Broughton Archipelago, B.C., 174
Bruat, Mount, N.W.T, 96
Brudenell Township, Ont., 95
Bruges, Lac, Qué., 98
Brussels, Ont., 81
Bruxelles, Man., 81
Buade, Isle, Ont., 186
Buies, Arthur, 131
Burbridge, Qué., 99
Burgeo, Nfld., 87, 89–90
Burgeo Islands, Nfld., 89–90
Burk's Falls, Ont., 62
Burstall, Mount, Alta., 184
Burton City, B.C., 111
Bury Head, P.E.I., 55
Bute Inlet, B.C., 174
butte, 6, 112–13
Buttermilk Creek, N.B., 96

Byers Bay, Ont., 5, 58

Caamaño Sound, B.C., 92
Cabot, John, 18, 47, 88-9
Cabotia, 14
Cadomin, Alta., 60
Caesarea, Ont., 47, 79
Cairo, Ont., 77, 83
Cairo Township, Ont., 77
Caledon, Ont., 50
Caledon Village, Ont., 50
Calgarian, 41, 43
Calgary, Alta., 6, 8, 45, 109,
    182-3
Calgary Southeast, Alta., 39
Calgary Southwest, Alta., 38
Calico City, Y.T., 112
Cambrai, Canton, Qué., 98
Cambrai, Mont, Qué., 98
Cambridge Bay, N.W.T, 139
Camel Chute, Ont., 57
Camelot Island, Ont., 187
Campbell's Bay, Qué., 61
Canaan, N.S., 78
Canaan, Ont., 77
Canaan Rapids, N.B., 78
Canaan River, N.B., 77-8
Canaan Road, N.B., 78
Canaan Station, N.B., 78
Canada, 3, 11-14, 15, 18
Canada Bay, Austr., 83, 104
Canada Day, 16-18
Canada East, 14
Canada Hill, Scot., 104
Canada Walk, Eng., 104
Canada Way, Eng., 104

Canada West, 14
Canadensia, 14
Canadian Bay, Austr., 83
Canadian Board on
    Geographical Names, 166,
    191, 216
Canadian Permanent
    Committee on
    Geographical Names, xi,
    xiii, 4, 21, 72, 119, 179, 186,
    217-18, 220, 226-7, 230
Canarican, Lake, Ont., 192
Canmore, Alta., 185
Canon Smith Lake, Alta., 231
Canora, Sask., 4, 50, 59
Canrobert, Qué., 96
Canrobert Hills, N.W.T., 6,
    96
Canso, N.S., 7, 148-51
Canso, Cape, N.S., 150
Canso Causeway, N.S., 151
Canso, Gut of, N.S., 150-1
Canso, Strait of, N.S., 150-1
Canusa, Lake, Ont., 192
Canyon City, Y.T., 112
Cap d'Espérance, Nfld., 19
Cap d'Espoir, Nfld., 19
Cape Aldrich, N.W.T., 20-1
Cape Bonavista, Nfld., 29, 89
Cape Breton, N.S., 28
Cape Breton Highlands, N.S.,
    24
Cape Breton Highlands-
    Canso, N.S., 36
Cape Breton Highlands
    National Park, N.S., 28

Cape Breton Island, N.S., 28
Cape Bretoners, 44
Cape Breton–The Sydneys,
   N.S., 36
Cape Canso, N.S., 150
Cape Chapeau Rouge, Nfld.,
   90
Cape Columbia, N.W.T., 4,
   20-1
Cape Fogo, Nfld., 89
Cape Fraser, N.W.T., 200
Cape Freels, Nfld., 89
Cape Mackenzie, N.W.T., 179
Cape Pine, Nfld., 89
Cape Race, Nfld., 88
Cape Ray, Nfld., 90
Capers, 44
Cape Spear, Nfld., 18, 88-9
Cape Split, N.S., 28
Cape St. Francis, Nfld., 89
Cape St. George, Nfld., 90
Cape St. Mary's, Nfld., 89
Cap-Pelé, N.B., 162
Caraquet, N.B., 162
Card Lake, N.S., 125
Cardigan Rocks, B.C., 95
Cardigan Strait, N.W.T., 95
Cariboo-Chilcotin, B.C., 35
Cariboo City, B.C., 111
Caribou City, Y.T., 112
Cario, Ont., 79
Carleton, Sir Guy, 48
Carleton, Thomas, 24-5, 102
Carleton, N.B., 48
Carleton Island, N.Y., 188
Carleton, Mount, N.B., 24-5

Carleton Place, Ont., 55
Carronbrook, Ont., 82
Carrot River, Sask., 121
Cartier, Jacques, 11-13, 27,
   35, 140-1, 162-3
Castle Butte, Sask., 112-13
Castle Junction, Alta., 74
Castle Mountain, Alta., 5,
   71-4, 227
Catalina, Nfld., 89
Cathcart, Ont., 96
Caubvik, Mount, Nfld., 24
cay, 118
Cayen, 42
Cedoux, Sask., 5, 55
Celista, B.C., 56
Celista Creek, 56
Celista Mountain, 56
Central Nova, N.S., 36
Centre East Pubnico, N.S., 30
Centre Woodlands Island,
   Ont., 192
Champagne, Pointe à, Qué.,
   121
Champlain, Samuel de, 48,
   55-6, 135, 141, 150, 156,
   160, 164
Chapeau Rouge, Cape, Nfld.,
   90
Chapleau, Qué., 34
Charité, L., Qué., 165
Charles Dickens Point,
   N.W.T., 121
Charlevoix, Fr. Pierre, 12, 19,
   185-6
Charlevoix, Qué., 36

Charlottetowner, 43

Château Laurier, Ont., 225

Chatham, N.B., 50

Chatham, Ont., 50

Chebucto, N.S., 134

Chester, Mount, Alta., 184

Chesterfield Inlet, N.W.T, 139

Chéticamp, N.S., 162

Chicoutimi, Qué., 135

Chilliwack, B.C., 53

Chin Coulee, Alta., 113–14

Chinamans Peak, Alta., 185

Chinguacousy Township, Ont., 135

Chocolate Cove, N.B., 125

Christmas Bay, Y.T., 120

Christmas Creek, Alta., 120

Christmas Creek, B.C., 120

Christmas Creek, Y.T., 120

Christmas Head, Nfld, 121

Christmas Hill, B.C., 120

Christmas Island, N.S., 121

Christmas Island, Ont., 120–1

Christmas Lake, Man., 120

Christmas names, 118–22

Christmas Point, B.C., 120

Christmas Pond, Nfld., 121

Churchill, Winston, 48, 65

Churchill Falls, Nfld., 49

Churchill Peak, B.C., 226

Churchill River, Man., Sask., 4, 48

Churchill River, Nfld., 4, 48–9

Circle City, B.C., 111

cities, 108–12

Clandeboye, Ont., 214

Clarkstown, Ont., 214

Closeleigh, Y.T., 33

Coaticook, Qué., 135

Cobalt, Ont., 31

Cocagne River, N.B., 100

Cochrane, Alta., 50

Cochrane, Ont., 50

Cockburn Island, Ont., 188

Codroy, Nfld., 90

Coffee Creek, Ont., 122

Colonia, 14

Colpoy's Bay, Ont., 62

Columbia, Cape, N.W.T., 4, 20–1

Columbia, Mount, Alta., 22

Columbia River, B.C., 22, 180, 199

Comeauville, N.S., 162

Comet, Mount, N.B., 119

Commission de toponymie du Québec, 24, 41, 54, 133, 137–8, 163, 166–7, 220

Committee Punch Bowl, Alta., B.C., 121, 195–6

Commonwealth Lake, Man., 85

Comox–Alberni, B.C., 39

Conception Bay, Nfld., 89

Conrad City, Y.T., 112

Conran Island, Ont., 188

Consort Peak, B.C., 209

Cook, Capt. James, 22, 91, 177–8

Coolan Deadwater, N.S., 116

Cootes Paradise, Ont., 101

Copenhagen, Ont., 82
Coral Harbour, N.W.T, 139
Cordova Bay, B.C., 92
Corkum Stillwater, N.S., 116
Cornwallite, 43
Corte-Real, Gaspar, 29, 88-9
Corte-Real, Miguel, 88
Cortes Island, B.C., 92
Côte-Saint-Luc, Qué., 108
Cougar Smith Creek, B.C.,
  231
coulee, 6, 113-15
Courcelette, Qué., 98
Courcelette, Lac, Qué., 98
Courtrai, Lac, Qué., 98
Cowdung Pass, Alta., B.C.,
  196
Cranberry Point, P.E.I., 121
Creighton, Sask., 170
Crimean War names, 93-7
Cross Lake, Ont., 69
Crotch Lake, Ont., 68-9
Crowfoot, Alta., 38
Crowsnest Mountain, Alta.,
  194
Crowsnest Pass, Alta., B.C.,
  193-4
Crystal City, Man., 109, 111
Cullite Cove, B.C., 68
Cummings Bridge, Ont., 214
Cupers Cove, Nfld., 157
Cupid Island, Ont., 123
Cupid, Mount, N.B., 119
Cupids, Nfld., 8, 123, 156-9
Cupids Cove, Nfld., 123,
  157-8

Cupids Rock, Ont., 123
Currie, Mount, Alta., 184
Cypress Hills, Alta., Sask., 23,
  114

Dagon, Mount, B.C., 129
Dain City, Ont., 110
Dalhousie, N.B., 45, 77
Dalhousie Township, Ont.,
  45
Dalhousie University, N.S.,
  45
Damascus, N.B., 77
Damascus, Ont., 77, 83
Dancer, Mount, N.B., 119
Dancing Hill, Man., 126
Dardenelles, Alta., 26
Daredevil Hill, Man., 128
Darragh, Ian, xi, xiii
Dartmouth, N.S., 35
Dartmouth-East Halifax,
  N.S., 35
Darwin Point, B.C., 206
Dasher, Mount, N.B., 119
Davis Corners, Ont., 84
Dawson, George M., 9, 183-5,
  194, 204-8
Dawson Bay, B.C., 206
Dawson Bay, Man., 207
Dawson Bay, Ont., 205
Dawson Channel, Ont.,
  205
Dawson City, B.C., 111
Dawson City, Y.T., 33, 50,
  112, 171-2, 204, 207
Dawson Cove, B.C., 206

Dawson Creek, B.C., 50, 204, 206
Dawson Harbour, B.C., 206
Dawson Head, B.C., 206
Dawson Inlet, B.C., 206
Dawson Inlet, N.W.T., 207
Dawson Island, Ont., 205, 208
Dawson Islands, B.C., 206
Dawson, Mount, B.C., 207
Dawson, Mount, Y.T., 207, 224
Dawson Point, B.C., 206
Dawson Range, B.C., 207
Dawson Range, Y.T., 207
Dead Man's Flat, Alta., 185
deadwater, 116
Deathdealer Island, Ont., 187
DeCosmos, Mount, B.C., 231
Delhi, Ont., 83
Demarcation Point, Y.T., 20
de Monts, Sieur, 48, 55, 160
Denain, Canton, Qué., 98
Denys, Nicolas, 100, 141, 150
De Rottenburg Island, Ont., 188
DesBarres, Joseph F.W., 151
Desceliers, Pierre, 13, 163
Des Joachims, Qué., 46
Devil Door Rapids, Ont., 128
Devilhole Creek, Y.T., 129
Devil Island, N.W.T., 129
Devil names, 7, 126–30
Devil Pike Brook, N.B., 127
Devil Shoepack Falls, Ont., 128
Devils Back Brook, N.B., 127

Devil's Bite, Alta., 128
Devils Burrow, The, N.S., 127
Devils Cellar Rapids, Ont., 128
Devils Claw Mountain, B.C., 129
Devil's Club Creek, Y.T., 129
Devils Club Mountain, B.C., 129
Devils Cove, Nfld., 126
Devils Cupboard, N.S., 127
Devils Dancing Place, Nfld., 126
Devils Dancing Table, Nfld., 126
Devils Den Lake, B.C., 129
Devils Dressing Place, Nfld., 126
Devils Elbow Rapids, N.B., 7, 127
Devils Elbow, Y.T., 129
Devils Funnel Stillwater, N.S., 116, 127
Devils Glen, Ont., 128
Devils Half Acre, N.B., 127
Devils Hand, N.B., 127
Devils Kitchen, Nfld., 126
Devils Knob, Nfld., 126
Devils Limb, N.S., 127
Devils Lookout Island, Nfld., 126
Devils Portage, Man., 128
Devils Punch Bowl, Man., 128
Devils Punchbowl Lake, Ont., 128

Devils Punchbowl Provincial
   Park, P.E.I, 127
Devil's Rectum, B.C., 129
Devils Spire, B.C., 129
Devils Thumb, Alta., 128
Devils Thumb, B.C., 129
Devils Tongue, B.C., 129
Devils Tooth, B.C., 129
Devil's Warehouse Island,
   Ont., 128
De Watteville Island, Ont.,
   188
Diable Bay, Nfld., 126
Diable, Crique du, Qué., 127
Diable, Pointe au, Qué., 127
Diable, Pont du, Qué., 127
Diable, Rapides du, Qué., 127
Diable, Rivière du, Qué., 127
Diable, Ruisseau du, Qué.,
   127
d'Iberville, Mont, Qué., 24
Dickinson Island, Ont., 192
Dickinsons Landing, Ont.,
   189-90, 192
Dickinson's Landing Station,
   Ont., 190, 212
Diefenbaker, John, 5, 73
Digdeguash River, N.B., 45
Dingle, Ont., 81
Dinner Place Creek, Man.,
   121
Disappointment, River,
   N.W.T., 178
disgusting names, 67-71
Distress, Nfld., 68
Dixon Entrance, B.C., 92

Dominion, 3, 15-18
Dominion, N.S., 18
Dominion, P.E.I., 18
Dominion City, Man., 18, 110
Dominion Day, 16, 18
Dominionville, Ont., 18
Donder, Mount, N.B., 119
Donnacona, 11
Dorsey Heath, N.B., 118
Dorval, Qué., 108
Douai, Lac, Qué., 98
Downie Island, Ont.,
   187
Drakes Perdue Bogan, B.B.,
   117
droke, 118
Drolet, Jean-Paul, xi, xiii
drook, 118
Dublin, Ont., 82
Dublin Shore, N.S., 82
Dubreuil, Ont., 57
Du Gua de Monts, Pierre, 48,
   55, 160
Dumfounder Island, Ont.,
   187
Dumpling Savannah, N.S.,
   118
Duncan City, B.C., 111
Dundas, Ont., 49
Dundas County, Ont., 49
Dundas Island, B.C., 175
Duplessis, Maurice, 17
Durham, Ont., 49
Durham, Regional
   Municipality of, Ont., 49
dyke, 118

East Pubnico, N.S., 30
Eastview, Ont., 214-15
East Woodlands Island, Ont., 192
Ebenezer, Ont., 78
Eden, Man., 76, 101-2
Eden, N.S., 76
Eden, Ont., 76, 101
Edenbridge, Sask., 102
Edenburg, Man., 102
Eden Grove, Ont., 76, 101
Eden Indian Reserve, Alta., 102
Eden Island, N.W.T., 102
Eden Lake, Alta., 102
Eden Lake, N.S., 76, 101
Eden Mills, Ont., 76, 101
Eden Mountain, B.C., 102
Edenvale, Ont., 76, 101
Edenwold, Sask., 76, 102
Edmontonian, 42
Edmonton Northwest, Alta., 39
Edmonton Southeast, Alta., 39
Edmonton Southwest, Alta., 39
Edmonton-Strathcona, Alta., 35, 39
Edmundston, N.B., 5, 51
Efisga, 14
Egypt, Ont., 77
Égypte, Qué., 77
Egypt Road, N.S., 77
Eisenhower, Mount, Alta., 5, 71-4, 227

Eisenhower Peak, Alta., 73-4
Electoral ridings, 34-40
Elginburg, Ont., 45
Elijaks Steady, Nfld., 116
Elizabeth, Lake, Ont., 192
Elizamerica, Lake, Ont., 192
Empress, Alta., 210
Endymion Island, Ont., 187
Engadine, Mount, Alta., 184
Entrada de Juan Pérez, B.C., 92
Erato Lake, Ont., 123
Eros Lake, Ont., 123
Eskimo Point, N.W.T, 139
Esquimalt–Juan de Fuca, B.C., 39
Espérance, Cap d', Nfld., 19
Espoir, Bay d', Nfld., 45-6
Espoir, Cap d', Nfld., 19
Esterhazy, Sask., 32
Estevan, Sask., 5, 59
Etobicoke, Ont., 46
Etzikom Coulee, Alta., 113-14
Eurydice, Mount, B.C., 125
Eve River, B.C., 125
Exshaw, Alta., 185
Eyremore, Alta., 111

Fagundes, Joo Alvares, 90
Fairhaven, Nfld., 68
Fairweather Mountain, B.C., 22
Famish Gut, Nfld., 68
Fanton Bogan, N.B., 117
Farbus, Lac, Qué., 98
Farmersville, Ont., 80

Farran Point Ont., 192
Farrans Point, Ont., 189–90, 192
federal ridings, 34–40
Fenwick, N.S., 95
Fenwick, Ont., 95
Fenwick Township, Ont., 95
Fermeuse, Nfld., 88
Fernandes, Joo, 18, 88
Ferryland, Nfld., 87–8
Festubert, Canton, Qué., 98
Fiddlers Elbow, Ont., 189
Fidéen, 42
Figure of Eight Rapids, N.W.T., 129
Fiji Island, N.W.T., 86–7
First World War names, 97–100
Fisher Range, Alta., 184
Flanders, Qué., 99
Flanders, Lac, Qué., 98
Flanders Mountain, B.C., 98
Flanders Township, Ont., 99
Flandre, Canton, Qué., 99
Fleming, Sir Sandford, 185, 196
Fleurbaix Creek, B.C., 98
Flin Flon, Man., Sask., 8, 168–70
Flin Floner, 43
Florence, Ont., 96
Florence, Mount, B.C., 96–7
Florenceville, N.B., 96
Flores Island, B.C., 92
flowage, 118
Flowers Cove, Nfld., 125

Foch, Mount, Alta., 184
Fogo, Cape, Nfld., 89
Fogo Island, Nfld., 89
foreign capitals, 79–83
Forest City, N.B., 110
Forillon National Park, Qué., 27
Forsey, Eugene, 17
Fort Alexandria, B.C., 181
Fort Chimo, Qué., 7, 138
Fort-Chimo, Qué., 138
Fort Chipewyan, Alta., 178
Fort Erian, 43
Fort Fraser, B.C., 199
Fort Norman, N.W.T, 139
Fort Saskatchewan, Alta., 50
Fort Smith, N.W.T., 229–30
Fortune Bay, Nfld., 90
Fort Victoria, B.C., 209
Foul Bay, B.C., 67
Foul Bay Road, B.C., 67
Foxboro, Ont., 230
Framboise Intervale, N.S., 6–7, 118
Franklin, Sir John, 8, 20, 84, 179
Fraser, Keith, x, xi, xiii, 200
Fraser, Robert, 200–1
Fraser, Simon, 180, 199
Fraser Bay, N.W.T., 200
Fraser Bay, Sask., 201
Fraser Brook, N.B., 203
Fraserburg, Ont., 202
Fraser Canyon, B.C., 200
Fraser, Cape, N.W.T., 200
Fraser, Chutes, Qué., 202

Fraser Crab, Ont., 203
Fraser Creek, B.C., 200
Fraser Creek, Man., 201
Fraser Creek, Ont., 202
Fraser Creek, Sask., 201
Fraser Creek, Y.T., 200
Fraserdale, Ont., 202
Fraser Falls, Y.T., 200
Fraser Glacier, Alta., 199
Fraser Island, B.C., 199-200
Fraser Island, Man., 201
Fraser Island, N.W.T., 200
Fraser Island, Sask., 202
Fraser, Lac, Qué., 202
Fraser Lake, B.C., 199
Fraser Lake, Man., 201
Fraser Lake, Nfld., 204
Fraser Lake, Sask., 201
Fraser Lakes, Sask., 201
Fraser Mills, N.S., 203
Fraser, Mount, B.C., 199, 200
Fraser Peak, B.C., 200
Fraser, Pointe, Qué., 203
Fraser Rapids, Sask., 201
Fraser Reach, B.C., 199
Fraser River, B.C., 9, 92, 180, 198-9
Fraser River, Nfld., 204
Fraser, Ruisseau, Qué., 203
Fraser Settlement, 203
Fraser's Grant, N.S., 203
Fraser Township, Ont., 201
Fraser Valley East, B.C., 39
Fraser Valley West, B.C., 39
Fraserville, Qué., 202-3

Fraserwood, Man., 201
Frederick Island, B.C., 19
Fredericksburg, Ont., 83
Fredericton, N.B., 36, 45
Frederictonian, 42
Freels, Cape, Nfld., 89
Frenchman Butte, Sask., 113
Frobisher Bay, N.W.T., 7, 136-7
Fundy, Bay of, N.B., N.S., 28
Fundy National Park, N.B., 27-8
Fundy-Royal, N.B., 35

Gabarus, N.S., 47
Gabarus Barachois, N.S., 117
Galatea, Mount, Alta., 184
Galiano Island, B.C., 92
Galilee, Ont., 78
Galtonian, 42
Ganaraska River, Ont., 230
Gander-Grand Falls, Nfld., 34
Gander-Twillingate, Nfld., 34
Ganong, William F., 24, 141, 149, 161
Ganounkousenot, Ont., 186
Garden of Eden, N.S., 76, 101
Garden of Eden, Ont., 76
Garden of Eden Barrens, N.S., 101
Gasburg, Alta., 147
Gaspé, Qué., 11, 35
Gaspésien, 41
Gastown, B.C., 175

Gatineau–La Lièvre, Qué., 34

Geary, N.B., 55

generic terms, 112–18, 202

gentilés, 4, 41

Geographic Board of Alberta, 52, 72

Geographic Board of Canada, 20, 52, 60-2, 67, 72, 91-2, 110, 137, 145, 153, 166, 171, 184, 221, 224

George River, Qué., 138-9

Georgian Bay Islands National Park, Ont., 27

Georgia, Strait of, B.C., 8, 92, 174

Georgina, Ont., 81-2

German Mills, Ont., 64

Gibsons, B.C., 62

Gibson's Landing, B.C., 62

Gift Lake, Alta., 125

Givenchy, Lac, Qué., 98

Glacier National Park, B.C., 26

Gleichen, Alta., 46

Glen Eden, Ont., 101

Glen Valley, P.E.I., 24

Gloucester, N.B., 35–6

Gods Lake, Man., 126

God's Mercie, Islands of, N.W.T., 126

Gods Mercy, Bay of, N.W.T., 126

Gonzales Bay, 67

Goshen, N.B., 77

Goshen, N.S., 78

Goshen, Ont., 77

Granbyite, 43

Gran Canal de Nuestra Señora del Rosario la Marinera, B.C., 92, 174

Grande Isle, Ont., 186

Grand Falls–Windsor, Nfld., 49

Grand lac Victoria, Qué., 210

Grand Miramichi, N.B., 141

Grand River, N.W.T., 178

Grants Point, Ont., 154

Granville, B.C., 176

Grasslands National Park, Sask., 27

Great Colinet Island, Nfld., 90

Great Devil Rapids, Sask., 128

Great Divide passes, 9, 193-7

Great River, N.W.T., 179

Great Slave Lake, N.W.T., 177-8

Great Whale River, Qué., 138

Greenwich, N.B., 45

Greenwich, N.S., 45

Greenwich, P.E.I., 45

Greenwood, B.C., 6, 109

Grenadier Island, Ont., 187-8

Grenville Channel, B.C., 175

Griffintown, Ont., 230

Griffith Township, Ont., 95

Gros Morne, Nfld., 28

Gros Morne National Park, Nfld., 28

Guelphite, 43

Guelph–Wellington, Ont., 37

Guie, Nicholas, 123, 158
gulch, 118
Gulf Islander, 44
gully, 115–16
gut, 118
Gut of Canso, N.S., 150–51
Guy, John, 123, 156

Hades Islands, Ont., 128
Hades, Lac, Qué., 128
Hague, Sask., 80
Ha Ha, Nfld., 132
Ha! Ha!, Qué., 131
Ha! Ha!, Baie des, Qué.,
   131–3
Ha! Ha!, Baie du, Qué., 130–1
Ha Ha Bay, Nfld., 132–3
Ha! Ha!, Lac, Qué., 131
Ha Ha Mountain, Nfld., 132
haha names, 7, 130–3
Ha! Ha!, Petit lac, Qué., 131
Ha Ha Point, Nfld., 132
Ha! Ha!, Rivière, Qué., 131
Ha Ha Rock, Ont., 132
Ha Ha, The, Nfld., 132
Halifax, N.S., 42
Haligonian, 41–2
Hall Beach, N.W.T, 139
Hamelin, Mount, N.W.T., 96
Hamiltonian, 42
Hamilton River, Nfld., 48–9
Hanging Heart Lake, Alta.,
   124
Hansen Township, Ont., 66
Happyland Creek, Sask., 126
Harmony Mills, N.S., 103

Haro Strait, B.C., 92
Harrington Lake, Qué., 8,
   165–8
Hastings, B.C., 175–6
Hastings, Ont., 49
Hastings County, Ont., 49
Hastings–Frontenac–Lennox
   and Addington, Ont., 37
Havre-Saint-Pierre, Qué., 42
Hawkesbury Island, B.C., 175
Hay Island, Ont., 187
Headforemost Tickle, Nfld.,
   116
Heart Island, N.Y., 188
Heart Lake Indian Reserve,
   Alta., 124
Heart Mountain, Alta., 185
Heart's Content, Nfld., 123
Heart's Delight, Nfld., 7, 123
Heart's Delight–Islington,
   Nfld., 123
Heart's Desire, Nfld., 123
Hearts Hill, Sask., 124
Heart Shoal, Ont., 124
Hearts Point, Nfld., 124
Heartstone Peak, B.C., 124
heath, 118
heavenly names, 100
Hebron, Nfld., 78
Hector, Dr. James, 71, 185,
   194–5
Hellangone Lake, Ont., 128
Hellcat Brook, N.B., 127
Helldiver Bay, Ont., 128
Helldiver Lake, Sask., 128
Hellfire Creek, Sask., 128

Hell Fire Pond, Nfld., 126
Hell Gate, B.C., 129
Hell Gate, N.W.T., 129
Hell Grapple Hill, Nfld., 126
Hell names, 7, 126–30
Hell Rackets, N.S., 127
Hell Raving Creek, B.C., 129
Hellroarer Creek, B.C., 129
Hell Roaring Creek, N.W.T.,
    129
Hell-Roaring Falls, Alta., 128
Hells Al, Nfld., 126
Hells Gate, B.C., 129
Hellsgate Rapid, Y.T., 129
Hells Gate Rapids, N.B., 127
Hell's Gate Rapids, N.W.T.,
    129
Hells Gates, N.S., 127
Hellsgate Slough, B.C., 129
Hells Kitchen, N.B., 127
Helluva Hole, N.S., 127
Helluva, Lac, Qué., 127
Hennepin, Fr. Louis, 12
Henry and Harry's Butte,
    Sask., 113
Hernando Island, B.C., 92
Hick Smith Stillwater, Nfld.,
    231
Hickey Island, Ont., 187
highest points, 4, 22–5
Hill Island, Ont., 188
Hillsborough, P.E.I., 35
Hills, Lake of , Alta., Sask.,
    177
Hochelaga, Qué., 14,
    162–3

Hochelaga–Maisonneuve,
    Qué., 40
Holy Land names, 75–9
homonyms, 47–50
Hood, Mount, Alta., 184
Howe Island, Ont., 186
Howse Pass, Alta., B.C., 193,
    195
Hudson Bay, 50, 60
Hudson Bay, Sask., 50, 60
Hudson's Bay Company, 60,
    137, 152, 196, 211, 230
Hudsons Hope, B.C., 62
Hudson's Hope, B.C., 62
Hudson Strait, 60
Humber–Port au Port–St.
    Barbe, Nfld., 35
Humber–St. Barbe–Baie
    Verte, Nfld., 35
Humboldt Island, Ont., 208
Huxley Island, B.C., 206
Hyperborean Sea, N.W.T.,
    178

Igluligaarjuk, N.W.T, 139
Ikaluktutiak, N.W.T, 139
Île Pauline, N.W.T., 216
Île Vanier, N.W.T., 216
Illecillewaet, B.C., 135
Indedom, Lake, Ont., 192
Indefatigable, Mount, Alta.,
    184
indigenous names, 134–40
Ingargarnekulluk Tickle,
    Nfld., 116
Ingleside, Ont., 9, 189, 191

Inglewood, Calif., 106
Inglewood, Ont., 106
Inkerman, Ont., 6, 94
Inkerman Parish, N.B., 6, 94
Inoucdjouac, Qué., 137–8
International Rift, Ont., 189
intervale, 117–18
Inukjuak, Qué., 138–9
Invincible, Mount, Alta., 184
Iqaluit, N.W.T., 7, 136–7
Iroquois, Ont., 189
Ishpatina Ridge, Ont., 23
Islanders, 44
Islands of God's Mercie, N.W.T., 126
Isle Buade, Ont., 186
Ivujuvik, Qué., 138

Janeville, Ont., 214
Jasper House Pass, Alta., B.C., 196
Jasper National Park, Alta., 26
Jasper Pass, Alta., B.C., 196
Jellicoe, Mount, Alta., 184
Jervis Inlet, B.C., 174
Jim Fiji Harbour, N.W.T., 86–7
Joffre, Mount, Alta., 184
Johnstone Strait, B.C., 174
Jordan, Ont., 78
Juan de Fuca Strait, B.C., 91–2, 174
Juan Pérez, Entrada de, B.C., 92

Judasville, 148
Jules-Léger, Lac, Qué., 9, 220–1
Juliet, Mount, B.C., 125

Kalaria Island, Ont., 189
Kaleden, B.C., 76, 102
Kaministiquia, Ont., 135
Kamloops, B.C., 35
Kamloopsian, 43
Kananaskis Provincial Park, Alta., 184
Kananaskis River, Alta., 183
Kanata, Ont., 191
Kangaroo Island, Man., 85
Kangiqsualujjuaq, Qué., 138–9
Kangiqsujuaq, Qué., 138–9
Kangirsuk, Qué., 138
Kars, Ont., 94
Karsdale, N.S., 94
Kars Parish, N.B., 94
Kars Township, Ont., 95
Kashagawigamog Lake, Ont., 135
Kashutl Inlet, B.C., 68
Kathryn, Alta., 55–6
Kazabazua, Qué., 47
Keewatin, Ont., 58–9
Kejimkujik Lake, N.S., 28
Kejimkujik National Park, N.S., 28
Kelownan, 42
Kennedy, John F., 10, 225–8
Kennedy, Mount, B.C., 226
Kennedy, Mount, Y.T., 227–8

Kenora, Ont., 4, 50, 58-9
Kenoraite, 42
Kent, Ont., 37
Keremeos, B.C., 7, 32-3, 134
Kertch, Ont., 95
Khartum, Ont., 81
Kicking Horse Pass, Alta.,
    B.C., 193, 195
Kicking Horse River, B.C.,
    195
Kidd, Mount, Alta., 184
Killiniq, N.W.T., 138
Kinburn, Ont., 94
King, Mackenzie, 5, 17, 72,
    227
King City, Ont., 109-10
Kipling, Rudyard, 146-8
Kiss, Lac, Qué., 126
Kitchener, Ont., 5, 64-5, 81
Kitley Township, Ont., 71
Kitsymenie Island, Ont., 189
Kitwanga, B.C., 32, 134
Kiwi Island, Man., 85
Klondike, Y.T., 33, 106-7,
    171-2
Klondike City, Y.T., 112
Klondike River, Y.T., 33,
    206-7
Kluane National Park, Y.T.,
    28
Knight Inlet, B.C., 174
Koartac, Qué., 138
Koartak, Qué., 138
Kokshittle Arm, B.C., 67-8
Koksoak, Rivière, Qué., 135
Koocanusa Lake, B.C., 59

Kootenay, B.C., 50, 53
Kootenay National Park,
    B.C., 26
Kootenay River, B.C., 26
Kouchibouguac, N.B., 30
Kouchibouguac National
    Park, N.B., 28, 30
Kouchibouguac River, N.B.,
    28, 30
Kowshet Cove, B.C., 68
Kuujjuaq, Qué., 7, 138-9
Kuujjuarapik, Qué., 138

Laberge, Lake, Y.T., 8, 170-1
Labrador, Austr., 83
Labrador, Nfld., 87-8
Labrador City, Nfld., 109
Labradorian, 44
Lacadie, 160
L'Acadie, Qué., 161
Lacey Point, N.W.T., 125
Lac des Arcs, Alta., 183
Lac Ha! Ha!, Qué., 131
Lachine-Lac-Saint-Louis,
    Qué., 36
Lac Jules-Léger, Qué., 9,
    220-1
Lac Meech, Qué., 165-8
Lacombe, Alta., 32
Lady Laurier, Mount, B.C.,
    224
Ladysmith, B.C., 231
Ladysmith, Ont., 231
Ladysmith, Qué., 231
Lake Athabasca, Alta., Sask.,
    177-8, 195

Lake Canarican, Ont., 192
Lake Canusa, Ont., 192
Lake Elizabeth, Ont., 192
Lake Elizamerica, Ont., 192
Lake Fleet Islands, Ont., 187
Lake Indedom, Ont., 192
Lake Laberge, Y.T., 8, 170–1
Lake Muskoka, Ont., 31
Lake of the Hills, Alta., Sask.,
    177
Lake St. Lawrence, Ont., 189,
    192
Lake Uscan, Ont., 192
Lake Utopia, N.B., 102
Lakeheader, 43
Lamaline, Nfld., 90
La Mauricie National Park,
    Qué., 27
La Nativité, Qué., 121
Langelier, Qué., 36
Langemarck, Lac, Qué., 98
Langemarck Township, Ont.,
    99
Langenburg, Sask., 46
L'Anse-Amour, Nfld., 125
L'Anse au Diable Brook,
    Nfld., 126
L'Anse au Loup Barasway,
    Nfld., 117
L'Anse aux Meadows, Nfld.,
    156
L'Ardoise, N.S., 46
Lasqueti Island, B.C., 92
Laurentia, 14
Laurier, Sir Wilfrid, 9, 221–5
Laurier, Man., 223

Laurier Avenue, Ont., 224
Laurier, Canton, Qué., 222
Laurier Cove, B.C., 224
Laurier Creek, Ont., 223
Laurier Creek, Y.T., 224
Laurier Island, Ont., 223
Laurier Island, Sask., 223
Laurier, Lac, Qué., 222
Laurier Lake, Alta., 223
Laurier Lake, Ont., 223
Laurier, Mont, Qué., 221
Laurier, Mount, B.C., 224
Laurier, Mount, Y.T., 207,
    224
Laurier Park, Qué., 225
Laurier Pass, B.C., 223
Laurier Rock, N.S., 223
Laurier Rural Municipality,
    Alta., 223
Laurier Rural Municipality,
    Sask., 223
Laurier Township, Ont., 223
Laurier-Station, Qué., 222
Laurierville, Qué., 221–2
Lax Kw'alaams, B.C., 139
lead, 118
Leatherhead Pass, Alta., B.C.,
    196
Leather Pass, Alta., B.C., 196
Lebanon, Ont., 77
Leek Island, Ont., 187
Leeville, Sask., 31
Léger, Jules, 9, 218, 220–1
Leman, Mount, Alta., 184
Lens, Canton, Qué., 98
L'Épiphanie, Qué., 121

Leroux Island, Ont., 188
Lescarbot, Marc, 150
Lethbridge, Alta., 69–71
Lethbridge River, Alta., 70–1
Lewes River, Y.T., 171
Lewis Hills, Nfld., 24
Lewis Pond, Nfld., 121
Lion Island, Man., 85
Lions Bay, B.C., 62
Lions Gate Bridge, B.C., 62
Lion's Head, Ont., 61–2
Lisgar–Marquette, Man., 37
Little Booth Island, N.W.T., 87
Little Canada, Minn., 104
Little Devil Rapids, Sask., 128
Little Egypt, Ont., 77
Little Heart's Ease, Nfld., 123
Little Heaven Island, Ont., 103
Little Saskatchewan River, Man., 31
Logan, Sir William E., 22
Logan Island, Ont., 208
Logan, Mount, Y.T., 22, 227–8
London, Ont., 80
Londoner, 43
Lone Eagle Butte, Alta., 112
Long Range Mountains, Nfld., 24
Long Sault, Ont., 9, 189, 191
Long Sault, Ont., Qué., 154
Long Sault Parkway Ont., 192

Long Sault Rapids, Ont., 190, 192
Longue Sault, Ont., 191
look-alikes, 47–50
Loos, Lac, Qué., 98
Lorette, Mount, Alta., 184
L'Orignal, Ont., 154
Lorneville, N.B., 68
Lougheed, Mount, Alta., 183
Louis-Hébert, Qué., 37
Love Lake, Man., 124
Love, Sask., 124
Lovers Cove, Nfld., 124
Lovers Cove, N.S., 7, 124
Lovers Creek, Ont., 124
Lovers Isle, Ont., 124
Lovers Lane, Ont., 124
Lovers Lane, Ont., 189
Lower Canada, 14
Lower East Pubnico, N.S., 30
Lower North Branch Little Southwest Miramichi River, N.B., 140
Lower Sackville, N.S., 49
Lower West Pubnico, N.S., 30
Lucan, Ont., 95
Lucan Islands, B.C., 95
Lucifer, Lac, Qué., 128
Lucifer Peak, B.C., 129
Lunenburger, 43
Łutselk'e, N.W.T, 139
Lyell Island, B.C., 206
Lynx City, Y.T., 112
Lys Creek, B.C., 98

McDonell Peak, B.C., 199

McDougall, Mount, Alta., 184
McGillivray, Mount, Alta., 185
Mackenzie, Alexander, Prime Minister, 179–80
Mackenzie, Sir Alexander, 8, 177–82, 199
Mackenzie, B.C., 180
Mackenzie, Sask., 38
Mackenzie Bay, N.W.T., 179
Mackenzie, Cape, N.W.T., 179
Mackenzie Delta, N.W.T., 179
Mackenzie, District of, N.W.T., 179
Mackenzie Highway, Alta., N.W.T., 180
Mackenzie, Mount, B.C., 181
Mackenzie Mountains, N.W.T., Y.T., 179
Mackenzie Pass, B.C., 181
Mackenzie Point, N.W.T., 179
Mackenzie River, N.W.T., 178–9
Mackenzie Valley, B.C., 181
Mackey-Smith, Lac, Qué., 231
MacLean Barachois, N.S., 6, 117
Madawaska, N.B., 135
Madawaska, Ont., 7, 135
Madawaska River, N.B., 56
Madawaska River, Ont., 56–7
Magaguadavic River, N.B., 45, 135
Main-à-Dieu, N.S., 127
Malakoff, N.B., 94

Malakoff, Ont., 94
Malaspina Strait, B.C., 92, 174
Malpeque Bay, P.E.I., 135
Manilla, Ont., 83
Maniwaki, Qué., 30–1
Manomin Island, Ont., 189
Mantario, Sask., 58
Marfleet, Alta., 60
Margaree, N.S., 46
Maricourt (Wakeham), Qué., 138
Mariposa, Ont., 83
Marne Township, Ont., 99
Mary Fraser Island, P.E.I., 204
Maryhill, Ont., 63–4
Marysvale, Nfld., 68
mash, 118
Massacre Butte, Alta., 113
Massey Island, N.W.T., 216
Maugerville, N.B., 46
Meach, Lac, Qué., 54
Meares, Capt. John, 91
Medicine Hat, Alta., 7, 10, 40, 145–8, 230
Medicine Hatter, 43
Meduxnekeag Intervale, N.B., 118
Meech, Lac, Qué., 54, 165–8
Meech Lake Accord, 54
Meech Lake, Qué., 8, 165–8
Meelpaeg Lake, Nfld., 135
Meetinghouse Rips, N.B., 7, 118
Meighen, Alta., 68

Melba Creek, Y.T., 86

Melbourne, Man., 87

Melita, Man., 47

Melville Island, Ont., 187

Menagoueche, N.B., 48

Mercer Lake, B.C., 206

Mercer, Mount, Alta., 184

Mercer Point, B.C., 206

Merrymeeting Point, Nfld.,
    124

Mersereau Bogan, N.B., 6, 117

Mesopelagia, 14

Messines, Qué., 6, 99

Messines, Lac, Qué., 98

Michener, Roland, 218-20

Michener Game Preserve,
    Norah Willis, N.W.T., 220

Michener, Mount, Alta., 9,
    218-19

Middle Barachois River,
    Nfld., 117

Middle East names, 75-9

Middle East Pubnico, N.S., 30

Middle Island, Ont., 19

Middle Sackville, N.S., 49

Middleton, Ont., 83

Middle West Pubnico, N.S.,
    30

Midnight Dome, Y.T., 172

Mille Roches, Ont., 189-90,
    192

Mineral City, B.C., 111

Mingan, Qué., 27

Mingan Archipelago
    National Park, Qué., 27

Minnedosa, Man., 31, 135

Minnedosa River, Man., 31

Minnetonka, Sask., 143

Minota Island, Ont., 189

Miramichi, N.B., 7, 36, 140-2

Miramichi, N.S., 140

Miramichi, Ont., 140

Miramichi Bay, N.B., 140

Miramichi-Newcastle, N.B.,
    140

Miramichi River, N.B., 141

mish, 118

Mississauga, Ont., 135

Mississaugan, 42

Mississippi River, Ont., 135

mistakes, 54-8

mocauque, 118

Moloch, Mount, B.C., 129

Monchy, Sask., 99

Monckton Township, N.B.,
    54

Moncton, N.B., 54

Monctonian, 42

Monkman Pass, Alta., B.C.,
    193, 196-7

Mons Peak, B.C., 98

Mons Township, Ont., 99

Mont Cambrai, Qué., 98

Mont d'Iberville, Qué., 24

Mont Laurier, Qué., 221

Mont-Laurier, Qué., 222

Mont Nebo, Sask., 78

Montreal, Ark., 106

Montreal, Mo., 106

Montréal, Qué., 8, 108-9,
    162-5

Montreal, Wisc., 106

Montréalais, 41
Montrealer, 41
Montréal-Est, Qué., 164
Montréal-Nord, 37, 164
Montréal-Ouest, Qué., 164
Mont Royal, Qué., 8, 163
Mont-Royal, Qué. 39
Mont Sir-Wilfrid, Qué., 222
Mont Sorrel, Qué., 98
Mont Vimy, Qué., 98
Moose Bath Pond, B.C., 7,
    155
Moose Creek, Ont., 154
Moose Ear Pond, Nfld., 155
Moose Factory, Ont., 152–3
Moose Factory Island, Ont.,
    152
Moosehide Hills, Y.T., 155
Moose Javian, 44
Moose Jaw, Sask., 7, 153
Moose Jaw River, Sask., 153
Mooseland, N.S., 154
Moose Mountain, Sask., 153
moose names, 151–5
Moose River Gold Mines,
    N.S., 154
Moose River, N.S., 154–5
Moose River, Ont., 152
Moosomin, Sask., 153
Moosomin Indian Reserve,
    Sask., 153
Moosonee, Ont., 7, 152
Morrisburg, Ont., 189
Morts, Anse aux, Nfld., 125
Moscow, Ont., 81
Moulinette, Ont., 189–90, 192

Mount Adam, N.S., 101
Mount Allan, Alta., 183
Mount Athabasca, Alta., 52
Mount Azazel, B.C., 129
Mount Beelzebub, B.C., 129
Mount Belial, B.C., 129
Mount Black Prince, Alta.,
    184
Mount Blitzen, N.B., 119
Mount Bogart, Alta., 184
Mount Brock, Alta., 184
Mount Bruat, N.W.T., 96
Mount Burstall, Alta., 184
Mount Carleton, N.B., 24–5
Mount Carmel, Ont., 78
Mount Carmel, P.E.I., 78
Mount Caubvik, Nfld., 24
Mount Chester, Alta., 184
Mount Columbia, Alta., 22
Mount Comet, N.B., 119
Mount Cupid, N.B., 119
Mount Currie, Alta., 184
Mount Dagon, B.C., 129
Mount Dancer, N.B., 119
Mount Dasher, N.B., 119
Mount Dawson, B.C., 207
Mount Dawson, Y.T., 207,
    224
Mount DeCosmos, B.C., 231
Mount Donder, N.B., 119
Mount Eisenhower, Alta., 5,
    71–4, 227
Mount Engadine, Alta., 184
Mount Eurydice, B.C., 125
Mount Florence, B.C., 96–7
Mount Foch, Alta., 184

Mount Fraser, B.C., 199, 200
Mount Galatea, Alta., 184
Mount Hamelin, N.W.T., 96
Mount Hebron, N.B., 78
Mount Hood, Alta., 184
Mount Indefatigable, Alta.,
   184
Mount Invincible, Alta., 184
Mount Jellicoe, Alta., 184
Mount Joffre, Alta., B.C., 184
Mount Juliet, B.C., 125
Mount Kennedy, B.C., 226
Mount Kennedy, N.B., 226
Mount Kennedy, Y.T., 227-8
Mount Kidd, Alta., 184
Mount Lady Laurier, B.C.,
   224
Mount Laurier, B.C., 224
Mount Laurier, Y.T., 207, 224
Mount Leman, Alta., B.C.,
   184
Mount Logan, Y.T., 22, 227-8
Mount Lorette, Alta., 184
Mount Lougheed, Alta., 183
Mount Mackenzie, B.C., 181
Mount McDougall, Alta., 184
Mount McGillivray, Alta.,
   185
Mount Mercer, Alta., 184
Mount Michener, Alta., 9,
   218-19
Mount Moloch, B.C., 129
Mount Nightingale, B.C.,
   96-7
Mount Nirvana, N.W.T., 23
Mount Orpheus, B.C., 125

Mount Peck, B.C., 66
Mount Penelope, B.C., 125
Mount Pétain, Alta., B.C., 65
Mount Pisgah, N.B., 78
Mount Prancer, N.B., 119
Mount Putnik, Alta., 184
Mount Revelstoke National
   Park, B.C., 26
Mount Rimmon, B.C., 129
Mount Robert Service, Y.T.,
   172
Mount Robert Smith, B.C.,
   231
Mount Robson, B.C., 23, 224
Mount Romeo, B.C., 125
Mount Roosevelt, B.C., 226
Mount Royal, Qué. 39, 165
Mount Rudolph, N.B., 119
Mount Rundle, Alta., 185
Mount St. Elias, Y.T., 20, 22
Mount St. Nicholas, N.B., 119
Mount Satan, B.C., 129
Mount Shark, Alta., 184
Mount Sir Alexander, B.C.,
   180
Mount Sir Donald, B.C., 230
Mount Sir James MacBrien,
   N.W.T., 23
Mount Smuts, Alta., 184
Mount Sparrowhawk, Alta.,
   184
Mount Stalin, B.C., 5, 66
Mount Torrens, Alta., 86
Mount Turner, Alta., 184
Mount Ulysses, B.C., 125
Mount Vancouver, B.C., 176

Mount Vanier, N.W.T., 217
Mount Vanier, Y.T., 217
Mount Vixen, N.B., 119
Mount Warspite, Alta., 184
Mount White-Fraser, B.C., 200
Mousseau, Lac, Qué., 8, 167-8
Mousseau, Ruisseau, Qué., 167
Mulcaster Island, Ont., 187
Murchison Island, Ont., 208
Muskoka, Ont., 7, 31, 135
Muskoka, Lake, Ont., 31
Musquodoboit, N.S., 135
Myers Island, Ont., 188

Nackawic, N.B., 30
Nackawic Stream, N.B., 30
Nahanni Butte, N.W.T., 113, 139
Nahanni National Park, N.W.T., 28
Nakiska, Alta., 183
Nanaimo-Cowichan, B.C., 39
Nanaimo Harbour, B.C., 92
Nanaimoite, 43
Nanisivik, N.W.T., 33
Nanticoke, Ont., 46, 50
Nares, Sir George, 20
Narrows, The, N.S., 134
National park names, 25-8
native names, 134-40
Navy Islands, Ont., 187
Nazareth, Qué., 79

Neddie Smiths Pond, N.S., 231
Needle's Eye, Ont., 189
negative connotations, 63-7
Nelson-Miramichi, N.B., 140
New Acadia, P.E.I., 161
New Albion, 14
New Brunswick, x, 16
New Canaan, N.B., 78
New Canaan, N.S., 78
Newcastle, N.B., 50
Newcastle, Ont., 50
New Dublin, Ont., 82
New Dublin Township, N.S., 82
Newfoundland, 46
Newfoundlander, 42
Newfoundland Geographical Names Board, 24, 133
New France, 14
New Germany, Ont., 63-4
New Harmony, P.E.I., 103
New Hermon, Ont., 78
New Kiew, Alta., 83
New London, P.E.I, 82
New Lunnon, Alta., 82
New Niagara, N.B., 55
New Salem, N.S., 78
New Sarepta, Alta., 79
New Stockholm, Sask., 82
New Zealand, P.E.I., 84
New Zion, N.B., 78
Niagara Fallsian, 43
Niagarentia, 14
Nicabong, Qué., 47
Nichols Lake, Ont., 61

Nickel Belt, Ont., 40
nicknames, 41
Nightingale, Mount, B.C.,
    96-7
Nineveh, N.S., 75
Nirvana, Lac, Qué., 103
Nirvana, Mount, N.W.T., 23
Nirvana Pass, B.C., 103
Noël, Lac, Qué., 121
Nolalu, Ont., 59
Nolan Point, B.C., 95
Norah Willis Michener Game
    Preserve, N.W.T., 220
Noranda, Qué., 59
Norland, 14
Norman, Ont., 58-9
North Bayite, 43
Northern Yukon National
    Park, Y.T., 28
North Gower, Ont., 46
North Pole Mountain, N.B.,
    119
North Pole Stream, N.B., 119
Northumberland–Miramichi,
    N.B., 36, 140
Notre-Dame-d'Ivugivic, Qué.,
    138
Notre-Dame-de-Koartac,
    Qué., 138
Nova Scotia, x, 16
nub, 118
Nunatsiaq, N.W.T., 40
Nutana, Sask., 144

Odessa, Ont., 95
Odlum, B.C., 65

offensive names, 67-71
Ogidaki Mountain, Ont., 23
Ogilvie, William, 207
Ogre Mountain, B.C., 7, 129
Okanagan, B.C., 5, 53
Okanagan Centre, B.C., 39
Okanagan–Similkameen–Merritt,
    B.C., 39
Oldman River, Alta., 69-71
Old Shop Steadies, Nfld., 116
Onoman, Lac, Qué., 136
Ontario, 134
Ontario, Calif., 6, 104
Ontario, Ont., 37
Ontario, Ore., 6, 104-5
Ontario Northland Railway,
    53, 152
Ophir, Ont., 77
Ophir Creek, Y.T., 76
Ophir Township, Ont., 77
Orignac, R de l', N.S., 155
Oromocto, N.B., 135
Orpheus, Mount, B.C., 125
Oshawan, 42
Osnabruck, Ont., 191
Ottawa, Ont., 136
Ottawa Centre, Ont., 37
Ottawa South, Ont., 37
Ouigoudi, N.B., 48
oven, 118
Owen Island, Ont., 187

padou, 117
Pakan, Alta., 209-10
Palliser, John, 69, 71, 153,
    183-4, 194

Paradise, Nfld., 6, 101
Paradise, N.S., 101
Paradise Arm, Nfld., 101
Paradise Brook, N.S., 100
Paradise Cove, Nfld., 101
Paradise Creek, Y.T., 101
Paradise Hill, Sask., 101
Paradise River, Nfld., 101
Paradise Sound, Nfld., 101
Paris, Ont., 80
Parkway, Ont., 64
Parrsboro Aboiteau, N.S., 118
Parr Town, N.B., 48
Partridge Berry Gully, Nfld., 116
Paska, Ont., 68
Paska Creek, Ont., 68
Paska Lake, Ont., 68
Paska Township, Ont., 68
Passchendaele, N.S., 99-100
passes, 193-7
Pauline, le, N.W.T., 216
Payne Bay, Qué., 138
Peace River, Alta., 39
Pearson, Lester B., 227
Peas Brook, N.S., 121
Peck, Mount, B.C., 66
Pelee Island, Ont., 19
Pelee National Park, Ont., 27
Pelee, Point, Ont., 19, 27
Peltry Barasway, Nfld., 117
Pembroke, Ont., 140
Penelope, Mount, B.C., 125
Penguin Islands, Nfld., 90
Penny Ice Cap, N.W.T., 28
Perth, Ont., 49

Perth County, Ont., 49
Perth-Wellington-Waterloo, Ont., 37
Petain, B.C., 65
Pétain, Canton, Qué., 66
Pétain, Lac, Qué., 66
Pétain, Mount, Alta., B.C., 65
Peterborough, Ont., 35
Peterburian, 43
Peter Lougheed Provincial Park, Alta., 184
Petitcodiac, N.B., 135
Petit lac Ha! Ha!, Qué., 131
Petit Miramichi, N.B., 141
Philippe, Lac, Qué., 167-8
Philp Coulee, Alta., 113
Pickards Padou, N.B., 6, 117
Pickering, Ont., 49
Pickering Village, Ont., 49-50
Picton, Ont., 42
Pictonian, 42
Picton Island, N.Y., 188
Pictou, N.S., 42
Picture Butte, Alta., 113
Pigeon Mountain, Alta., 185
Pincher Creek, Alta., 32
Pinchgut Tickle, Nfld., 6, 116
Pine, Cape, Nfld., 89
Pisarinco, N.B., 68
Pisgah, Mount, N.B., 78
Pitt Island, B.C., 175
Place du Québec, Fr., 6, 105
Plaza de Québec, Mex., 105
Pocomoonshine Deadwater, N.B., 6, 116

Pocowagamis Deadwater, N.B., 116

Pointe-à-l'Orignal, Ont., 154

Point Pelee, Ont., 19, 27

Poirier, Jean, 163

political corrections, 63–7

Poperinghe, Lac, Qué., 98

portage, 112

Port Brabant, N.W.T., 137

Port Burwell, N.W.T., 138

Port Dalhousie, Ont., 45

Porte d'Enfer Rapids, B.C., 129

Port Harrison, Qué., 137–8

Port Hope, Ont., 230

Portland Canal, B.C., 175

Portneuf, Qué., 36

Port-Nouveau-Québec, Qué., 138

Port Simpson, B.C., 139

Portuguese, 12, 29, 18–19

Portuguese names, 18–19, 55, 87–90

Port Williams, N.S., 94–5

possessive names, 60

Poste-de-la-Baleine, Qué., 138

Potato Creek, Y.T., 121

Pouce Coupe, B.C., 46

prairie, 112

Prancer, Mount, N.B., 119

Premier Range, B.C., 224

Prescott, Ont., 49

Prescott County, Ont., 49

Président-Kennedy, Avenue du, Qué., 226

Président-Kennedy, Route du, Qué., 226

Prince Albert National Park, Sask., 26

Prince Albert, Sask., 26

Prince Edward Island, x

Prince Edward–Hastings, Ont., 37

Prince of Wales, 9, 211–13

Prince of Wales, N.B., 212

Prince of Wales College, P.E.I., 212

Prince of Wales Drive, Ont., 213

Prince of Wales Falls, Ont., 213

Prince of Wales Highway, The, Ont., 213

Prince of Wales Hotel, Alta., 213

Prince of Wales Island, N.W.T., 211–12

Prince of Wales Mountains, N.W.T., 212

Prince of Wales Northern Heritage Centre, N.W.T., 9, 213

Prince of Wales Reach, B.C., 212

Prince of Wales Road, Ont., 213

Prince of Wales's Fort, Man., 211

Prince of Wales Strait, N.W.T., 212

pronunciation, 44–7

Provost, Alta., 47
Pubnico, N.S., 29, 162
Pudding Burn, B.C., 121
Puerto de Revillagigedo,
    B.C., 92
Pukaskwa National Park,
    Ont., 27
Pukaskwa River, 27
Purgatory Glacier, B.C., 129
Putnik, Mount, Alta., 184

Qausuittuq, N.W.T, 139
Qu'Appelle-Moose
    Mountain, Sask., 154
Quadra and Vancouver's
    Island, B.C., 92, 175
Quadra Island, B.C., 92, 175
Quaqtaq, Qué., 138
Quebec, Eng., 6, 105
Québec, 50, 134
Québec City, Qué., 11, 50, 108
Québec-Est, Qué., 36
Quebeck, Tenn., 105
Quebecker, 42
Québécois, 42
Québec-Ouest, Qué., 36,
    215-16
Québec, Place du, Fr., 105
Québec, Plaza de, Mex., 105
Queen Charlotte, B.C., 112
Queen Charlotte City, B.C.,
    112
Queen Charlotte Islands,
    B.C., 19-20, 205-6
Queen Peak, B.C., 209
Queen Victoria, 9, 208-11

Quesnel, B.C., 46
Quetico Provincial Park,
    Ont., 59
Quirpon, Nfld., 46

Rabbit Creek, Y.T., 172
Race, Cape, Nfld., 88
Rada de Valdés y Bazan, B.C.,
    92
Ragged Range, N.W.T., 23
Raglan, Ont., 95
Raglan Point, B.C., 95
Raglan Range, N.W.T., 95
Raglan Township, Ont., 95
Raleigh, Nfld., 132
Rancheria, Y.T., 47
Rand, Rev. Silas, 149
Ranfurly, Alta., 84
Rankine Islands, B.C., 206
Rapid City, Man., 110-11
Rapide-à-l'Orignal, Qué., 222
Rat Portage, Ont., 58-9
Rattling Brook Steadies,
    Nfld., 116
Ray, Cape, Nfld., 90
R de l'Orignac, N.S., 155
Redan, Ont, 94
Red Island, Nfld., 90
Regina, Sask., 9, 210, 144
Reginan, 44
Regina-Lumsden, Sask., 38
Regina-Qu'Appelle, Sask.,
    38
Regina-Wascana, Sask., 35
Rencontre, Nfld., 46
Renews, Nfld., 88, 157

Renfrew County, x
Resolute, N.W.T, 139
Restigouche, N.B., 35
Restigouche–Chaleur, N.B.,
 35
Restigouche River, N.B., 141
Revelstoke, B.C., 26
Revillagigedo, Puerto de,
 B.C., 92
Reykjavik, Man., 83
Richards, Capt. George, 174,
 199
Richmond, B.C., 85
Richmond–Wolfe, Qué., 36
Rideau City, Ont., 230
Riding Mountain, Man., 27
Riding Mountain National
 Park, Man., 27
Riga, Sask., 83
Rimmon, Mount, B.C., 129
Rimouski–Témiscouata,
 Qué., 35
Rio Florida Blanca, B.C., 92
rips, 118
River Disappointment,
 N.W.T., 178
Riversdale, Sask., 144
Rivers Inlet, B.C., 174
River Styx, Ont., 128
Rivière-du-Loup, Qué.,
 202
Rivière Ha! Ha!, Qué., 131
Robert Service Creek, Y.T.,
 172
Robert Service, Mount, Y.T.,
 172

Robert Smith, Mount, B.C.,
 231
Robson, Mount, B.C., 23, 224
Rocky Barachois Bight, Nfld.,
 117
Rocky Mountain Pass, Alta.,
 B.C., 196
Rocky Mountain passes, 9,
 193-7
Rocky Mountains, Alta.,
 B.C., 179
Rocky Mountains Park, Alta.,
 25
Romaine, Rivière, Qué., 136
romantic names, 122-6
Romeo, Mount, B.C., 125
Roosevelt, Mount, B.C., 226
Roseau, Man., 110
Rosseau, Ont., 110
Rothesay, N.B., 212
Rouge River, Ont., 39
Royal, Mont, Qué., 8, 163
Royal Roads, B.C., 92
Royal Victoria Hospital,
 Qué., 208
Rudolph, Mount, N.B., 119
Rundle, Mount, Alta., 185
runround, 118
Rustico, P.E.I., 30
Rustico Bay, P.E.I., 30

Saanich–Gulf Islands, B.C.,
 39
Sackville, N.B., 49
Sackville, N.S., 49
Saglouc, Qué., 138

Saguenay, Que., 135
St. Arnaud Hills, N.W.T., 96
St. Brides, Nfld., 68
St. Catharines, Ont., 5, 37, 51
St. Catharinite, 43
Sainte-Élisabeth, Qué., 42
Sainte-Foy, Qué., 42
St. Elias, Mount, Y.T., 20, 22
St. Elias Mountains, Y.T., 22, 227–8
St. Francis, Cape, Nfld., 89
St. George, Cape, Nfld., 90
Saint-Jean-sur-Richelieu, Qué., 48
Saint John, N.B., 4, 45, 47–8, 109
Saint Johner, 43
St. John River, N.B., 47–8
St. John's, Nfld., 4, 5, 43, 45, 47–8, 61, 89
St. Johns, Qué., 48
St. John's East, Nfld., 35
St. Johnsian, 43
St. John's West, Nfld., 35
St. Julien Township, Ont., 99
St. Laurent, Louis, 17
St. Lawrence, Nfld., 90
St. Lawrence Island, Ont., 187
St. Lawrence Islands National Park, Ont., 27, 188
St. Lawrence, Lake, Ont., 189, 192
St. Lawrence Provincial Park, Ont., 192–3

St. Lawrence River, 11
St. Lawrence Seaway, Ont., 189
Saint-Louis-du-Ha! Ha!, Qué., 7, 130–1
St. Mary River, Alta., 70
St. Marys, Ont., 62
St. Mary's Bay, Nfld., 89
St. Mary's, Cape, Nfld., 89
St. Mary's District Municipality, N.S., 61
St-Maurice, Rivière, Qué., 27
St. Nicholas, Mount, N.B., 119
St. Nicholas Peak, B.C., 7, 120
Saint-Nicolas, Qué., 121
Saint-Noël, Qué., 121
Saint Pierre and Miquelon, 89
Saint-Pol, Lac, Qué., 98
St-Quentin, N.B., 6, 98–9
Saint-Valentin, Qué., 122
Saint-Wilfred, N.B., 223
Salem, N.S., 78
Salem, Ont., 78
Salem Corners, Ont., 78
Salem Road, N.S., 78
Salliq, N.W.T, 139
Salluit, Qué., 138
Sandon, B.C., 109
Sanirajak, N.W.T, 139
Santa Lake, Ont., 120
Santa's Village, Ont., 120
Santy Lake, Sask., 120
Sarcee Butte, Alta., 112

Sardis, B.C., 79
Saskatchewan City, Man., 110-11
Saskatonian 42
Saskatoon, Sask., 7, 142-5
Saskatoon-Clark's Crossing, Sask., 38
Saskatoon Drive, Ont., 145
Saskatoon-Dundurn, Sask., 38
Saskatoon Hill, Alta., 145
Saskatoon-Humboldt, Sask., 38
Saskatoon Island Provincial Park, Alta., 145
Saskatoon Lake, Alta., 145
Saskatoon Lake, Sask., 145
Saskatoon Mountain, Alta., 145
Satan, Mount, B.C., 129
Saugeen, Ont., 135
savannah, 118
Scarlett Point, B.C., 95
Scilly Cove, Nfld., 68
Schreiber, Ont., 47
Sebastopol Township, Ont., 94
Secret Creek, Y.T., 126
Semiwagan Deadwater, N.B., 116
sensitive names, 67-71
Service, Robert, 8, 170
Sevogle, N.B., 226
Shark, Mount, Alta., 184
Sharon, Ont., 79
Shawvillite, 42

Sheaffe Island, Ont., 188
Sheba, N.B., 77
Sheba, Ont., 77
Sheba Township, Ont., 77
Shefford, Qué., 36
Sherbrooke, Austr., 83
Sherridon, Man., 60
Shippagan, N.B., 53
Shippegan, N.B., 53
Shippegan Bay, N.B., 53
Shippegan Beach, N.B., 53
Shippegan Channel, N.B., 53
Shippegan Harbour, N.B., 53
Shippegan Parish, N.B., 53
Shippegan Park, N.B., 53
Shippigan, N.B., 53-4
Shubenacadie River, N.S., 161
Sidney, B.C., 50
Sidney, Man., 87
Signal Hill, Nfld., 156
Siloam, Ont., 78
Silver City, Y.T., 112
Simcoe, John Graves, 80
Simcoe, Ala., 107
Simcoe, Ont., 49
Simcoe County, Ont., 49
Simcoe North, Ont., 37
Similkameen, B.C., 134
Simon Creek, Alta., 199
Simon Glacier, Alta., 199
Simon Peak, B.C., 199
Sipweske, Man., 68
Sir Alexander Mackenzie Provincial Park, B.C., 181

Sir Alexander, Mount, B.C., 180

Sir Donald, Mount, B.C., 230

Sir James MacBrien, Mount, N.W.T., 23

Sir-Wilfrid, Mont, Qué., 222

Skeena, B.C., 40

Skidegate, B.C., 47

Slocan, B.C., 111–12

Slocan City, B.C., 112

Smallwood, Joseph, 48

Smith, Ross, xi, xiii, 10

Smith Coulee, Sask., 231

Smithfield, Ont., 230

Smith-Jones Lake, Sask., 231

Smith Lake, Sask., 231

Smith names, 228–31

Smith Peninsula, Sask., 231

Smith Point, P.E.I., 229

Smith's Creek, Ont., 230

Smiths Falls, Ont., 5, 61, 229–30

Smiths Shanty Hill, Ont., 231

Smiths Slough, Man., 231

Smith Sound, N.W.T., 230

Smith Township, Ont., 230

Smith-Windsor Islands, Sask., 231

Smithville, Alta., 10, 147, 230

Smithville, Ont., 230

Smuts, Mount, Alta., 184

Snafu Creek, Y.T., 60

Snowdrift, N.W.T, 139

soi, 118

Sointula, B.C., 6, 103

Somme Creek, Y.T., 100

Somme, Lac, Qué., 98

Somme, Rivière, Qué., 98

Somme Township, Ont., 99

Sooite, 43

Sooke Inlet, B.C., 92

Sorcerer Mountain, B.C., 129

Sorcier, Mont du, Qué., 128

Sorel, Qué. 30

Sorrel, Mont, Qué., 98

sound-alikes, 47–50

Souris, Man., 45

Souris, P.E.I., 45

Souris–Moose Mountain, Sask., 154

South Nahanni River, N.W.T., 28

South Saskatchewan River, 69–71, 142–3

South Seas names, 83–7

Southwest Miramichi, N.B., 140

South West Nova, N.S., 36

Spanish names, 90–2

Sparrowhawk, Mount, Alta., 184

Spear, Cape, Nfld., 18, 88–9

spelling, 50–4

spelling mistakes, 53–4

Spence Bay, N.W.T, 139

Spilsbury Island, Ont., 187

Spinneys Heath, N.S., 118

Split, Cape, N.S., 28

Springfield, Ont., 81

Spud Islanders, 44

Squaw Island, Ont., 187

Stadacona, 11

Stalin, Mount, B.C., 5, 66
Stalin Township, Ont., 66
Star City, Sask., 111
Statesmen Range, B.C., 226-7
steady, 116
Stefansson, Vilhjalmur, 86,
    137
stillwater, 116
Stockholm, Sask., 82
Stouffville, Ont., 46
Stovin Island, Ont., 188
Strait of Canso, N.S., 150-1
Strait of Georgia, B.C., 8, 92,
    174
Straits of Anian, 90
Stratfordian, 43
Strathcona, Alta., 230
Strathcona Sound, N.W.T.,
    230
Strathgartney Provincial
    Park, P.E.I., 30
Stupendous Mountain, B.C.,
    181
Styx Glacier, B.C., 125
Styx Mountain, B.C., 129
Styx, River, Ont., 128
Sudburian, 43
Sugar Island, Ont., 187
Sugar Island Padou, N.B.,
    117
Sugluk, Qué., 138
Summersider, 43
Suni, Ont., 68
Suni Creek, Ont., 68
Suni Lake, Ont., 68
Suni Township, Ont., 68

Sunnyvale, Ont., 191
Superior, 14
Sutherland's, Ont., 77
Swastika, Ont., 65
Swift Current-Maple
    Creek-Assiniboia, Sask., 35
Sydney, N.S., 50
Sydneynite, 43

Tabusintac Gully, N.B., 116
Taloyoak, N.W.T, 139
Tarfu Creek, Y.T., 5, 60
Tasmania Islands, N.W.T., 84
Témiscaming, Qué., 53
Témiscamingue, Qué., 39, 53
Témiscamingue, Lac, Qué. 5,
    53
Témiscouata, Qué., 135
Temiskaming and Northern
    Ontario Railway, 53, 152
Terra Nova National Park,
    Nfld., 28
Terrebonne, Qué., 36
Texada Island, B.C., 92
Tête Jaune Cache, B.C., 196
Tête Jaune Pass, Alta., B.C.,
    196
The Forks, Ont., 81-2
Thompson, David, 195, 199
Thompsonite, 43
thoroughfare, 118
Thousand Islands, Ont., 8,
    185
Three Sisters, The, Alta., 185
thrum, 118
Thunder Bayite, 43

Thwartway Island, Ont., 187
tickle, 114-15
Tidds Island, Ont., 187
Tilleys Gullies, Nfld., 116
Timiskaming, Ont., 50, 135
Timiskaming, District of,
    Ont., 53
Timiskaming-French River,
    Ont., 39
Timiskaming, Lake, Ont., 5,
    53
Timmins, Ont., 6, 109
Timmins-Chapleau, Ont., 35
Tiny Tim Lake, B.C., 7, 120
Tip Top Mountain, Ont., 24
Tofino Inlet, B.C., 92
tolt, 118
Tom Howes Gully, Nfld., 116
Toniata, Ont., 187
Torngat Mountains, Nfld.,
    Qué., 24, 126
Toronto, Austr., 83, 106
Toronto, Ind., 6, 106
Toronto, Iowa, 6, 105-6
Toronto, Kans., 6, 106
Toronto, Mo., 6, 106
Toronto, Ohio, 6, 105
Toronto, Ont., 45, 80, 109,
    230
Toronto, Tenn., 6, 106
Torontonian, 41
Torrens, Mount, Alta., 86
townies, 43
Tracadie Bay, P.E.I., 161
Transatlantica, 14
Transcona, Man., 60

Transylvania, 14
Tremont Island, Ont., 187
Trepassey, Nfld., 47
Trifluvien, 42
Trinity Bay, Nfld., 89, 157
Trois-Rivières, Qué., 39, 42
Trout Lake City, B.C., 111
Troy, N.S., 79
Troy, Ont., 79
Tsawwassen, B.C., 47
Tthenaagoo, N.W.T, 139
Tuktoyaktuk, N.W.T., 137,
    139
Tulit'a, N.W.T, 139
Tumbler Ridge, B.C., 197
Tupona, 14
Tuponia, 14
Turk's Gut, Nfld., 68
Turkey Point, Ont., 121
Turner, Mount, Alta., 184
Tuurngatalik Island, N.W.T.,
    129
Twillingate, Nfld., 29

Ucluelet, B.C., 47
Ulysses, Mount, B.C., 125
undesirable names, 67-71
Upper Canada, 14
Upper Canada Village, Ont.,
    192
Upper Christmas Pond,
    Nfld., 121
Upper Sackville, N.S., 49
Upper West Pubnico, N.S., 30
Uranium City, Sask., 111
Urbainville, P.E.I., 162

Ursalia, 14
Uscan, Lake, Ont., 192
Utopia, Ont., 6, 102
Utopia Lake, B.C., 102-3
Utopia, Lake, N.B., 102

Valdes Island, B.C., 92
Valdés y Bazan, Rada de,
    B.C., 92
Valenciennes River, B.C., 98
Valentine, Ont., 125
Valentine Creek, Sask., 122-3
Valentine Hill, B.C., 122
Valentine Lake, N.B., 123
Valentine Lake, Nfld., 122
Valentine Lake, Ont., 122
Valentine names, 7, 122
Valhalla, Alta., 103
Valhalla, Man., 103
Valhalla Lake, Ont., 103
Valhalla Mountain, N.W.T.,
    103
Valhalla Ranges, B.C., 103
Valpy, Michael, 17
Van Horne, William, 59, 146,
    176, 208
Vancouver, Capt. George, 8,
    91-2, 173-6
Vancouver, B.C., 50, 175-6
Vancouver Bay, B.C., 176
Vancouver Island, B.C., 50,
    92, 175
Vancouverite, 41, 43
Vancouver, Mount, B.C., 176
Vancouver-Quadra, B.C., 39
Vancouver River, B.C., 176

Vancouver Rock, B.C., 176
Vanier, Georges, 9, 213-18
Vanier, Ont., 6, 9, 109, 214-15
Vanier, Qué., 9, 215-16
Vanier College, Qué, 217
Vanier Cup, 217
Vanier, le, N.W.T., 216
Vanier Institute of the
    Family, 217
Vanier Medal, 217
Vanier, Mount, N.W.T., 217
Vanier, Mount, Y.T., 217
Vanier Park, B.C., 217
Varna, Ont., 95
vault, 118
Verdun Glacier, B.C., 98
Verdun, Lac, Qué., 98
Verdun Township, Ont., 99
Vermilion Pass, Alta., B.C.,
    193-4
Verrazzano, Giovanni de, 159
Vesperia, 14
Victoria, Queen, 9, 16, 208-11
Victoria, Alta., 209-10
Victoria, B.C., 9, 209
Victoria, Nfld., 210
Victoria, Ont., 96, 210
Victoria, P.E.I., 210
Victoria, Sask., 210
Victoria and Albert
    Mountains, N.W.T., 211
Victoria Avenue, Ont., 208
Victoria Beach, Man., 210
Victoria Corners Ont., 210
Victoria County, N.B., 210
Victoria County, N.S., 210

Victoria County, Ont., 210
Victoria Cross, P.E.I., 210
Victoria General Hospital,
  Man., 208
Victoria General Hospital,
  N.S., 208
Victoria, Grand lac, Qué., 210
Victoria Harbour, N.W.T.,
  209
Victoria Harbour, Ont., 210
Victoria Island, N.W.T.,
  210-11
Victoria Lake, Man., 210
Victoria Lake, Ont., 210
Victorialand, 14
Victorialia, 14
Victorian, 42
Victoria Peak, B.C., 209
Victoria, Pointe, Qué., 209
Victoria Springs, Ont., 210
Victoria Square, Ont., 210
Victoria Township, Ont., 210
Victoria University, Ont., 208
Victoriaville, Qué., 210
Victoria West, P.E.I., 210
Vienna, Ont., 82
Viking, Alta., 68
Ville-Marie, Qué., 164
Vimy, Alta., 98
Vimy Barracks, Ont., 97-8
Vimy, Canton, Qué., 98
Vimy Lakes, B.C., 98
Vimy, Mont, Qué., 98
Vimy Peak, Alta., 98
Vimy Ridge, Alta., 6, 98
Vimy Ridge, B.C., 6, 98

Vimy Ridge, Ont., 98
Vimy Ridge Island, Ont., 98
Vixen, Mount, N.B., 119

Waddington, Mount, B.C.,
  22
Wakeham Bay, Qué., 138
Walbran, Capt. John, 91
Wales, Prince of, 9, 211-13
Wales, Ont., 189-92, 212
Wales Island, N.W.T., 212
Walhalla Creek, Y.T., 86
Wanapitei, Ont., 47
Wanderers Channel, Ont.,
  189
Wapta River, B.C., 195
Wardsville, Ont., 229
Warrior Mountain, Alta.,
  B.C., 184
Warsaw, Ont., 80
Warspite, Mount, Alta., 184
Wascana, Sask., 135
Waterloo, Ont., 37, 64-5
Waterton Lakes National
  Park, Alta., 26
Wauchope, Sask., 47
Wawanesa, Man., 31, 68, 135
Welland Junction, Ont., 110
Welland-St. Catharines-
  Thorold, Ont., 37
Wellesley Island, N.Y., 188
Wellington, Ont., 49, 94
Wellington-Grey-Dufferin-
  Simcoe, Ont., 35, 37
Wendigo Beach, Man., 128
Wendigo Lake, Ont., 128

Wendigo Point, Man., 128
Wendigo River, Man., 128
West Dublin, N.S., 82
Western Arctic, N.W.T., 38
West Islanders, 44
Westlock, Alta., 60
Westmorland-Kent, N.B., 36
West Paradise, N.S., 101
West Pubnico, N.S., 30
West Road (Blackwater)
    River, B.C., 181
West Saskatoon, Sask., 143
West Woodlands Island, Ont.,
    192
Wetaskiwin, Alta., 35
Whapmagoostui, Qué., 138
White-Fraser, Mount, B.C.,
    200
White Hill, N.S., 24
Whitehorse Rapids, Y.T., 33
Whitehorse, Y.T., 33, 171
Whonnock, B.C., 52
Wild Rose, Alta., 38
Wilfrid Island, Ont., 223
Wilfrid, Lac, Qué., 222
Wilfrid Laurier University,
    Ont., ix, 224
William Henry, Qué., 30
Wind City, Y.T., 112
Wind Mountain, Alta.,
    183-84
Windigo Island, Ont., 128
Windigo Lake, Man., 128
Windigo Lake, Ont., 128
Winding Stairs Rips, N.B.,
    118

Windsor, N.B., 49
Windsor, N.S., 49
Windsor, Ont., 49
Windsor, Qué., 49
Windsor Mountain, Alta., 72
Windtower, Alta., 184
Windy Mountain, Alta., 183
Winnipeg, Man., 135
Winnipegger, 41, 43
Winnipeg North Centre,
    Man., 37
Winnipeg South Centre,
    Man., 37
Winnipeg-Transcona, Man.,
    35
Winston, Ont., 65
Winterton, Nfld., 68
Winthuysen, Bocas de, B.C.,
    92
Witch Spirit Lake, B.C., 129
Wolfe Island, Ont., 186
Wood Buffalo National Park,
    Alta., N.W.T, 26
Woodlands, Ont., 189-90, 192
Woodlands Islands, Ont., 192
Woods Lake, Ont, 61
Woodstonian, 42
Wunnammin Lake, Ont., 136

Yahk, B.C., 53
Yarmouthian, 43
Yellowhead Highway, Man.,
    Sask., Alta., B.C., 196
Yellowhead Pass, Alta., B.C.,
    193, 196
Yellowknife, N.W.T., 33

Yellowknifer, 43
Yoho National Park, B.C., 26
Yoho River, B.C., 26
York, Ont., 80
Yorke Island, Ont., 187
York–Sunbury, N.B., 36
Ypres, Canton, Qué., 98
Yser, Lac, Qué., 98
Yukon, Y.T., 35
Yukon River, Y.T., 135, 171
Yukon Territory, 171
Yule Lake, B.C., 120

Yule Rock, B.C., 7, 120
Yuletide names, 118–22

Zealand, Ont., 84
Zealandia, Sask., 6,
   84
Zeballos Inlet, B.C., 92
Zion, Ont., 78
Zion Hill, Ont., 78
Zion Line, Ont., 78
Zionville, N.B., 78
Zone Mills, Ont., 96